Advance Praise

"Patti DeNucci has done it again! She has filled her latest book *More Than Just Talk* with hundreds of powerful ideas and techniques that anyone can use to converse and connect more proactively, positively, and personably in just about any setting. You'll want to put it at the very top of your personal and professional reading list!"

—Steve Harper
Speaker, Entrepreneur, and Author of *The Ripple Effect: Maximizing the Power of Relationships for Your Life and Business*

. . . .

"If you are looking to motivate, influence, and take relationships to the next level, this book is a MUST! Patti has created an interactive and fun read that will challenge, inspire, and elevate your interactions. I cannot wait to put her ideas into action!"

—Christine Cashen, M.A.E.D., C.S.P.
Speaker Hall of Fame and Award-Winning Author

. . . .

"With *More Than Just Talk*, Patti DeNucci has really done her research. She's also woven in her upbeat, often humorous conversational style and personality. The result is a useful, fun-to-read guide from an expert communicator and networker. This book not only tells us why we should be having better conversations, but also how to do it more naturally, graciously, and effectively."

—Jill Griffin
Author of six business books, including *Earn Your Seat on a Corporate Board* and the international best-seller, *Customer Loyalty: How To Earn It, How to Keep It*

"Reading *More Than Just Talk* is like sitting with Patti DeNucci around a warm campfire on a crisp fall evening, having an enjoyable and sometimes funny discussion about good conversation. So much of the wisdom Patti shares is both affirming and enlightening. Even after a 50-year communications consulting career, I still experienced new insights and aha's."

—Lindy Segall
Communications Coach and Consultant, Professionally Speaking: "Prepare to be Quoted"

. . . .

"In nearly every industry and profession, the ability to talk and listen to others is a huge part of being likable, influential, and successful. *More Than Just Talk* delivers expert and well-researched advice on the topic of conversation in an engaging and often entertaining way."

—Scott Rake, D.M.D.
President of Dakota Valley Maxillofacial Surgery, Past President of the Minnesota Thoroughbred Breeders Association, and Past President of the Minnesota Horseman's Association

. . . .

"*More Than Just Talk* is a well-written, researched, and curated book that offers remarkable insights and timely value to anyone who wishes to become better at conversations."

—Kent Nutt
Marketing Director at Santa Fe Innovates

. . . .

"The art of conversation has been virtually lost in today's digital-centric culture. *More Than Just Talk* provides a practical blueprint to spark, manage, and benefit from all types of conversations, regardless of your social personality. We need this book now, more than ever before."

—Ed Gandia
Business Coach for Writers, Host of the "High-Income Business Writing" Podcast

"In *More Than Just Talk*, Patti DeNucci offers practical insights and strategies on a topic where most of us could use some help: conversation. The section on listening is particularly helpful, as the test of a good conversation—social or professional—begins with a commitment to listen."

—Doug Hall
Owner, W.D. Hall Company

. . . .

"As an introvert, the thought of improving social interactions can be daunting and scary. With an upbeat tone, Patti DeNucci's book *More Than Just Talk* does an excellent job of walking you through helpful, thought-provoking exercises. She also provides simple, useful techniques you can implement in your day-to-day interactions immediately."

—Natasha Gorski, M.S., P.M.P.
Proposal Manager for the BioDiscovery Institute at the University of North Texas

. . . .

"Regardless of where you are on the conversation continuum, you will learn valuable, practical insights from *More Than Just Talk*. The conversational, friendly tone is much like listening to nuggets of wisdom from a treasured friend. When you buy the book, be sure to pick up a copy for someone you know!"

—Darla Akin
Donor Engagement Manager, Meals on Wheels, Inc., of Tarrant County (Texas)

. . . .

"Grab your highlighter! Patti DeNucci's *More Than Just Talk* is an enjoyable and timely read that delivers insight and practical, actionable tools you can put to use today to have more interesting and meaningful conversations, both personally and professionally."

—Kymberli S.J. Speight
Professional Speaker and Author of *I Need To Know You: How to Meet Ordinary, Extraordinary People and Improve Your Life*

"Patti DeNucci seems to be in the business of illuminating the obvious. When I read *The Intentional Networker* years ago, the lights went on for me about things I should have already known as a professional psychologist. Patti has done it again with *More Than Just Talk*. She encourages us to get past 'the seductive mirage of social media' and delivers practical, applicable, and psychologically sound principles of real conversation and how to enjoy it more often."

—Paul H. Jenkins, Ph.D.
Psychologist, Speaker, and Author of *Pathological Positivity*

. . . .

"Patti DeNucci has taken on the seemingly impossible task of developing a comprehensive guide about how to improve conversations. Her latest book, *More Than Just Talk*, accomplishes this masterfully. It's filled with stories, tips, and simple exercises that will make you think and completely upgrade your conversations—even the difficult ones. Oh, to be in a room full of people who have read this book!"

—Mike O'Krent
Founder of LifeStories Alive, LLC, and ConvoMasters

. . . .

"*More Than Just Talk* is a wonderful collection of sage advice, meaningful real-life examples, and supportive research. As an experienced fundraiser and now nonprofit consultant, I found myself agreeing and nodding 'YES!' throughout Patti's book. This is a must-read for anyone who wants to enhance their conversations."

—Michelle Crim, C.F.R.E.
Founder and President of Dynamic Development Strategies, LLC

"*More Than Just Talk* is a highly readable, motivating, and flexible field guide to better communication. The stories, techniques, and exercises can help you vastly improve how you approach, engage in, and even close your conversations. Whether you're already a savvy socializer or find socializing difficult or draining, this is a must-have for your personal or professional library."

—Matthew Pollard
Author of the Best-Selling *Introvert's Edge* Series

. . . .

"Patti's book brilliantly covers not only what good conversation is and why it's important, but also how people can actually become successful at building connections and community through conversation. I especially love the 'Try this!' challenges she includes throughout the book. They get readers thinking—and acting—through small, simple activities to immediately practice the conversation techniques Patti recommends. *More than Just Talk* is a great resource for everyone looking to improve communication."

—Marny Lifshen
Speaker and Author of *Some Assembly Required: A Networking Guide for Women*

. . . .

"*More Than Just Talk* is a must-have resource for every professional! The bite-sized chapters provide heavy-hitting strategies for enjoying more meaningful conversations with those around you. I highly recommend this book for anyone looking to fine-tune their communication skills or who wants a refresher on the fundamentals of intentional relationship development."

—Stephanie Sherman, M.S.
Center for Transforming Lives, Fort Worth (Texas)

MORE THAN JUST TALK

The Essential Guide for Anyone Who Wants to Enjoy Better Conversations

Patti DeNucci

Edited by Susan Priddy

 **ROSEWALL PRESS**
Austin, TX

MORE THAN JUST TALK
The Essential Guide for Anyone Who Wants to Enjoy Better Conversations

© 2023 Patti DeNucci
All rights reserved.

Published by:
Rosewall Press
5114 Balcones Woods Drive 307-430
Austin, TX 78759
512-970-8129

Editing: Susan Priddy (www.SusanPriddy.com)
Cover Design & Interior Layout: Kendra Cagle (www.5LakesDesign.com)
Cover Background Painting: Patti DeNucci (www.PattiDeNucci.com)
Proofreading: Marjo Rankin
Indexing: Russell Santana (www.e4Editorial.com)

Library of Congress Control Number: 2022922732

Publisher's Cataloging-in-Publication
(Provided by Cassidy Cataloguing Services, Inc.)

Names: DeNucci, Patti, author. | Priddy, Susan, editor.

Title: More than just talk : the essential guide for anyone who wants to enjoy better conversations / Patti DeNucci ; edited by Susan Priddy.

Description: Austin, TX : Rosewall Press, [2023] | Includes bibliographical references and index.

Identifiers: ISBN: 978-0-9835461-5-3 (paperback) | 978-0-9835461-6-0 (Kindle) | 978-0- 9835461-7-7 (ePub)

Subjects: LCSH: Conversation. | Interpersonal communication. | Business communication. | Social skills. | Listening. | LCGFT: Self-help publications. | BISAC: SELF-HELP / Communication & Social Skills. | BUSINESS & ECONOMICS / Business Communication / General.

Classification: LCC: BF637.C45 D46 2023 | DDC: 153.6--dc23

Patti DeNucci | www.PattiDeNucci.com | pattidenucci@gmail.com

About the Cover

....

Did you notice the abstract design in the background on the cover?

I did that!

Most people who know me professionally don't realize that I'm not just a professional writer and speaker. I'm also an artist. In college, I majored in Clothing, Textiles & Design (with emphases on journalism, marketing, design, and business) and minored in Art. For many years, when I was busy building my business and raising a son, I admit that I neglected my artistic side. (Who had the time?)

Then, at my class reunion in 2017 (never mind which one), my high school art teacher Dennis Borich asked me if I was doing any painting. When I said no, he gave me that look of total disappointment. "But you were so good!"

That got me thinking about painting again. I bought some art supplies, which mostly just sat on the shelf. Hey, I was busy writing a book—*this book!*

In 2020, as you will vividly recall, the pandemic and subsequent lockdowns hit, and I received "the message" again. On Easter Sunday, I resurrected my visually creative side, sat down with my paints at the kitchen table, turned on some music, and quickly remembered how much I enjoyed and missed this part of myself.

Since then, I have created more than 100 pieces. Some are ink and watercolor, others are mixed-media abstracts. I began sharing my work on Facebook where family, friends, and followers have been extremely encouraging.

Next thing you know, I've subscribed to a few online classes from Tracy Verdugo (TracyVerdugo.com). Oh my gosh, I so love her sweet, playful spirit and beautiful alumni community!

Among the many things Tracy has taught me: Never waste leftover paint; have fun swishing and splattering it on any extra paper that's handy; make interesting marks with everyday objects (chopsticks, jar lids, wine corks, toilet paper tubes, etc.); create interesting contrasts; loosen up and get playful; take a piece you don't like and play with it until you do; and (most importantly) let go of perfection and don't criticize what's not yet finished. These philosophies not only helped me with my painting, but they have helped with my writing and speaking, too!

All that said, what you see on the cover of this book was one of those playful pieces where I totally let go of any expectations. I only knew I wanted to use my branding colors and apply circles to the paper in some way to represent the idea of social circles and conversational interactions.

My editor Susan Priddy and my designer Kendra Cagle were both on board with the outcome. So here we are. I couldn't be more pleased to share this book and my artistic side with you!

Dedication

. . . .

This book is dedicated to
the memory of
Jan B. King,
a gifted conversationalist
and a great source of inspiration
and insight to authors such as me.

JAN B. KING
May 11, 1942—March 3, 2015

Table of Contents

Section Seven:
Dealing with Drainers and Downers (D&Ds) ..319

Foreword
By **Sara Canaday**

. . . .

If there's anyone who has actually mastered the art of the conversation, it's Patti DeNucci.

I've had the pleasure of knowing Patti as a friend and colleague for more than a decade, and her ability to connect and communicate with others is in a class by itself. She spent the better part of her professional life formally connecting people as the owner of a prestigious talent bureau, and her award-winning book about networking is still a go-to resource for people in virtually every industry.

The common thread that runs throughout her career is her capacity to engage in productive, meaningful conversations with others, so I'm delighted she is now sharing her wisdom in this area with all of us.

Beyond her innate skills, Patti did extensive research on the topic of conversations to fill this book with heart-warming examples, funny analogies, and actionable tips. This project truly became a labor of love for her, and the results are fascinating.

Patti found a creative way to dissect brilliant conversations into bite-size chunks so readers can methodically elevate the quality of their interactions. She doesn't just describe the parts of the conversation, but she shows us how to make measurable improvements. Her compelling (and often humorous) stories bring her smart strategies to life, and she knows how to gently hold up the mirror to help us see some of our own habits that might be working against us.

The timing for Patti's book also couldn't be better. Just like many things that were overlooked during the global pandemic, our conversation muscles may have atrophied a bit during months of social isolation. If small talk wasn't our strong suit before, now it's probably become a liability. Patti is providing exactly the guidance and inspiration we need to get back out there and get talking.

Whether we are struggling to begin a conversation or desperately trying to end one, we can find the advice we need in Patti's book. It is essentially an engaging and entertaining action plan from an industry pioneer. I can confidently say that this book will change the way people think about having conversations and give them the tools they need to do it with extraordinary outcomes.

SARA CANADAY *is a leadership expert, keynote speaker, and award-winning author based in Austin, Texas. For more information, visit www.SaraCanaday.com.*

Preface

....

Hello and welcome!

This book has been a long time coming. While in some ways I have been working on it all my life, it took nearly a decade for what you now hold in your hands to come into the world. Once I dove into the subject, it captured my fascination. I soon discovered so much helpful and interesting information to share, I couldn't stop writing! Thank goodness for my good friend, fellow wordsmith, and sharp-as-nails editor Susan who helped me trim, organize, and polish the massive amounts of content I initially generated!

I would have loved to publish this book sooner, but sometimes Divine Timing has its own way. As it turns out, a post-pandemic release seems to be perfect, since friends and colleagues keep telling me the world *needs this book—right now!*

So here it is!

Introduction

....

You might be wondering why you should take the time to read this book. Well, I'll tell you why...

Imagine what it would feel like to have the skills, strategies, tools, and confidence to have better conversations on a regular basis, with almost anyone, and in virtually any setting.

These exchanges could be short or long; light-hearted or deep; social or professional; in groups or in one-on-one settings; with people you know well or with strangers you're meeting for the first (and possibly only) time.

Now imagine what it would feel like to have the power and diplomacy to effectively manage (or *graciously exit*) discussions you find uninteresting, unpleasant, unproductive, or contentious. Or the ones that are simply going on for *way too long*. (You're envisioning these exact scenarios right now, aren't you? Uh-huh. We've all been there.)

If all this isn't totally ringing your bell, imagine what it would feel like to be the person others find likable and even *fascinating*. What's more, you're experiencing vast improvements in your overall mood, productivity, personal and professional relationships, creativity, career, and health!

Sound unlikely? Impossible? Ridiculous?

It's not!

Whatever your current attitudes, abilities, or challenges concerning your daily interactions with other people, if you're interested in learning how to become better at conversation and want to experience more of the joys and rewards of successful socialization—this book is for *you!*

My vision was simple: to create a guide that could inspire more people to enjoy better conversations, more often.

In some respects, it's the prequel to my first book, *The Intentional Networker: Attracting Powerful Relationships, Referrals & Results in Business.*

That book focuses on how to attract success in business (and in life) not by networking *more*, but by networking *better*. It was also an award winner, sweeping the nonfiction category of the Indie Reader Discovery Awards and chosen among thousands of entries as a ForeWord Review Book of the Year Finalist. Most importantly, *The Intentional Networker* earned enthusiastic reviews from readers of all ages, from all industries, and from all walks of life. Many tell me *The Intentional Networker* didn't just change the way they network, it changed how they approach their careers and lives. (Gotta admit: That's pretty satisfying!)

The book you're reading now offers similar epiphanies and possibilities, but with a focus on conversations.

So if you had to explain how you, personally, feel about conversations right now, what words would you use? What phrases? How would you describe yourself?

- A seasoned conversationalist who loves people and socializing.
- Someone who avoids human interaction at all costs because it feels so…awkward, boring, draining, or unpleasant.

- ⁑ Someone between these two extremes who socializes well but wants to keep improving.
- ⁑ Someone who, on any given day or in any given situation, could be any of the above.

Depending on the circumstances or the people involved, I could fit into any of these categories. In other words, *I get it.* Which is why I use "we" a lot in the following pages. We are all learning and improving!

As you go through this book, you'll find strategies, stories, facts, inspiring quotes, expert opinions, resources, discussion prompts, exercises, best practices, diagrams, and a wealth of juicy tidbits you can put to use immediately.

And here's something really refreshing:

You have the freedom to reflect on and decide what good conversation looks like, feels like, and sounds like for *you.*

Plus, you'll discover time-tested principles and practices that contribute to enjoyable exchanges for most people, in most settings. (Because, let's face it, good conversation has to be *mutually enjoyable!*)

In the pages ahead, you'll read about these important topics:

- ⁑ Why social interaction is so vital to your success and quality of life.
- ⁑ Obstacles and barriers that may be preventing you from having better conversations.
- ⁑ The advanced prep work that will ensure your success.
- ⁑ The mindset, skills, and practices in every good conversationalist's toolkit.

- ☀ How to begin a conversation with almost anyone—and keep it going with ease, authenticity, and confidence.

- ☀ The simple (but surprising and exceedingly rare) skill that can make you the most charming and memorable conversation partner ever.

- ☀ How to keep conversations on a positive track.

- ☀ How to shift, manage, or exit conversations that aren't working for you.

- ☀ And much more!

> You'll soon discover why the quality of your conversations goes well beyond what you say, how much you say, or how you say it. *It's also about what you do and how you do it.*

Rest assured...

This is NOT a book that will try to transform you into a flitty social butterfly or a dashing bon vivant who strives to be the life of the party. This isn't about how to capture (or hog) the spotlight or "work the room" like an ambitious politician up for re-election. It's definitely not about how to be a slick schmoozer who manipulates others for her own gain. And for sure it's not about trying to be "impressive" or perfect or becoming someone you're not.

Far from it. In fact, you'll see that being genuine, humble, and imperfect are traits that are likable and appreciated in most interactions.

Additionally, this book doesn't offer a one-size-fits-all, cast-in-stone, miraculous, oversimplified, cookie-cutter "system" that's supposed to work for everyone. (I'm not even sure that's possible!) But it does contain lots of ideas and tools that will help you be more socially savvy, confident, and gracious.

So go ahead. Dig in. Read this book from cover to cover. Or keep it handy so you can pick it up, take in a few pages, and reflect on or practice what you've read. You might even try popping this book open to the page you're meant to see at this very moment. Or zero in on the topic you find most interesting—or vexing.

Highlight away. Scribble notes in the margins. Flag pages that speak to you. Keep a journal. And then, don't miss out on the opportunities to begin applying your new knowledge and insights. In many sections of the book, you'll find some simple exercises titled, *Try this!* Give them a whirl—and then give yourself a gold star for every technique you try.

You might even find it interesting to discuss what you're learning with family, friends, and co-workers. And, by all means, keep a few extra copies on hand to share with people *who clearly need this book.*

Do what makes sense for you. Read and use this book your way!

I'm confident you'll start noticing a difference in the quality of your conversations (and in how you feel about having them), day by day. One page, one step, one conversation at a time.

One little caveat: Some people are much easier (and more pleasant) to talk with than others. That's just the way of the world. But once you know how to avoid, shift, manage, or bid a gracious adieu to people and exchanges that aren't your cup of tea, you will feel totally liberated.

You will also be pleasantly surprised to notice that people you were certain you wouldn't enjoy talking to are actually good conversation partners with interesting ideas, stories, and lives. You also will see what's energizing to you—and what might be uncomfortable or draining.

Whatever sections, pages, or ideas in this book you find most helpful, I hope they get you thinking, offer you intriguing techniques, ease you out of your comfort zone, and help you experience good conversations that make everything about your world better.

With that, I sincerely hope you enjoy this book and find rich, practical, and life-changing value in it!

·····································

Understanding
The Benefits of
Good Conversation

·····································

*When I think about all the
incredible things that have
happened to me because
I chose to engage in a
conversation, my head
almost blows up.*

Let's talk about the advantages.

Maybe you've noticed this phenomenon. Here we are, living in an age where we have so many ways and opportunities to connect with others. Even people who live hundreds or thousands of miles away. And yet, many of us seem to work rather hard at avoiding social engagement whenever and wherever possible. When we do choose to engage, our conversations often never move beyond the surface-y level. Or we interact in ways that aren't necessarily conducive to (and might even erode or extinguish the possibility of) true connection.

But the rulings are in.

According to many researchers and numerous studies, positive social interaction—even a few seconds of friendly banter with people we don't know and may never see again—can offer significant benefits in many facets of our lives and careers. We're talking benefits you may not even know about!

So before diving headfirst into the how-tos of good conversation, let's invest some time into fully understanding why and how conversations with our fellow humans are so vital to our happiness, success, and even our health and survival.

CHAPTER 1

Boost Your Mood and *Enhance* Your Life

If your goal is to pack more joy and satisfaction into your life, better conversations have the power to do just that.

Get those happy brain chemicals flowing

You probably know that being the recipient of a cheery greeting, a kind word, an engaging question combined with a few moments of friendly banter, or a shared laugh can brighten someone's day. But did you know that if you're the person *offering* these regular bits of jovial conversation, you get a little boost, too?

That's right! Being friendly isn't just a kindness that benefits others. It's a legit mood-lifter for *everyone* involved!

Here's why: Even a very brief greeting or positive chat creates a little burst of *oxytocin* in our bodies. This hormone, sometimes called the "tend and befriend hormone," elevates our mood. It also enhances our ability to communicate, collaborate, establish trust, and bond with others.

I swear, waving at and hollering a cheery "Hello! Good morning! How are you doing today?" to my fellow neighborhood walkers during the pandemic saved my soul and sanity. Sure, getting out of the house and enjoying some physical exercise were great. But I could literally feel the happy oxytocin boosts after each little conversation. (Not to mention I now know a lot more of my neighbors. Who, as it turns out, are really nice and interesting people!)

But here's the bummer about the oxytocin buzz: It doesn't last very long. This means we need to find ways to keep it going and flowing.

The obvious solution?

Initiate, participate in, and enjoy more friendly, positive interactions throughout the day. With family, friends, neighbors, casual acquaintances, colleagues, customers, the mailman, the lady with the pretty spaniel who's out walking each morning, the Amazon delivery woman, the garbage truck driver—pretty much anyone.

Barbara L. Fredrickson, Ph.D., author of *Love 2.0: How Our Supreme Emotion Affects Everything We Feel, Think, Do, and Become* and a professor who studies positive emotions, calls these pleasant and essential exchanges "micro-moments of connection." I call them simply "being friendly."

Per Dr. Fredrickson, these lovely micro-moments are "momentary up-wellings of three tightly woven events," which I'm paraphrasing here:

1. **You share warm feelings.** ("Hello! Good morning!" "How are you doing?")

2. **You "sync up," maybe as you acknowledge something you have in common at that moment.** ("Gorgeous day out there!" "Yes, it sure is!")

3. **You express mutual care and interest in each other's well-being.** ("Hope you enjoy your day!" "You, too!")

TRY THIS!

Watch for oxytocin in action!

See if you can spot the friendly micro-moment trifecta in your casual interactions today. Warm feelings. Brains syncing up. Interest in the other's well-being. Notice how they impact your mood. We tend to think these are no big deal, but they are important for our overall mental and physical health!

◀ ▲ ▶

Putting more friendliness out into the world is a simple habit that can make life better for you and for everyone you encounter.

According to researchers, such as behavioral scientists Nicholas Epley and Juliana Schroeder, people who make a deliberate effort to be social with those around them (whether they are family, friends, colleagues, or strangers) often report feeling happier than when they keep to themselves.

The oxytocin bursts are part of it. But here's another reason: When we talk to strangers and casual acquaintances, we tend to show a friendlier, warmer, and happier version of ourselves. Ever noticed this?

Let's say you're in a bit of a funk or yelling at your kids or grumbling about a work issue one moment. Then suddenly you're smiling and laughing with the checkout clerk or your neighbor. Your entire mood has pivoted. This is similar to what happens when you smile (*even when you don't feel like smiling*). You start to feel a little more chipper. Once again, the actions of being friendly and smiling literally shift our brain chemistry, even though we didn't start out feeling happy.

Researchers Katherine L. Fiori, Chair of the Gordon F. Derner School of Psychology at Adelphi University, and Karen L. Fingerman, Professor of Human Development and Family Sciences at The University of Texas at Austin, have published some interesting findings on this topic.

Their discoveries? While close friends are certainly important, casual acquaintances (also known as "weak ties") offer us instant stimulation and community. They provide us with a sense of belonging, as well as variety and novelty. They give us a chance to move past the "shorthand" and predictable interactions we have with our loved ones. And the impact runs deeper than you might expect.

Spontaneous conversations with these acquaintances have the power to stimulate our brains and lift our moods.

This effect becomes even more pronounced and beneficial as we age.

It's a lot like musicians getting together to just riff. Jazz saxophonist Stan Getz observed that random, spontaneous conversation is the only art form other than jazz that can create so much satisfaction.

One way to sum this up perfectly comes from the little slip of wisdom I found inside a Chinese fortune cookie and have kept in my wallet for years: "Say hello to others. You will have a happier day." Sounds positive and powerful to me!

Spread the good vibes

On a similar note, ever noticed that the good feelings we give and get from a quick dose of friendly banter can be "contagious?" Experts have verified that these good feelings can resonate for at least three layers of interaction. Maybe even further.

Let's say you offer a friendly hello to your neighbor as he's putting out the trash. You continue to engage in a quick, cheery chat. Doesn't have to be anything special. He goes inside and says something loving and upbeat to his wife. (Always a good idea!) Now she's in a good mood, so she says something extra sweet and supportive to their child as she heads off to school. From there, the child sits with and shares her breakfast muffin with a new friend on the bus.

Who knows where the good vibes will go from there?

When I think of someone who made a lifelong habit of greeting and initiating short, happy conversations with everyone he met, I think of Kenneth Davis. He was the greeter at one of my neighborhood grocery stores for nearly 20 years. He had a bright smile and a friendly word for everyone. He also knew many of the regulars, including me, by name.

Kenneth had a consistently upbeat, cordial attitude. Not just because it was his job, but because he knew it made people happy, including him. Now that he's retired, going to the store has lost some of its luster and personality. He is definitely missed!

TRY THIS!

Identify your conversation role models.

Think of people you know (or encounter regularly) who are consistent in their friendliness and bring joy to others.

What do you enjoy most about these people?

_____

_____

What benefits do they bring to others?

_____

_____

What rewards do you think they enjoy for being friendly?

_____

_____

How could you follow their good example?

_____

_____

◂▴▸

Dive deeper for even more value and connection

Brief encounters have their place and value, but let's not discount the amazing benefits of longer, deeper discussions. These can be with new acquaintances—presenting opportunities to get to know each other better—or they can be regular visits or in-depth discussions on mutually interesting topics with loved ones, friends, and colleagues.

Handled with care and sincerity, longer exchanges can create meaningful and profound levels of enjoyment and satisfaction. They help us learn, explore, build understanding, find common interests, and strengthen bonds.

If you've ever enjoyed a long, leisurely visit with a loved one, a colleague, or even someone you've just met, you may know what I'm talking about. It's not just a good way to pass the time. It's a memorable and meaningful experience. You may walk away feeling uplifted, energized, amused, inspired, or even enlightened. You look forward to doing it again.

Also, when you spend time diving deep into a topic of mutual interest or "getting real" with another person, you may discover you're not the only one who has had a specific experience or has struggled with a certain challenge. Or you finally find someone who shares a similar philosophy or viewpoint—or a completely different one that's no less interesting.

It expands your world.

And, of course, you might also find that, yes, there is indeed someone on this planet who shares the same wacky (or subtle) sense of humor you do. Or has the same hobbies or dreams.

You'll learn about ways to create and enjoy more of these deeper and potentially rich conversations in the chapters ahead.

Meanwhile, consider this from Ruth Whippman, a British author and journalist who studies and writes about the impact of social isolation: "Study after study shows that good social relationships are the strongest, most consistent predictor there is of a happy life. This finding cuts across race, age, gender, income, and social class so overwhelmingly that it dwarfs any other factor."

Private chef Louis Cloete adds that enjoying good conversation goes beyond mere happiness for him. "Human connection leaves me with a satisfied feeling of having had a wonderful 'meal'—a feeling of happy contentment, like things are right and my soul has been fed."

To sum up: The frequency, depth, and quality of our conversations matter to our happiness and satisfaction with life. But there's more. Lots more.

Listen for, learn from—and savor—the wisdom and inspiration

While many conversations can be pleasant and fulfilling, some can have a more significant impact on us. These interactions can happen with almost anyone. They might even be the only (or last) conversation we have with this person. And yet, the words spoken cling and resonate, impacting or changing us in some special way.

A conversation that has stayed with me throughout my adult life is one I had with my grandfather just before I graduated from college and moved to Texas.

Grampa was in ill health and wheelchair-bound, but he listened with interest to news I shared about school, my move, my fiancé, and my new career prospects. It was clear he was sad to see me moving to a different state, yet very proud of me and excited for my future.

As we said our goodbyes, I gave Grampa a gentle hug and a kiss. But before I could turn to leave, he reached for my hand one last time, gave it a firm squeeze, and looked at me with eyes glistening. With all the energy, enthusiasm, and love he could muster, he said, "You have a *good* life!"

This was so much more than a wish. It was a blessing. Perhaps even an assignment. Or an *order*.

Apparently, Grampa knew something I didn't. Within the year he contracted pneumonia and didn't recover. I never saw him again. His last words to me suddenly took on even greater significance.

"You have a *good* life!"

So many of our conversations, long or short, have the power to give us what we need in the moment—or to prepare us for what's up ahead.

This brings to mind one of my very favorite quotes from author, Holocaust survivor, and heroine Corrie ten Boom. She wrote these words in her autobiographical book, *The Hiding Place:* "Every experience God gives us, every person He puts into our lives is the perfect preparation for the future that only He can see."

Ms. ten Boom didn't say specifically "every conversation," but I think you get what I mean. Experiences and people matter, but every conversation—and the words, wisdom, and energy they contain—matters, too.

High-impact conversations.

Ever had an interaction that touched you in a profound and lasting way?

Perhaps this experience...

- Gave you reassurance, motivation, or strength.
- Helped you get through a challenging moment or situation.
- Lifted your mood at a critical time.
- Provided you with a much-needed reality check.
- Offered you an important piece of information or feedback.
- Revealed a profound truth or new perspective.
- Sparked a fresh idea.
- Led you to an opportunity, resource, connection, or relationship.
- Left with you a lasting and happy memory of a loved one.
- Presented you with some other benefit.

Reflect on the conversation. Who was the person you spoke with and what were the circumstances?

_____

_____

_____

What was said?

_____
_____
_____
_____

How did it impact you?

_____
_____
_____
_____

Why do you suppose that is?

_____
_____
_____
_____

◂▴▸

NOTES:

_____
_____
_____
_____
_____
_____
_____
_____

CHAPTER

2

Build *Connection*
and Community

Think about the friendships and connections you've developed over the years. It's amazing to think that every one of them began with a conversation!

TRY
THIS!

The roots of friendship.

Let's deconstruct some of your current relationships—the ones you find valuable and enjoyable. Where and how did these conversations and connections begin?

See if you note any patterns.

The person	How we met	Our first conversation(s)
_____	_____	_____
_____	_____	_____
_____	_____	_____
_____	_____	_____

◂▴▸

Find your tribe—and seek out some variety, too

Conversations can help us uncover common (or contrasting) backgrounds, interests, experiences, beliefs, and connections. As we share who we are—where we're from, what we've experienced, what's important to us, what we are working on, where we're going, who we know, and so on—the bonds between us can grow and strengthen. This can give us an immediate sense of connection and community.

> It's natural to seek out and gravitate toward the people with whom we immediately identify and resonate.

This can be comforting and sometimes even relieving. We've experienced a touchpoint.

- ※ "Really? You love Saturday morning hikes? Me, too!"
- ※ "No way! The town where you grew up is just four miles down the road from where I grew up!"
- ※ "Oh, yeah! I'm also a huge fan of bluegrass music!"
- ※ "Absolutely! Sauvignon blanc over chardonnay any day!"

※ "You're kidding! You've been to Loutro? Most people have never heard of it."

※ "What? You collect PEZ dispensers, too?"

Speaking of PEZ dispensers, I know someone who actually collects them: author and speaker Mike Robertson. "I don't often run into someone who collects PEZ and knows anything about them," he said. "But when I do, there's an instant connection. I know we are going to have an enjoyable conversation."

Conversation also can help us discover and experience entirely new worlds as we listen to others who have seen, done, and experienced things we haven't or couldn't even imagine.

Or perhaps we hear about beliefs, ways of life, careers, or connections that are vastly different from ours. This brings us a much-needed perspective and adds to the diversity of our conversation range and portfolio. It can benefit almost any group or community. You'll learn a lot more up ahead about how to better engage in (and hopefully enjoy) conversations with people who aren't just like you.

"Special interest" discussions offer yet another advantage—especially if we are interested in expanding our learning, experience, or practice in certain areas. Associations and clubs form this way and can be based on personal or professional interests.

I might decide I want to learn more about wine. If I join a wine club, take a wine class or tour, or host a wine-tasting party, it's quite likely that the experience will expand my knowledge and give me forums where I can converse with people who share this interest.

The same could go for any number of topics or areas of focus. PEZ dispensers. Surgery. Plumbing. Writing books. Reading books. Hiking. Needlework. Learning a new language. History. Weaving. Painting. Fly fishing. Ceramics. Golf. Birdwatching. Outdoor yoga with baby goats.

The list is endless.

Want to increase the chances of being among people who share your interests? Host a gathering that centers around one of those interests and see who shows up.

My friend Connie hosted a very successful, one-time book discussion that centered around Viktor Frankl's beautiful book, *Man's Search for Meaning*. I fondly recall what a poignant evening that was, primarily because those who attended were book lovers and had actually read the book!

Another friend, Sherry, created a group that studied and discussed the nine Enneagram personality types. "It was a fast-track way to get to know each other because we all took the Enneagram profile test, discussed the results, and got to know and understand each other on a deeper level."

And I can't resist adding this one: My friends Robert and Julie hosted a wine-tasting party where guests were asked to "bring a bottle of wine and a story." We could share a specific tale about the wine we selected, a general story involving wine, or whatever we wanted. There were no formal presentations, but everyone showed up with wine and conversations ready to flow. It was delicious!

And speaking of delicious conversation, it won't surprise you to learn that I enjoy hosting conversation salons. Here, I invite diverse groups of friends, colleagues, and neighbors for an evening gathering. The participant list and discussion topics are different every time. We have a few casual guidelines and a loose format. Other than that, the conversation wanders wherever it will. Everyone who shows up loves good conversation, and we explore many fascinating topics together.

TRY THIS!

On your mark, get set …

Maybe it's time for you to host or help organize an event that will generate the good conversations you're wanting to enjoy.

What conversations are you craving? What are your interests or areas to explore?

_____

_____

_____

_____

When, where, and how could you do this?

_____

_____

_____

_____

Who would you like to invite?

_____

_____

_____

_____

◄ ▲ ►

When you think about it, almost every interaction—whether that involves two people or several—could be mapped out on a Venn diagram. You are discovering how you are similar and how you are different.

If you're not familiar with Venn diagrams, they consist of two or more circles that intersect to illustrate where there is contrast as well as common ground. (And trust me, there's always common ground. Are you breathing? Are you human? Do you eat food? Boom! That's three things in common right there.)

Remember the compare-and-contrast thing your teacher made you do in English or literature class? Venn diagrams are like that.

Illustration by Jessica Hagy (www.JessicaHagy.info)

Just say Venn!

Dig out and dust off your compare-and-contrast skills to generate a conversation or discussion that helps you get to know another person. Simply explore with a conversation partner:

- What do we have in common?
- How are we different?

This is particularly fun as an icebreaker game at a gathering where a lot of people don't know each other. Each person pairs up with someone and starts having a conversation. Your task is to discover at least three things you have in common and three ways you are different before you move on to your next conversation partner.

You'll likely generate some smiles and laughs as you discuss obvious (and not-so-obvious) similarities and uncover some fascinating differences.

Celebrate it all! Bonus points if you actually jot these down in Venn-diagram style and share with the larger group later.

◂▴▸

Comparing and contrasting is not only fun and easy, but it also has the power to make your conversations a lot more interesting and multidimensional.

You will see up ahead how this can go a long way in helping you attract and generate better conversations.

Build bridges and strengthen teams

Conversations can help us get to know each other and build bonds. If we build those bonds with sincerity and care, they can lead to many benefits. These include a more cohesive, cooperative, and trusting group dynamic. This matters immensely in sports teams, families, organizations, committees, neighborhoods, and other "collections" of people.

Simply put, a well-bonded group has far less distrust and drama. Plus, it will likely feature a better overall culture, which increases satisfaction and performance.

If you need a good example, consider the movie, "Remember the Titans" (2000). It's based on a true story about a newly integrated high school football team in Arlington, Virginia, in the 1970s.

In one scene, Coach Herman Boone (played by Denzel Washington) is leading summer training camp and trying to find ways to build unity while reducing conflict and distrust within the team. He knows his players have the talent and the potential to come together and win the state championship. But racial tensions, egos, and an array of bitter feelings are generating drama and creating destructive power struggles that will prevent the team from winning any games, let alone performing at the ultimate level.

To remedy this volatile situation, Coach Boone issues an order. Every team member is required to have a one-on-one conversation with every other player before camp ends.

The boys begin to talk with and listen to each other, reluctantly at first. Then things shift. Unlikely bonds and friendships begin to form. Understanding, appreciation, and camaraderie emerge. It's no surprise that the team starts playing a *lot better.*

I won't ruin the outcome for you if you haven't seen the movie, but I think you can guess the results.

Keep memories alive and create new ones

Talking about shared memories is a favorite pastime for many people, especially at meetings, gatherings, and reunions where we can rehash highlights of our common experiences and histories. These interactions could be with family members, friends, classmates, peers, and co-workers.

Wakes, funerals, and memorials for those we love offer special versions of this opportunity. Everyone shares their fond memories of the person who has passed.

These can be profound and heart-warming conversations that may prompt us to tear up or even find ourselves laughing together.

One of my favorite lines from the movie "Steel Magnolias" (1989) is when Truvey Jones (played by Dolly Parton) says, "Laughter through tears is my favorite emotion."

Mine, too. It can be *very* affirming and healing.

And who hasn't enjoyed the fun of reviewing in extensive detail the interesting (okay, maybe even outrageous) details of a party the night before? It's fun and satisfying as we recall, compare, and analyze what happened to further strengthen our bonds and collective memories.

If we are having new conversations and new experiences together while we are sharing memories, we are creating new memories in the process.

As a footnote: I'm primarily referring to happy, positive memories that we share and revive on occasion. Some negative or traumatic memories are best put behind us or worked through with the help of a professional. And I certainly don't recommend conversations that keep us stuck in the past.

TRY THIS!

Next stop: Memory Lane.

How does it feel for you to rehash fond memories and mutual experiences with colleagues, classmates, friends, or family members? Do you find value in these conversations? Why or why not?

_____

_____

_____

_____

◂▴▸

Make others feel welcomed

Ever been the new person in a group, neighborhood, organization, or class? Ever been a guest at a gathering where you didn't know a soul? Perhaps you've attended a professional meeting or industry conference for the first time. You were standing off by yourself, awkwardly holding a cup of coffee or a glass of questionable zinfandel and wondering, *"Now* what am I supposed to do?" Maybe you felt like you had the word "Newbie" tattooed in red ink across your forehead.

We've all been there.

It can be uncomfortable, intimidating, and lonely to feel like the odd person out. Especially when everyone else seems to be talking and having a great time.

This means it can feel *really good*—like you've just been rescued—when someone approaches you with a smile, introduces themselves, welcomes you, introduces you to others, and shows you around.

I can feel a sense of welcome relief just writing about this!

Can you see how easy it is to become an instant hero simply by being the one who is willing to initiate a friendly chat and help someone feel more at ease? You'll find lots of ways to be that person in the pages ahead.

In the meantime, I'll share a quick story.

I vividly recall meeting my high school classmate, Lori, for the first time at the start of our junior year. It was third-period American History class with Mrs. Rukavina.

As I entered the classroom, I chose a seat next to a pretty blonde girl I'd never seen before. As I sat down, I did what seemed like the right thing to do: I introduced myself.

"Hi, I'm Patti. You new here?"

Indeed, she was. We began to chat. Within seconds, we discovered how much we had in common. Her dad had once worked at my dad's auto dealership. How cool was that? The visit was short because we only had a few moments before the class bell rang. But the emotional imprint was there.

How do I know?

More than two decades later at our 20th class reunion, Lori and I had the chance to visit again. In addition to 20 years of news and updates, Lori told me how much my friendliness that first day of school had meant to her. In turn, Lori's gratitude touched my heart.

It's so easy to think that kind words and thoughtful actions are no big deal, go unappreciated, or are quickly forgotten. But I can assure you, they aren't. The choice to be friendly and welcoming to others *matters*.

I can tell you that Lori's words of appreciation at our reunion meant the world to me. But they would take on even more meaning a few years later, when Lori died of cancer.

It's worth noting: What impression or imprint do you create and leave behind? What might others appreciate about you, even if you never hear about it? How will your words and conversations matter to others?

Good conversation is so much more than simply choosing what words to say. It's also about *how* we say them and the intention, attitude, and spirit we bring to each interaction.

Daniel Goleman—psychologist, science journalist, and acclaimed author of *Social Intelligence: The Revolutionary New Science of Human*

Relationships—notes that a "life well lived" means "conducting ourselves in ways that are beneficial *even at the subtle level* for those with whom we connect."

The Vietnamese monk and peace activist Thich Nhat Hanh says this another way, calling mindful speaking a "deep practice" because "the way we speak to others can offer them joy, happiness, self-confidence, hope, trust, and enlightenment."

What a gift! And it doesn't cost us a single penny.

. . . .

Elevate Your Professional and Personal Success

. . . .

Conversations can definitely bring a richer tapestry of colors to our personal lives, but they can also give us a distinct professional edge. This is true whether you work for an organization or run your own business. It's also valid whether you are just beginning your career, a leader at the top, or anywhere in between.

I've found plenty of evidence in my life and career to enthusiastically agree with American actor, writer, lawyer, and commentator Ben Stein when he says, "Personal relationships are the fertile soil from which all advancement, all success, all achievement in real life grows."

Robert Wolcott and Michael Lippitz, co-authors of *Grow from Within: Mastering Corporate Entrepreneurship and Innovation,* reiterate that same point: "Having a robust network is one of the most important factors in succeeding as an innovator or entrepreneur, inside or outside a large corporation."

And, of course, you can't build your relationships and networks if you're not having conversations. So, let's unpack this.

How can conversations impact your career and your success?

Become more visible and likable

Every warm and positive interaction with colleagues and customers, whether it's about work or something *totally unrelated* (yes, you read that right), has the potential to make an impression and create a memorable connection. Some of these connections can turn into powerful relationships that positively impact (and also transcend) work.

Even if you don't become best friends with your peers and clients, your conversations on both work and non-work topics still establish and solidify how people see and experience you. This ultimately impacts your likability, reputation, influence, and success. You've made an emotional imprint and an impact.

Several studies reveal that people who regularly partake in conversations on a variety of topics at work are often viewed as more likable and successful than people who keep to themselves.

Of course, job performance is still key. But being a friendly and considerate co-worker who can chat about more than just "shop talk" is a big plus.

Daniel Threlfall, CMO and co-founder at KosmoTime, notes, "What really matters, I have discovered, is conversation. The chatter around the water cooler. The small talk before the meeting. The huddle in the cubicle. The update in the elevator. These small [exchanges] are where leadership becomes evident, culture is formed, and success is born."

But what if you're someone who prefers to keep to yourself at work, staying focused, nose to the grindstone, getting things done, and all that? You're saving any socializing energy *strictly* for close friends and family.

Sorry to break it to you, but the all-work-and-no-conversation mindset can work against you.

Your co-workers (and your boss) may misinterpret your social selectivity and solitary "work ethic" as aloofness or disinterest in being part of the group and a team player. In other words, they may see you as unfriendly and disinterested.

Just saying.

By the way, this can be detrimental to your personal life as well.

Sophia Dembling, author of *The Introvert's Way: Living a Quiet Life in a Noisy World,* writes, "One of the risks of being quiet is that the other people can fill your silence with their own interpretation: You're bored. You're depressed. You're shy. You're stuck up. You're judgmental. When others can't read us, they write their own story—not always one we choose or that's true to who we are."

Related to this...

Boost your intelligence and creativity

Not sure who started this rumor or philosophy, but many of us are led to believe that top performers and prolific creators are loners. They are tethered to their keyboards or workstations and rarely have (or make) time to socialize. They may argue: "Who has the bandwidth for unnecessary interruptions or really wants to engage in random, mindless chit-chat? Can't you see we're *busy* trying to come up with brilliant ideas and *get things done?*"

Sure, solitude is part of the success equation. It gives us time and space to reflect, focus, think, create, and move through our To-Do Lists. I'm a total fan of that, and maybe you are, too.

Yet if you look at the *actual* workstyles and routines of famous, brilliant, and prolific geniuses, innovators, and leaders throughout the centuries, you'll quickly see that stimulating conversations played a role in their success.

Gatherings were critical to jumpstarting, enhancing, and sometimes even offering a revitalizing break from just about any type of intellectual or creative work.

Some of these peak performers even created little groups—clubs, masterminds, associations—that met regularly over the course of years. This gave them much-needed and regularly scheduled socialization, including opportunities for conversations that further enhanced their thinking, creativity, and output.

Studies such as the 1995 *Myth of the Lone Genius* project reveal that, in the long run, successful people generally create and accomplish more and do better work when they blend in social time with people who can inform, inspire, energize, mentor, and support them. And yes, sometimes distract them for brief periods.

Who among us couldn't benefit from a little inspirational "refresh," an interesting new perspective, or an enjoyable session of *non-work* socializing? Over a meal or a beverage or around a fire? How about during a walk, a game of golf, or a leisurely Sunday drive?

And it's worth emphasizing:

Some of our conversations should be with people who aren't exactly like us so we can gain access to different views, experiences, ideas, and creative options.

These vastly expand our ability to do our jobs and create at a higher level.

No doubt this is why conferences (think of the word *confer*—to discuss, talk, or converse) and conventions (think of the word *convene*—to meet or assemble as a group) are so vital to various industries. The formal learning sessions often held at these events can be outstanding for professional development. But many will agree that it's the spontaneous banter that takes place during breaks and receptions—and in the hallways, elevators, bars, and cafés—that are the most interesting and memorable.

Nineteenth century sociologist Émile Durkheim coined a term for the excitement, amplified energy, and emotion generated by a group experiencing something together: "collective effervescence."

I'll take a big, frosty glass of that!

You could argue that you're just not social and prefer to learn from books, videos, and other sources. These are certainly helpful and put a lot of information at our fingertips. But real-time conversations are different. They give us the opportunity to have a spontaneous and real-time *dialogue*. A back-and-forth. A tête-à-tête. We can think out loud, pose questions, hear other views, test theories, debate key points, get a reality check, laugh at our own foibles, and potentially shift our perspectives.

Socializing stimulates our brains very differently than reading or watching a video.

We also may have one of those amazing, synchronistic moments when we hear something that seems totally irrelevant but, for whatever *crazy reason*, it reminds us of something else.

Neurons in a previously mothballed section of our brain come alive. We receive the answer we've been seeking. We bring this awareness into the discussion. The lights flash, the dots connect, another epiphany presents itself, the angels break into song, and we experience a zesty zing of creativity. Or we get a glimpse of the precious answer we've been relentlessly seeking. Likewise, we may say something that sparks a valuable new idea or epiphany for another. Finally!!

In his book, *The Art of Creative Thinking*, Wilfred A. Peterson notes, "Brainstorming is thinking together, harnessing imaginative power. It is mental teamwork, going into a creative huddle… Wherever you are, whoever you are, whatever your project, brainstorming will widen the horizons of your thinking."

And, finally, an anonymous-but-spot-on Chinese proverb reinforces this whole idea:

"A single conversation across the table with a wise person is worth a month's study of books."

Now *there's* a shortcut I could support!

Still a bit skeptical?

It's been proven time and again that well-networked, conversationally astute people tend to produce a higher quantity and quality of ideas because their knowledge comes from a wide variety of sources.

They spend far less time grinding away in the doldrums, stuck in their own minds, and enjoy far more breakthroughs.

Jeff Goins—American author, blogger, speaker, and founder of Tribe Writers, an online community for (you guessed it!) writers—adds, "Every success story is really a story of community."

And I can't help but share this from Oxford scholar Theodore Zeldin:

"Conversation is a meeting of minds with different memories and habits. When minds meet, they don't just exchange facts. They transform them, reshape them, draw different implications from them, engage in new trains of thought. Conversations don't just reshuffle the cards. They create new cards."

Conversation before creativity.

Next time you're "stuck" on a project or feeling burned out or maybe creatively challenged, schedule a visit—in person or by phone—with someone you know, like, trust, and are inspired by.

- ☀ Tell them what you're working on (or let them see it).
- ☀ What *constructive* thoughts do they have for you?

Just as important: Discuss other unplanned and unrelated topics.

- ☀ Share news and stories.
- ☀ Vent a little.
- ☀ Find things to laugh about.
- ☀ Let your brain loosen up.
- ☀ Meander across random topics.
- ☀ Let the conversation *flow*.

See what transpires afterward.

- ☀ How do you feel?
- ☀ How's your energy level?
- ☀ What has shifted?
- ☀ Any new ideas emerge?
- ☀ What are you able to accomplish?

◂▴▸

Build your ability to motivate and influence

Whether you're the boss trying to motivate your team, an entrepreneur launching a new product or service, a philanthropist trying to recruit donors and patrons, or even an author selling her new book (*ahem*), conversations are effective ways to educate, enroll, inspire, influence, motivate, and persuade.

When we actively learn about and spend time practicing to become better conversationalists, this process can boost our confidence and credibility. It's also the key to helping us have more powerful and persuasive discussions.

Be in the know

Want to stay up to the minute with the latest industry news and trends, hear about potential opportunities (before everyone else!), or discover the best resources and expertise without having to speculate or go through the usual channels or guesswork?

Conversations are your ticket.

Sure, we can get some of our information and intelligence via mass media, social media, online forums, bulletin boards, and other resources. But well-timed, face-to-face conversations can often lead us to all kinds of timely and valuable details and opportunities that we might not otherwise hear about. This is what makes some people "insiders"—and others, the ones who get left in the dust.

I'm guessing you'd prefer to be the former rather than the latter.

In the same vein, if you've ever been traveling or are new to a community or organization, you may know that gathering intelligence and helpful tips from the locals and experts is a powerful practice. You quickly learn the "dos" and "don'ts," avoid mistakes and missteps, and slide up and over the learning curve a lot faster than if you were totally on your own.

Improve your productivity and performance

How many misunderstandings, delays, or other problems are created when we don't talk to each other, forget to share important information, or communicate vaguely? I'm sure you can think of quite a few instances when not being in touch in a timely way created tensions and issues. Maybe even catastrophic problems.

And, as you read earlier in the story from "Remember the Titans," conversations help teams communicate, cooperate, bond, build understanding and trust, get things done, and function better. These teams enjoy higher morale and better overall productivity. In addition, the work environment becomes more efficient, pleasant, and less stressful. Which in turn can reduce absenteeism and turnover, lower costs, and create happier customers.

What about the value of constructive feedback? It's not always what we want to hear. But gentle yet honest, solutions-oriented conversations and critiques from our team members, customers, and others we trust can be invaluable. And, of course, we want to hear the good feedback, too!

Some organizations host once-a-week meetings offsite where there are "no secrets." Here, the managers or executives give their staff members permission to ask anything and the freedom and support to honestly share what others really need to know—the good, the bad, and the ugly. Among the questions asked:

- "What do I need to know?"
- "What's the good news we can celebrate?"

- ☀ "Where are we making progress?"
- ☀ "What's the not-so-good news we need to work on?"
- ☀ "What questions do you have for us?"
- ☀ "How can we help / support you?"

The secret to making these sessions effective is to:

- ☀ Keep the conversations on track (so they don't turn into whining sessions).
- ☀ Give everyone equal time to speak.
- ☀ Encourage clarifying questions.
- ☀ End all discussions on a positive note.

Imagine what something like this could do for any team, organization, committee, family, friendship, partnership, or marriage!

Attract champions who build your confidence

We can all use some concentrated and capable guidance as we navigate our careers, build our businesses, solve problems, and tackle big projects. If we are willing to partake in a variety of discussions with a range of peers (there's that value-in-variety thing again), we are far more likely to discover and get to know those special people who can inspire and mentor us, show us the ropes, fill in the gaps of what we don't know, and support our efforts on a regular basis.

The conversations and connections we have with these special advocates and wise experts can boost our confidence, reduce our anxieties, motivate us, rekindle our enthusiasm, and keep us forging ahead toward success, even when the going gets tough or the path is unclear.

Professional speaker, speaking coach, and author Jim Comer aptly refers to these treasured connections as "major supporters." They are priceless, and they don't just instantly appear in our lives. We have to work at finding them, attracting them, building bonds with them, and earning their loyalty, one conversation at a time.

Create priceless opportunities in the moment

Sometimes conversations and the connections they generate can prompt or create an opportunity that otherwise wouldn't exist.

Consider this story from Debra Fine, author of *The Fine Art of Small Talk: How to Start a Conversation, Keep It Going, Build Networking Skills, and Leave A Positive Impression.*

While waiting in the TSA security line at Denver International Airport, Fine realized she was standing just a few feet away from Barry Peterson, the international and national correspondent for CBS News. She could have just said to herself, "Huh, that's cool" and continued on her way. But she didn't. She walked over to him, extended her hand, and introduced herself.

"I asked where he was going and what he was working on," says Fine. "We had a pleasant conversation that resulted in him doing a segment on small talk for CBS Sunday, with me as the featured interview."

What a great opportunity for an author!

And all it took was gathering the courage to say hello, introduce herself, ask Mr. Peterson what he was working on, listen, and let the exchange flow from there.

Similarly, here's what actor Sam Stinson does when he runs into a peer, especially one who is famous or successful. Rather than freezing up or requesting a photo or autograph, he starts a conversation. He often asks a career-related question: Any good advice to share? Got any tips on handling rejection or bouncing back after a failure? What helped you take your acting career to the next level?

"These generate some of the most helpful and meaningful conversations I've ever had," Stinson says.

> *A good lessen to remember.*
>
> When we encounter someone who is our senior at work, who is a decision-maker, or who we perceive to be more important or famous or otherwise "above" us, knowing what to ask or say can be a conversation game-changer. With the right conversation intentions, confidence, and tools, which you'll discover in the coming pages, you'll be comfortable talking to just about anyone!

Embark on a journey of greater self-discovery

As we speak and connect with others, we have the opportunity to process perspectives, issues, and challenges out loud. When we do this, something interesting and unexpected can take place: We learn more about *ourselves.*

We catch ourselves in odd thought processes and loops. We spot and unravel our quirks, failings, and more. *Hopefully* this awareness helps us develop into better versions of ourselves.

As an added bonus, this can improve our relationships with others and bring our future conversations to a whole new level.

Harriet Lerner supports this idea wholeheartedly. She's a clinical psychologist and author of numerous books on relationships, including *The Dance of Intimacy, The Dance of Connection,* and *Marriage Rules.*

"Only through our connectedness to others can we really know and enhance the self," Lerner says. "And only by working on the self can we begin to enhance our connectedness."

This is why our friends, our peers, and the people in our support groups, coaching sessions, and masterminds can be so helpful as we are dealing with challenges.

When we share what's happening, how we feel about it, and what we hope to do about it, we are experiencing ourselves in powerful new ways.

As we listen to and consider what others share and what they are doing, we can compare, clarify, or possibly even soften or shift our own perspectives, opinions, and beliefs. We may even build a newfound sense of confidence or identity. We have learned, discovered, and grown, both personally and professionally.

Ron J. West, executive coach and creator of The Chrysalis (Vertical Leadership Development) Program®, believes in the power of conversation, both in his work and in his personal life. He notes, "Good conversation stretches me. It sparks new thinking, deeper thinking. It helps me reframe my own thoughts, ideas, and opinions. I find it energizing and inspiring."

The brilliant American physician, poet, and polymath Oliver Wendell Holmes, Sr., also believed in the power of conversations as a way to self-examine, to re-examine, and to transform.

"I talk half the time to find out my own thoughts, as a school-boy turns his pockets inside out to see what is in them," he said. "One brings to light all sorts of personal property he had forgotten in his inventory."

Considered one of the greatest writers of his time, Holmes was a member of the Fireside Poets group. Can you imagine him attending the meetings, sharing his thoughts, listening to what others in the room had to say, and enjoying the many dazzling exchanges that likely took place?

Oh, to be a fly on the wall during one of their discussions!

TRY THIS!

Holmes, sweet Holmes!

Consider the wisdom of a great poet. Holmes believed that "a mind once stretched by a new idea never regains its original dimensions." Do you find this to be true? Can you think of an instance where listening to or participating in a group conversation shifted something in you that changed you forever? Reflect on and write about that experience.

_____
_____
_____
_____
_____
_____
_____
_____

◄ ▲ ►

Become a better role model

What happens when we avoid, miss out on, or even mishandle opportunities to acknowledge and talk with others in positive and engaging ways? In other words, what's the result when we are oblivious to someone's presence or treat them as if they are "beneath" us?

For starters, we may hurt feelings. Secondly, we may be building a reputation as an unfriendly and disrespectful person. Most importantly, we are missing the chance to set good examples and standards for what courtesy, friendliness, kindness, and respect can look and sound like.

This "good example" is part of what Jan Goss, founder of Civility Consulting, calls "showing up well."

Showing up well is a choice that can make a dramatic difference, not just to us, but also to our colleagues, customers, everyone in our professional and personal spheres, and anyone with whom we come in contact. Even more vital, it's critical that we act as good social examples for our loved ones, especially young people.

Psychologist Richard Weissbourd, Ed.D., of the Harvard Graduate School of Education notes that our children are powerfully—perhaps even permanently—impacted by how we treat others socially.

"Children learn empathy, not just by how we treat those closest to us, but also by how we acknowledge the strangers around us," says Weissbourd. "They notice if we appreciate the server in a restaurant and say hello to the mail carrier. They also notice if we treat them like they're invisible or inferior."

"See the light in others, and treat them as if that is all you see."
—Wayne W. Dyer
Motivational Speaker and Author

When we engage courageously and warmly with others, we are demonstrating to our young people—and to everyone in our midst—how to "humanize others across the usual divides."

This is a valuable skill and practice that we owe them and must model to them.

CHAPTER 4

Improve Your Health and *Longevity*

You've read about the ways conversations can make life and work better while stimulating and expanding our thinking. Now let's examine all the ways they can impact our health and life expectancy.

Research tells us that people who regularly engage in meaningful and varied forms of socializing—while also maintaining an upbeat outlook—tend to enjoy better health and live longer, fuller lives.

More specifically, sociable people tend to experience less pain and inflammation, develop fewer illnesses and chronic diseases, and recover from sickness and other health challenges more successfully. They also have a slower rate of cognitive decline and maintain their zest for life.

I'm all over that! How about you?

Help to extend your own life (yes, really!)

In case you think this longevity and good health business is just luck, consider the following story.

My friend Karen Cortell Reisman invited close friends and family members to keep her company during her chemo sessions when she had breast cancer. In that way, she transformed what might have been depressing and difficult treatments into positive, social opportunities that she could look forward to. Karen says her sessions went by faster with the well-chosen company. She also felt stronger and more supported than if she'd gone through them alone.

Karen recovered completely, lives a full and vibrant personal and professional life, and has remained cancer-free.

This isn't just a happy accident. It's backed by study after study.

The Nurses' Health Study, one of the largest investigations into the risk factors for major chronic diseases among females, showed that women with 10 or more friends had a *three times* greater likelihood of *surviving* breast cancer than those without personal support systems.

Along these lines, the work of Sharon Toker, Ph.D., and her colleagues at Tel Aviv University, reveal that people with a high level of social support at work had a 22% lower chance of developing diabetes.

Researchers at both Northwestern Medicine and the Harvard T.H. Chan School of Public Health also see links between positive social relationships and a significantly reduced risk of cognitive decline.

All this circles back to what you read earlier about conversations.

Even short affable exchanges with people we encounter throughout our days can improve our mood and stimulate our thinking.

We use it and, therefore, we don't lose it.

Age gracefully

It's questionable whether there is indeed a Fountain of Youth, but being interested, friendly, and social are valuable and time-tested secrets to staying young. A woman who participated in one of the studies mentioned earlier offers these everyday tips for aging well and staying vibrant. See how many you practice faithfully (and how many you could work on).

- Offer a smile and greeting to everyone.
- Be cordial to all, even people you don't know yet.
- Learn and use names.
- Show people you care.
- Maintain friendships no matter what is happening in your life.
- Get involved in a variety of activities.

What a coincidence! These are all basic social graces and more demonstrations of "showing up well." In stark contrast, research subjects who didn't fare well in terms of health and aging exhibited these traits. They generally:

- Kept to themselves and avoided talking or sharing.
- Told the same stories over and over.
- Complained repeatedly.
- Had a negative outlook.
- Never listened to others.

As a final note, Chris Crowley and Henry S. Lodge, M.D., co-authors of the *New York Times* best-selling book *Younger Next Year,* agree that remaining both active and social are keys to extending the number of years you can enjoy good mental, emotional, and physical health.

They offer this simple, but stern warning: "Disconnect at your own peril."

. . . .

It's pretty tough to find the downside to engaging in positive interactions with others on a regular basis. And yet, there are so many reasons and excuses why we don't do it as often as we could. Let's explore those next.

Recognizing the Barriers and *Obstacles*

The best conversations are interesting and uninterrupted. Too bad most of us haven't had one of those since 1997.

So, what stops us?

As you read in the previous section, positive interactions of all types can offer us a huge range of compelling benefits. Yet there seem to be numerous barriers and obstacles that stop us from having quality conversations and gaining the advantages.

A survey from the U.S. Bureau of Labor Statistics revealed that, on any given day, the average person spends a meager *four minutes* attending social events and *less than an hour* engaged in interaction with another person. And this was before we experienced the global pandemic!

Let's take a look at the major obstacles and barriers that prevent us from engaging. Some you might be practicing subconsciously or simply out of habit. Others you might be utilizing ingeniously and intentionally as a way to stay disconnected.

As with many changes we want to make in life, truthful awareness of the problem and its sources is critical. When we take a moment to identify and examine the obstacles and barriers that hinder our socializing, consider how they got there, and choose to be accountable, we can then find ways to address, manage, reduce, or even eliminate them.

Let's begin with ...

CHAPTER 5

Our
Lifestyles

Some of the biggest barriers to good conversations—or any human interaction at all—come about because of how we've designed our daily lives or allowed them to become.

Extreme busyness (real, created, or imagined)

Hoo, boy! We are busy, busy, *busy!* What can we say about modern life? It can get really hectic, really distracting, and really intense. That is, if we let it. And we seem to be exceptionally good at doing this.

We have demanding jobs, active families, packed schedules, endless to-do lists, and a lot of big ambitions, dreams, and responsibilities. These eat up our limited time, attention, and energy. Which means we can quickly and regularly become overwhelmed and drained.

Our inability or unwillingness to manage or slow
the pace of life can put a big blockade in front
of any possibility for quality interaction.
With anyone and everyone.

I'll be the first to admit that I'm not a fan of the feelings I get when I'm rushed, stressed, or over-scheduled and my power pack has once again been drained. I'm cranky, my stomach knots up, and my head starts to throb.

Socializing and being pleasant are the last things on my mind. I just want a nap and a soothing cup of tea! Preferably in the privacy and comfort of a quiet room in my own home. No people. No one talking. Yes, that would be perfect.

Sound familiar?

When our lives stay in crazy-busy mode, we probably aren't getting out into the fresh air to take walks or work in our yards as often as we could. And, hey! Either of these simple activities could result in a lovely impromptu chat with our neighbors.

"Neighbors? What neighbors? I have neighbors? I don't even know them."

My point exactly.

What about having people over?

"What? Entertain guests? Oh please. You've got to be kidding!"

Right.

First, who has time? Second, our homes are a wreck (or so we think). And third, it's just too much work and too expensive and elaborate.

Martha What's-Her-Name, Pinterest, Instagram, and all those glossy home lifestyle magazines have made us feel terribly inadequate. It's just too hard to live up to those standards.

So, we don't even bother to invite anyone over.

Worst of all, we are often barely present with our families and closest friends. Because we are so terribly busy. And stressed.

"Beware the barrenness of a busy life," noted the wise, socially savvy, and fully accurate Greek philosopher Socrates, who lived way back in the years 470 to 399 BC.

Has that epic wisdom stood the test of time or what?

Interaction overload

Many of us live in highly populated cities, work in big organizations, serve the general public, teach huge classes, attend big conferences, go to entertainment events, and travel through bustling airports and train stations. That means our lives are jam-packed with people. Every single day.

We're constantly surrounded by our peers, customers, patients, friends, family, neighbors, and fellow citizens on the sidewalks or in the grocery store aisles or at the dry cleaners. On top of that, we are likely receiving and responding to dozens of phone calls, emails, texts, and other messages. Maybe even watching and listening to way too much news.

Let's get real here. By the end of the day, we may have reached the point of interaction overload.

We're totally peopled-out. Especially if some of our interactions have been less than pleasurable. (Some people can be so demanding and rude! And there's so much bad news in the world!)

Sadly, we are wired to remember negative experiences far longer than positive ones.

The last thing we want to do in that moment is socialize with friends or loved ones, let alone chit-chat with casual acquaintances and strangers. In fact, we want to escape! We are so *done*.

Wouldn't it be easier to go home to an indifferent cat, a frozen dinner or some leftovers, a cold beer, and a little Netflix?

Uh-huh. Sounds perfect.

Social regulation mixed with a dash of self-absorption

What happens when we mix a heaping cup of interaction overload with a giant pot of extreme busyness? That concoction can quickly prompt us to regulate our socialization (or avoid it altogether), maybe under the empowering guise of needing "me" time.

We opt to work remotely, even after the pandemic. We pass on invitations to coffee, lunch, events, or gatherings. We secretly celebrate when a friend has to cancel lunch or dinner plans. Before we know it, our sense of independence and noble commitment to "self-care" (which might just translate into way too much solitude) have turned us into modern-day hermits.

That's how it happens.

Suddenly we need more and more alone time. We're caught up in our own little worlds. And, frankly, we kinda like it there.

We want to stay in control of our time, space, and energy. It's a state of mind that is all about us—and eventually inhibits conversation and connection. Instead of taking the time to engage with others and hear their stories, we stay hyper-focused on ourselves.

And then... our social muscles atrophy. We totally forget how to socialize and converse.

Can *you* relate to that?

Limited opportunities to engage

Now for the other end of the spectrum. And this one gets a hall pass. What about those who aren't retreating from hectic lives? Some of us live in isolation not by choice, but by circumstance in small towns and rural areas. There simply aren't enough opportunities to interact with others because there just aren't that many people around.

Some of us experience varying degrees of isolation due to age, chronic illness and disability, lack of transportation, extreme weather, a language / cultural barrier, concerns for safety, or other factors. Maybe even an antisocial spouse.

Also consider this: The formal groups that used to bring people together regularly are losing popularity. Fewer and fewer people belong to organized church communities, clubs, orders, or associations. In the previous century, these were all standard and reliable ways to stay connected. They were an enjoyable, vital part of community life.

The reality is, many natural platforms for socializing are quickly disappearing.

Today it's up to us to come up with more of our own ways to get together. If we don't take that proverbial bull by the horns, we won't be engaged in many conversations at all. Our social skills will dwindle further. Sooner or later, it's easier to camp out with the television or a book or a video game than it is to pursue what we assume will be an awkward, draining, or unpleasant interaction.

CHAPTER

6

. . . .

Settings and *Situations*

. . . .

Some settings and situations are perfect for having a good conversation. And yet there are also scenarios where it's almost impossible to have *any* type of conversation.

Loud music and poor acoustics

Don't get me wrong. I love a lively party and *really* love to dance. Crank up the music, and I'll likely be the first one on the dance floor. Except...when my goal is to enjoy good conversation. Following is an example that still has me shaking my head.

I was at a lovely party one evening. It was a housewarming for a dear friend. She had invited a fun and interesting array of guests, and we were enjoying some really good wine and delicious appetizers prepared by a friend who is a professional chef. It was all very pleasant and civilized. The discussions were stimulating and fun. The environment was beautiful, classy, and relaxed. I felt like I was making a whole new set of friends and relishing the process.

Until one of the guests decided to "get this party started."

Suddenly the music shifted from soft, easy jazz to something obnoxious and more suited to a frat party or hockey game. Those of us engaged in conversation had to start yelling to hear each other. Very irritating! The mood and social ambiance were totally obliterated, monster-truck style.

And we had been having such a pleasant time!

Before long, many of us who had been engaged in enjoyable discussions decided to make gracious (but decisive) exits. We agreed to meet at another, more subdued spot down the street where we could hang out and continue the evening.

Ahhh. **Relief!**

The sudden music apocalypse at my friend's otherwise-charming party had the opposite effect the self-proclaimed D.J. had intended. It didn't get the party started. It brought it to a hasty conclusion.

The lesson here: The setting and ambiance matter when it comes to the type and quality of your conversations.

If you want to engage in enjoyable, relaxed conversation, choose an environment that's not too loud and has good acoustics. And if you want your party guests to enjoy socializing and getting to know each other, choose your playlist and set up the environment accordingly. This goes double if you or those you are socializing with have any hearing challenges!

Distractions and interruptions

Any discussion of conversation obstacles must include the annoyance of constant interruptions and distractions. Ever tried to have a chat with someone who is constantly checking their phones or taking calls? Or while people keep knocking on the door to ask a question? Or the coffee grinder, drink blender, or kitchen noises are clanging right in your ear? Or the kids need something *right now*? Or diners at the next table are speaking in their "outdoor voices" while their children are running around the restaurant like little hooligans?

Ugh! It can be maddening.

Distractions and interruptions not only ruin the flow of a good visit, but they also create tension, dissonance, and frustration.

At that point, a conversation is neither enjoyable nor relaxing. We can't (nor should we) eliminate all distractions and interruptions, but we can be aware of them and avoid them when necessary.

On a side note... If you're looking for a creative way to guarantee some interruption-free conversations, check out what one of our Founding Fathers did to give everyone their time in the spotlight.

Ever heard of the "Jeffersonian-style" dinner party? Thomas Jefferson hosted these frequently, hence the name. Here's how it works: A topic, theme, or question is posed by the host. Then, each person at the dinner table takes a turn speaking *uninterrupted* on this topic or question. All other dinner guests listen respectfully *with no side talk*. This allows all views to be heard respectfully and without interruption. (Yes, I have a feeling Mr. Jefferson did a bit of facilitating to keep any filibustering windbags under control.)

While we're on the subject of interruptions, it's worth a quick mention here that our widespread and chronic inability to listen—and listen well—is a massive barrier to good conversation. Since poor listening is so pervasive (and good listening so important to good conversation), I've devoted an entire section to it later in this book.

Let's explore a few more obstacles first.

A hectic or rushed atmosphere

Whether it's a crowded café where they want you in and out as fast as possible or a coffee date with someone who keeps checking the time, a hurried or frantic atmosphere does little to encourage an engaging and leisurely exchange. Unless, of course, you prefer to make it quick, for whatever reason. (Yes, in some situations that can be a legitimate exit strategy!)

Philosopher, speaker, and photographer Matthew Ferrara says when he wants to enjoy a long, unhurried visit with a friend, especially one he hasn't seen in a long time, he books dinner at a favorite restaurant where he knows the service is attentive (but never rushed), the ambiance is relaxed and welcoming, and the menu has something for everyone.

"Time flies by and the conversation flows when we choose the right venue," Ferrara says. "We can suddenly lose six hours over a good meal!"

Six hours. Now that's a lot. But even one hour at a burger joint or favorite watering hole can be great if the atmosphere is comfortable and conversation-friendly.

Foursomes are fabulous.

As a side note, one of my favorite ways to enjoy good conversation (other than one-on-one over coffee or a drink) is with a carefully curated foursome. Four people can comfortably sit around a modest table and be just close enough for everyone to talk and listen easily. It's a large enough group for the conversation to stay lively, yet small enough for each person to share and listen. It can be energizing and fun, without being "too much."

Four on Friday.

Embrace the practice of inviting three friends or colleagues to lunch (or breakfast, coffee, happy hour, dinner) on Fridays (or whatever day works for you). Mix things up and make it an opportunity to connect or reconnect with people in your family, neighborhood, network, or company. One of my client organizations began this practice after I shared it with them in a workshop. Employees from every department can sign up each week. Foursomes are chosen by drawing, so it's always a surprise to discover who your "Four on Friday" coffee or lunch companions will be. Based on the feedback I've received, these little gatherings have created a more connected and cohesive organizational culture.

◂▴▸

Location, location, location.

Reflect for a moment on the situations and settings that, in your experience, have provided a comfortable and conducive backdrop for great conversations. How can this awareness help you seek out better locations for your interactions with others?

_____

_____

_____

◂▴▸

Our homes and neighborhoods

It's a little ironic that our homes and neighborhoods, the places meant to encourage community and connection, have inadvertently evolved to restrict it. For instance, ever notice that many newer homes are designed with no front porches? Where are we supposed to sit with our favorite beverages and perhaps wave and say hello to the neighbors walking by on a pleasant evening?

Speaking of which, a lot of people don't get out to walk anymore, whether for transportation, pleasure, or fitness. And kids playing outside? Not nearly as common as it used to be. Crime is on the rise, and the days of parents yelling, "Be back before the streetlights come on," are long gone.

What about the addition of garage door openers and air conditioning? With the press of a button, we can skitter into our garages quickly, often nearly *undetected*! And having air conditioning means we can get (and remain) comfortable indoors at all times, even in the summer.

Great inventions? Sure! But they do reduce our moments of human contact.

The same goes for automatic lawn irrigation systems. This miraculous convenience eliminates the need to stand outside on a balmy summer evening to water the lawn, garden, flowers, or shrubs. Another missed opportunity to offer a quick hello to Mr. Gonzalez next door, to meet the Redmonds' puppy, or to catch up on how Mrs. Schlabotnik's new grandbaby is doing.

In all fairness, some architects, interior designers, and decorators are paying more attention to the social dynamics of homes. But many are still designed for privacy and arranged to accommodate our "stuff" rather than guests.

Chat-room check!

How is your home environment set up? Is it conducive to socializing and conversation? Or not so much? What could you do to make it better?

‹ ▲ ›

Stressful (even toxic) work environments

We spend a sizable chunk of our waking hours at work, which can be a hectic, demanding, and competitive place.

Who wants to engage and socialize when everyone is stressed out, maxed out, irritated with their boss or co-workers, and maybe even competing with them for the same promotion?

This reminds me of a large corporate client that hired me to help improve its internal culture and get its employees talking and more connected. The irony here was that the everyday culture, from the top down, was one that actually discouraged (maybe the word is *punished*) any non-work-driven interactions among its people during the workday.

"Productivity! Efficiency! Keep your eyes and fingers firmly glued to your laptop screens and keyboards at all times! Deadlines! Quotas! Work, work, work!"

This wasn't emblazoned on a sign in the hallway or on the latest company T-shirt, but it might just as well have been.

Let me paint a more detailed picture. One employee revealed to me that, if you were told to attend a meeting, there was an unspoken commandment: discussing anything non-work-related is off limits. No chatting with other attendees before the meeting begins. Don't introduce yourself. For goodness sakes, don't ask how everyone's weekend was!

If you lost your mind and broke these rules? You would quickly receive the stank eye. Or many stank eyes. Break it twice? Enjoy your stint as the office pariah. And any chance of advancement? Hah! Forget it.

This level of hostility blew my mind.

"You have no idea who you're sitting with in those meetings," said my contact with an air of total frustration. "You don't know what department they work in, or what their titles or job responsibilities are. Questions are strongly discouraged. It's like being in a very unfriendly and anonymous echo chamber."

Admittedly, not every company has such a toxic culture.

Many organizations tend to hyper-focus on productivity and the bottom line. The fact that workplaces are *human communities* can get lost in the shuffle.

That's a shame, since you read earlier that socializing and positive relationships have the power to create a much more supportive, motivating, efficient, and productive environment.

The irony there is unreal.

If companies want to improve performance, profitability, customer service, reputation, and more, they need to foster a friendly, collaborative culture that gets their people conversing and connecting! And it all begins at the top.

CHAPTER

7

....

Technology

....

You knew I'd get to this one, didn't you? In today's world, many people would say the need for technology is right up there with the need for air. Unfortunately, that technology also has the potential to choke the life out of our conversations.

Screens, screens, and more screens!

First, I will say that our amazing digital devices have opened up so many new worlds for us! Who doesn't love that? If we own a phone, tablet, laptop, or TV classified as "smart," we can instantly watch streaming media, take classes, listen to concerts, shop, play games (alone or with people miles away), make art, take photos, use an amazing array of apps, watch videos, see almost any movie or television show ever made, look up *anything*, navigate our way around unfamiliar regions, and on and on and on. We can also follow and interact with family, friends, and just about anyone with an online presence.

Truth is, we have more computing power and information at our fingertips today than the NASA astronauts had when they landed on the moon in the 1960s!

It's really rather incredible.

And yet, our smart electronic devices can be big-time conversation barriers.

They are the reason the term "phubbing" (the combination of "phone" and "snubbing") was coined. Another term for this? "Technoference" (technology interference).

> **Phubbing:** the practice of ignoring one's companion or companions in order to pay attention to one's phone or electronic device.
>
> **Technoference:** the potential interference smartphones and other technologies can have on our face-to-face interactions.

Just look around next time you're in a restaurant, coffee shop, or bar. People are positively glued to their devices, often ignoring others sitting right at their table.

These phenomenal tools that hold the promise of making us more connected than ever before are actually leaving us isolated, anxious, and addicted. They are stunting us socially and emotionally. And don't even get me started on the issues they can cause with our hands, wrists, eyes, necks, backs, and shoulders.

I will admit, I love my electronic devices as much as the next person. But I constantly have to remind myself that it's no substitute for real-world, in-person, face-to-face relationships and communications.

Along these lines…

The not-so-secret signal of earbuds and headphones

It's inevitable. Where there are digital devices, there are often earbuds and noise-cancelling headphones. These are positioned as courteous companions to the screens that prevent everyone else from having to listen to our choice of music or program.

How thoughtful! Well, yes…

Unfortunately, having anything in or on our ears is also pretty much the universal symbol for "DO NOT DISTURB." As in, "I'm busy. Take your conversation somewhere else, buddy." Or worse, "Hey! I'm plugged in, so you don't exist."

A solid social barrier, indeed.

Each time you pop your little pals into your ears or headphones over them, please consider your true intentions. Ask yourself:

- Am I wearing these to be courteous?
- Am I really wanting to repel any possibility of social interaction?
- If so, what's up with that?
- Am I willing to hit "pause" if someone approaches me?
- What could I miss out on if I continually "plug in" and "tune out"?

The seductive mirage of social media

Let's talk pros and cons on this one.

Pros? Social media has been a saving grace for those who want to stay connected to family, friends, and colleagues who are miles away. It's also a practical way to meet and get to know people we haven't yet met in person but find interesting or entertaining. As one example, I'm currently in several abstract art painting groups on Facebook that are incredibly inspiring! I love these people! Our brains are actually wired for connection, and social media makes it so easy. Almost too easy.

TRY THIS!

The luscious lure of connection.

What do you relish most about social media? What makes it so enticing?

_____

_____

_____

◂▴▸

Cons? Despite the allure, there are some obvious downsides to social media. You've probably noticed it has spawned a lot of self-absorption, as well as the trend of people habitually sharing impulsive and often poorly-thought-out posts and comments. From heavy vanity and snarky sarcasm to political pontification, judgy-ness, and downright contentious insults, many interactions are neither productive nor uplifting.

Think of all the things people feel compelled to do and say online that they'd never do or say in person! Kind of mind-boggling.

There's more. When people choose to engage heavily with social media (in a positive or negative way), they may convince themselves that they're popular or smart and influential. They may also believe they are having lots of "conversations" with many different people. But don't be seduced by the illusion!

According to Elisabeth Netherton, M.D., a psychiatrist with the Menninger Clinic in Houston, Texas, spending too much time on social media not only gobbles up your time, attention, and energy, but it also has the power to erode your sense of well-being. Plus, it can easily thwart real-time, in-person conversations and negatively impact your relationships.

The "endless scrolling" style is especially hypnotic and potentially harmful, says Dr. Netherton. And here's the kicker: The older you are, the worse the impact!

There's hope though.

A 2018 study revealed that participants who limited their social media time to *30 minutes a day* had a significant improvement in well-being and less loneliness and depression compared to participants who used social media as much as they wanted.

In short, if we believe that social media is an instant and fail-proof replacement for in-person, real-time, back-and-forth conversations (it isn't!), we are not only creating our own pesky roadblocks for meaningful, face-to-face interactions but also negatively impacting our mental health.

TRY THIS!

A dark and slippery slope.

What negative effects do you experience when you find yourself sucked into the social media vortex?

_____

_____

_____

To combat those effects, try following these expert tips for using social media more sensibly and courteously:

- Be mindful and purposeful about why and how you use it.
- Curate your feed accordingly.
- Establish a daily time limit.
- Pay close attention to how social media makes you feel.
- Participate in meaningful, two-way exchanges rather than a lot of drive-by, one-way commentary.
- Don't let social media become a substitute for real, in-person exchanges.

◄▲►

Head Chatter and *Cultural* Messages

We all have them: those pervasive and sometimes-annoying voices in our heads that convince us to do certain things and avoid others. Regardless of their origins, these inner voices can be intensely ingrained and very powerful. They play over and over and over again, for better or worse. What's more, they often influence our socializing protocol.

Societal and cultural messages

Much of what's stuck in our heads regarding social interaction and communication comes from our lifelong "membership" in society. What I mean is, all the messages and programming we received (directly and indirectly) from our parents, families, teachers, communities, and authority figures over the years.

We have also been bombarded with endless streams of media and marketing messages that get lodged in our brains. What resonates with us may differ depending on our unique cultures, our upbringing, our genders, our personalities, and many other factors.

- ❋ Don't speak to strangers!
- ❋ You should be seen and not heard.
- ❋ No talking in class!
- ❋ Girls shouldn't argue; it's not polite.
- ❋ If you can't think of anything nice to say, don't say anything at all.
- ❋ It's not safe out there! Everyone's a weirdo!
- ❋ You're not good / attractive / smart / rich enough!

While a few of these directives may have served a purpose at the time, most are outdated (because we are now adults, thank you). Yet some still "stick" and prevent us from engaging in good conversations.

As a disclaimer, if you want to sharpen your intuition and safety sense when in the presence of strangers, check out this book: *The Gift of Fear: Survival Signals that Protect Us From Violence* by Gavin DeBecker. It's an eye-opening, valuable read. I highly recommend it.

Uncertainty

Unless we have a crystal ball, we can't accurately predict how every social encounter will go. There's an unknown there. A giant question mark. For some people, that's what makes socializing fun. But for others, it can produce some anxiety. Okay, a lot of anxiety. The kind that can leave us feeling weak in the knees, sick in the stomach, and stuck on the sidelines of life.

- ❋ I have no idea what to say.
- ❋ What questions should I ask?

- ☀ How do I even get a conversation started?
- ☀ What if I say something stupid?
- ☀ What if they're rude to me?
- ☀ What if they reject me?
- ☀ What if they're boring?
- ☀ What if the other person gloms on to me and never stops talking?

Let's get logical about this for a moment.

Honestly, would you really want to know *exactly* how your day—every day—was going to go in advance? Or how your life was going to unfold? Do you want to know how everything is going to turn out before it happens? How every conversation will be? That actually sounds rather unpleasant! No, actually terrifying!

As for me, I prefer being surprised and delighted. Wouldn't life be boring if everything were known, guaranteed, and predictable?

And yet, a lot of us view conversations as uncertain, anxiety-producing events. So we avoid them.

In his book, *Uncertainty: Turning Doubt and Fear into Fuel for Brilliance,* best-selling author and founder of The Good Life Project® Jonathan Fields writes, "When you run from uncertainty, you end up running from life. From evolution. From growth. From friendship. From love."

He's so right. Nothing ventured, nothing gained.

Spiritual teacher and author Eckhart Tolle adds, "When you become comfortable with uncertainty, infinite possibilities open up in your life."

My recommendation? Think of every interaction as a game of possibilities.

Embrace the unknown. Say to yourself, "I wonder how this will go…" Substitute excitement, anticipation, and even amusement for the worry and anxiety. Sometimes you'll win. Sometimes you'll lose. And that's okay.

Negative thinking

Most people wouldn't purposely enter a social setting or work event with a bad attitude, but it happens. And when it does, conversations don't stand a chance.

- It's been a terrible day, and I'm in no mood to talk to anyone.
- I'd rather be anywhere else right now.
- I'll never see any of these people again. What's the point?
- I'd prefer a root canal over small talk with these losers.
- They won't like me.
- I'm so terrible at this!

If the little voice in your head is repeating any of these lines, it is attempting to give you full permission to keep to yourself.

The score? Grumpy Solitude 1, Conversation 0.

But remember what happens when we interact? Go back to Section One for the reminder about how conversations will likely make you feel better, even if you don't start out feeling that way.

False assumptions

Another leading cause of premature death for potentially fabulous conversations is false assumptions. (You know, those little instant judgments we make that often turn out to be completely *wrong*.) Once again, cue the little nagging voice:

- ☀ She looks tired / overwhelmed. She doesn't want to chat right now.
- ☀ He's far too busy / important to talk with me.
- ☀ I can already tell I would have nothing in common with her.
- ☀ He's so smart, and I would just sound like an idiot.
- ☀ I've known these people for years, and there's nothing left to say.
- ☀ That person? Are you kidding me? We probably couldn't agree on what time it is.

Any of those internal messages and excuses can derail an exchange before it ever starts. And sadly, many of them may not be founded in truth.

More *Complex* Issues

The last category of conversation roadblocks includes issues that are simultaneously more concrete *and* more challenging. I will also add, I'm not an expert on any of these. Not by a long shot. But they still deserve a brief mention.

Language barriers

Ever tried to have a conversation with someone who doesn't speak the same language or dialect or has a particularly thick accent? Listening and sharing in a natural way is difficult. You might quickly exhaust your capacity to communicate via gestures and movements that look like a game of Charades. And as we often forget, *talking louder doesn't help!* The language barrier can be tough to overcome.

Speaking habits

How we speak certainly impacts what others hear. This includes our intent, our tone, the words we use, and the way we approach others in conversation. These are all subtle (or not-so-subtle) factors that can make or break our conversations.

For example, I once worked with someone who spoke in a shrill, grating tone that was very off-putting. Kind of like (you guessed it) fingernails on a chalkboard. I know it wasn't intentional on her part. But everything she said (even the positive stuff) came across like a dramatic "poor-me" crisis.

I also knew someone whose tone and choice of words often veered toward the style of an aggressive interrogator. When that person spoke to me, I couldn't help but feel like I'd done something wrong—*even if I hadn't!*

> Can you see how these and other less-than-appealing speaking styles can make conversations unpleasant?

The good news is, they can be remedied with vocal awareness and training. A fantastic resource here is the book, *Vocal Power: Harnessing the Power Within,* by Arthur Samuel Joseph, M.A., founder and chairman of the Vocal Awareness Institute, Inc.

Intelligence

This one may surprise you—or maybe not. People who are highly intelligent sometimes have trouble being successful socializers.

This is not a joke. There's a reason behind it.

Highly intelligent people can sometimes be…shall we say, enamored with their intelligence. They may also thrive on gathering and sharing lots of overly detailed information, shifting into problem-solving mode prematurely, over-analyzing, or jumping to the "right" answer. They also may launch into unnecessarily complex technical or intellectual discussions that leave others in the dust.

And because smart people have minds that often operate at a much faster pace, they may get impatient or bored and interrupt frequently. They may also be stellar lecturers and sentence-finishers.

We've all been around these folks. Or maybe we are the ones making these conversation faux pas. We are so human! With patience and practice, we can learn to restrain these tendencies. But until we do, our conversation IQ won't match our intellectual brilliance.

In his *Book of Awakening,* poet and spiritual advisor Mark Nepo speaks to what happens when we let our intellect run the social show. "To always analyze and problem solve and observe and criticize what we encounter turns our brains into heavy calluses. Rather than opening us deeper into the mystery of living, the overtrained intellect becomes a buffer from experience."

And likely a buffer from good conversations and true connection as well.

To sum things up: If you insist on being the smartest person in the room, you just might end up being the *only* person in the room.

Physical and neurological conditions

Sometimes more specific and unfortunate barriers can get in the way of good conversations. First, it's a challenge to summon the motivation to initiate a conversation or go out and socialize if you're not feeling well or are experiencing chronic pain, fatigue, or depression. A speech impediment or difficulty hearing can also impair a person's conversations, as can severe shyness, autism, and Asperger's syndrome.

These are complex issues and are studied and written about by specialists who may have solutions and suggestions. If you or someone you love is dealing with any of these, professional and specialized guidance may be helpful.

TRY
THIS!

Roadblock alert!

Can you think of other obstacles and barriers that prevent you (and others) from initiating and enjoying conversations?

_____
_____
_____

What messages and internal voices keep you isolated or give you permission to avoid conversations? Where did these come from?

_____
_____
_____

◄▲►

. . . .

Now that you've been introduced to (or reacquainted with) some of the powerful forces, habits, and beliefs that can put the skids on initiating or enjoying conversations, let's roll up our sleeves and explore some initial strategies and tools that can pave the way for conversation success.

. . . .

Preparing
To *Succeed*

. . . .

*Whether you tend to be a
hermit, a social butterfly, or
something in between, prepare
to experience that glowing
ray of hope for a better
conversation tomorrow.*

Confidence starts with preparation.

Pop quiz time! What do academic tests, athletic competitions, first dates, bar mitzvahs, weddings, dinner parties, driving tests, holiday celebrations, sales presentations, vacations, weddings, and other "special events" have in common?

Massive amounts of stress? Well, yes. There's that.

These are all occasions for which most of us choose to prepare. We want to feel ready, confident, well-practiced, and "in shape." We want things to go smoothly and turn out well. We don't want to feel anxious, awkward, overwhelmed, or embarrassed. We don't want to fail. We want to succeed and feel *good*.

So we decide what success looks like and design our action plan. We adjust our attitude if needed and make the commitment to go for it. Then we study, take lessons, train, plan, practice, and get all jazzed up so we can achieve the success we're dreaming of. We focus on the outcome as we invest our time, skills, energy, and resources. We may even hire coaches and experts (or—*ahem*—read their books) to learn and gain an edge.

You probably know where I'm going with this.

Having better and more meaningful conversations is similar. For some, it *seems* to come naturally and without any effort. In truth, becoming a skilled and confident conversationalist requires every step you just read above. That's right. Even for the people who seem to be naturals. The reality is, they probably had excellent teachers and role models, and they took the steps I've mentioned at some point in their lives.

In her book, *How Winning Works: 8 Essential Leadership Lessons from the Toughest Teams*, American endurance and adventure racer Robyn

Benincasa writes, "Without preparation, there is no luck."

How's that for truth?

Louis Pasteur, the French chemist and microbiologist whose work has saved countless lives, said it another way: "Chance favors only the prepared mind."

Slight shift of words, but similar message.

You're likely reading this book for a reason. You want luck on your side as you strike up and engage in conversations. *You're preparing for success.*

Ironically, some of the steps you'll take during the preparation phase, especially in this section, won't involve talking or hanging out in social settings. They involve reflection and contemplation. Which means you'll do this prep work *alone*. You can certainly discuss some of the work with loved ones, friends, and colleagues. But initially, it's a solo gig.

Ironic, yes. But *very* important.

Why?

Because everything you do in this chapter will likely impact everything else you read in this book: how you think about it, respond to it, digest it, apply it, and tweak it. It's absolutely foundational! So please don't be tempted to skip this part!

Let's get to it: the first step in preparing for your conversation success.

....

Get to Know
Your *Social* Self

....

Sounds like another great topic for Greek philosopher Socrates. He believed that "knowing thyself is the height of wisdom."

Did you take that in? The *height* of wisdom!

Centuries later, Socrates' advice is still accurate. Self-awareness is a huge factor in your conversation wisdom—and success.

Keeping that in mind, let's begin with an obvious question that specifically pertains to this book:

What's your social personality?

If you've taken a personality profile such as the Myers-Briggs Type Indicator® (MBTI®), you know a few things about yourself, including your behavioral preferences and social tendencies.

For example, you know whether you are an introvert, extrovert, or a blend of both, which is an ambivert. (I happen to be an ambivert, which is why I can relate to introverts and extroverts alike.)

Even if you've never taken the Myers-Briggs, you may have a pretty good idea of where you fall on the introvert/extrovert scale. For good measure, check out these three simple questions:

- Are you energized by being with people? (If so, you could be an extrovert.)
- Are you energized by solo time? (You might be an introvert.)
- Do you enjoy and need a combination of both? (The signs point to ambivert.)

While some psychology experts argue that it's impossible to categorize humans with precise labels and that personality indicators are a bunch of hooey, there's no denying we have innate social tendencies, preferences, and patterns.

These tendencies matter when it comes to conversations and social situations, and they impact the following:

- How we feel before, during, and after socializing.
- When, how often, and how long we like to socialize
- What social styles, settings, and situations we prefer.

Want a few more details to help you decide your social personality? Here you go.

Which of the following best describes you?

Introverts

- ❋ Tend to be quiet, reserved, private, and introspective (although some introverts can be quite chatty!).

- ❋ Are inward-turning: focused on internal thoughts and feelings.

- ❋ Crave solitude to balance out and recharge after social time.

- ❋ Think before speaking and speak only when they have something to say.

- ❋ Have natural tendencies to listen, focus, and pose questions.

- ❋ Need time to process what they've heard.

- ❋ Are uncomfortable in large groups or with strangers.

- ❋ Choose friends carefully and have smaller social circles.

- ❋ Prefer deep, rich discussions and one-on-one interactions.

Is being introverted the same as being shy?

No. Introversion and shyness are different. People who are shy often suffer from pronounced feelings of fear, anxiety, and tension when they are around other people. What's more, they may have a hard time turning these feelings off.

Introverts, on the other hand, can "borrow extroverted energy" and become comfortable in social settings for a certain amount of time. Then they need a quieter setting (preferably alone) in which to rest, reflect, and recharge.

Some studies suggest that people who are shy as children often outgrow their shyness. But once an introvert, always an introvert.

If shyness is an issue for you, I hope this book will be helpful. I also encourage you to take advantage of the great resources and professionals out there to support you along your journey.

Extroverts

- ☀ Are energized by people, activity, and socializing.
- ☀ Find isolation unpleasant and draining.
- ☀ Tend to be outgoing and easy to get to know.
- ☀ Enjoy meeting new people and having a wide circle of friends.
- ☀ Strike up conversations easily.
- ☀ Solve problems and express themselves out loud.
- ☀ Enjoy group work.
- ☀ Look to others and outside sources for ideas and inspiration.

Perhaps you resonate with both the introverts and extroverts? You're not alone! Some experts believe ambiverts—people with a blend of both tendencies—represent up to two-thirds of the population. Maybe, like me, you're one of them. Let's find out!

Ambiverts

- ☀ Have a mixture of introverted and extroverted traits.
- ☀ Vacillate between needing social and solo time to recharge.
- ☀ Are socially flexible—comfortable in social situations or being alone.
- ☀ Tend to have a circle of close friends, but also many acquaintances.
- ☀ Are adaptable and can adjust their social approach to fit the situation.
- ☀ Are sometimes torn between going out and staying in.
- ☀ Enjoy having a "wingman" when out socializing.

Discovering I was an ambivert was a welcome epiphany. It helped me understand why I might crave social interactions one moment, then "hit the wall" and need alone time the next. These mixed and sometimes unpredictable feelings were not only normal, but totally okay. They are part of being an ambivert. Since I recognize that about myself, I adapt my life and socializing opportunities accordingly.

My self-awareness also helps me understand that I have to rest and practice good self-care so I can "show up" better for others when it's time to socialize, host gatherings, give presentations, and facilitate workshops. It also gives me full permission to plan solo time or make a gracious retreat when my social battery is drained. Or even when I crave some solo time to do things such as reflect, create, read, write, and prepare.

Understanding our social personalities can give us a huge edge as we plan for conversation success.

That knowledge allows us to better honor and leverage our natural tendencies and preferences, while managing our energy more effectively.

Evaluate *Your* Conversation Skills

Introvert. Extrovert. Ambivert. We are what we are. And, despite any labels, we are all unique human beings. Most of us are capable of learning how to evaluate, monitor, and even expand our conversation skills and *social intelligence.*

Social intelligence? Wait! What's that?

It basically means:

- Your awareness and management of your social behavior.
- How well you pay attention to the social cues of others.
- How well you interpret and act on those social cues.

In short, social intelligence is socializing well and generously.

Unlike your intelligence quotient (IQ), which you're born with and will not change, social intelligence is a learned and buildable skill. You accumulate it from your experiences with other people, beginning in your childhood. As an infant, you begin learning what works and what doesn't as you interact with others. You try out new methods and make course corrections accordingly.

And this tidbit is big:

If you are open to it, your social intelligence skills continue to build all throughout your life! It's something you can always work on and improve.

How affirming and exciting is that?

Plus, the world and workplace are filled with people of all ages—from small children to 90-somethings and beyond. This means we have to be ready to socialize, work, and converse with people who are much younger and older than we are. Developing, building, and practicing our *generational intelligence* is also vital to good conversation and to creating a better world.

And there's one more intelligence that's essential to our conversations: *emotional intelligence. Psychology Today* defines emotional intelligence as "our ability to perceive, use, understand, and manage emotions and to handle interpersonal relationships judiciously and empathetically."

Cheryl Jones, author of *Emotional Self-Mastery: The Best Book on Regaining Personal Power, Self-Confidence, and Peace,* expands on that definition. She adds that "individuals with a high level of emotional intelligence are aware of what they are feeling and what caused them to feel that way. Instead of reacting impulsively, they have the self-control to return to a balanced emotional state. In other words, they don't let negative emotional energy continue any longer than necessary."

As you might imagine, all three of these types of intelligence (social, generational, and emotional) combine to make great conversations and connections a reality.

So, let's see how you currently rate your conversational intelligence. Take the casual quiz below to find out.

TRY THIS!

Determine your conversational intelligence.

- ☐ I am confident in my ability to begin conversations with others.

- ☐ I have good conversations regularly—the kind that make me feel positive, inspired, energized, heard, accepted, affirmed, appreciated, and uplifted.

- ☐ I am often pleasantly surprised at the positive effects a conversation can have on me.

- ☐ Others have told me their conversations with me have been enjoyable, valuable, or impactful.

- ☐ I believe I've had a positive impact on people with whom I've interacted.

☐ My current circles include people with whom I enjoy good conversation.

☐ I am open to expanding and diversifying my circles so I can enjoy a wider variety of conversations.

☐ I use conversations to deepen my relationships with friends and family.

☐ I feel it's possible to have good conversations with most people.

☐ I am learning, feeling inspired, and expanding the possibilities in my life through good conversation.

☐ I like who I am in conversation.

☐ I know I can always improve my level and skill at good conversation.

Scoring: Easy! The more boxes you checked, the more confident and skilled you likely are in your preferred conversation settings—*at least from your own perspective.* Pay close attention to the boxes you didn't check. Those represent your greatest opportunities for growth.

But what if you checked every box? Should you stop reading now? No! You can still develop and expand your conversation awareness and skills in ways you may not have imagined.

◂ ▴ ▸

Not into quizzes? Or want another way to self-assess?

In your own words.

Take stock of your conversation strengths and areas with potential for improvement, and jot down your answers to the questions below.

Conversation strengths: What do you believe you do well and what comes easily to you in conversation? Where do you shine?

_____

_____

Conversation areas for growth: Where in your interactions do you have difficulties or feel less-than-successful? What would you like to learn, change, or improve? What do you wish were different or better?

_____

_____

Next steps to improvement: What do you really need to learn?

_____

_____

◂ ▴ ▸

Don't stop just yet! There's another important dimension involved with discovering your current level of interaction savviness. Since conversations involve you and at least one other person, it's time to ask others for their thoughts—*about you.* This feedback could give you a whole new perspective.

Take a ride on the feedback loop.

Add to your awareness by asking others for input about your conversation skills. It may sound daunting. Maybe even terrifying. You may even be thinking, "Pffft! Right. Totally unnecessary." But try it anyway: Ask trusted and supportive friends, family, and peers for their objective opinions. Have them describe how they see and experience you in conversations and in social settings. To be more specific, you could ask:

- "What words or phrases would you use to describe me socially or in conversation?"
- "What are my conversational strengths and gifts?"
- "What do you enjoy most about conversations with me?"
- "What could I do better or differently in my conversations?"
- "What other helpful insights would you like to share with me to help me improve?"

Worried about what they might say? Totally normal. Yet constructive feedback can be priceless, even life-changing. Think about it. You could have your eyes opened to *that one little thing* you do that could be holding you back (and would be so easy to correct). What's more, you might receive some really positive and encouraging feedback that delivers a whole new level of confidence and enthusiasm.

The more open you are to new ideas and constructive conversation feedback, the more benefits you can receive.

Some thoughts on asking for and evaluating feedback. Longtime friend, colleague, and collaborator Lindy Segall of Professionally Speaking shared this advice with me years ago. When it comes to asking for and evaluating feedback or criticism, follow these steps. They will keep you grounded, lead you to what's most helpful, *and* allow you to identify the truth.

1. Be specific about what type of feedback you're seeking.

2. Ask that all comments be kind, relevant, and constructive.

3. Toss out the worst, ugliest, most stinging criticism. (It's likely more about them than you.)

4. Ditto on the gushiest praise and compliments. ("Mom!! Really??? How embarrassing!")

5. Consider everything else in between, which is likely closer to the truth.

6. Be gentle with yourself most of all, and remember we are all learning!

◀ ▲ ▶

Now, for the next step. It's time to design your Vision for your conversations. In other words, what's the big picture for how you will define "success?" Where would you like to see yourself down the road when it comes to your interpersonal interactions?

CHAPTER

. . . .

Create Your *Vision* for Conversation Success

. . . .

Every person is unique. Not just in who they are, but also in what they want and what "success" means to them. So naturally, each of us has a special Vision for what better and more meaningful conversations look, sound, and feel like.

While I may be seeking witty, light-hearted banter over a cocktail at a lively bar, you may prefer serious intellectual debate on global topics over coffee or bourbon in a much more relaxed and leisurely setting.

Although Clara could talk for hours about books and movies, Ken may enjoy discussing the pros and cons of the latest technology or the subtle nuances of last night's basketball game. And Jasmine may be interested in solution-oriented exchanges that can help grow her business or career. Meanwhile, Manuel, the nature lover and outdoorsy type, wants some new ideas for where to go hiking and camping on a trip next weekend.

Then there are people who enjoy conversing about many different topics in a wide variety of settings, but they simply want their conversations to be pleasant, intelligent, and respectful. They want to feel confident while having them and be free to exit them with ease when it's time. Still others are trying to make friends, find partners, get to know co-workers, or win clients.

> Creating your definition of success—your Vision—is one of the very first steps in making it a reality.

After all, it's nearly impossible to hit a target if you don't know what or where that target is! Certainly, it's fun to just go with the flow and be open to whatever. But having some idea of your destination is vital.

I particularly love this definition of Vision: "The ability to think about or plan the future with imagination or wisdom."

You ultimately get to decide and define what success means for you and in as much detail as you wish. This will take some reflection and effort, but it can be very satisfying, too. And once you've established your Vision, amazing things can begin to happen. Let's take a look at the reason behind that.

Why is having a clear Vision so important?

That's an excellent question! And I have answers.

It's neuroscience: We can "tune" our brains to what we're seeking.

Our brains have an awesome feature called the Reticular Activating System (RAS). One of its many complex purposes is to serve as our personal radar and filter. We can't possibly take in and process every little piece of information and all the stimuli coming at us at any given moment. That would drive us completely crazy. So the RAS helps decide what we will notice and what we can filter out and ignore.

The really cool thing is we can deliberately calibrate or "tune" our RAS. Yep, you read that right. In fact, we do it all the time, both consciously and subconsciously. At any moment, we can decide (or be influenced by) what we are seeking or focusing on.

Stuck thinking about all the negative things in your life? Problems, issues, situations, and people that annoy you. Grudges, pet peeves, and perceived injustices. Everything that's going wrong in the world. I guarantee, the more focus you put on these, the more you'll see, experience, and suffer.

Who wants that?

In delicious contrast, you can choose to focus on all the positive things in your life. What's going well. All the little blessings. All your exciting hopes and dreams for the future. The good news. Yep, that's right. Make that choice, and you'll see more of those.

Let's look at an everyday application of this.

Say you're looking for that certain brand of laundry detergent or peanut butter on the grocery store shelves. You'll probably go right to it, especially if you know what aisle it's on and what the packaging looks like.

Likewise, ever had to pick out your child on the playground or spot a friend in a crowd? Chances are, you found them fairly easily unless their appearance changed (or they were wearing a disguise).

Another example: I often see "doppelgangers" (the twin!) of my sweet goldendoodle Maggie, who was my sidekick for more than 15 years. Medium sized with a sleek, elegant build. Dark, soulful eyes. Curly, cream-colored fur. Puppy cut. Always wagging that fluffy tail.

Think that's my RAS at work? You bet. My RAS will forever be tuned to my canine companion.

But back to the logic here. You get to *decide and focus* on what you want to sense and recognize. More specifically, you can also make choices about the following:

- How would you describe "good conversations"?
- What do you want to talk about and experience?
- How do you want to feel in your conversations?

Once you're very clear, you'll be far more likely to attract, recognize, and instigate better conversations. You'll also recognize (and this is big) when you're not in a good conversation. Up ahead I'll share all the ways you can do something about that.

More powerful reasons why it's good to be clear on what we're seeking.

It's a social thing: When we can tell others what we want, they can help us.

Generally, our loved ones, friends, colleagues, and even random strangers are interested in and willing to help us get what we want. At the very least, they're usually willing to steer us in the right direction. But first, we have to be able to tell them what that direction is.

Let's say you're interested in having more conversations about cross-country skiing, organic gardening, or learning to play the piano. Whatever it might be. You could start bringing up the topic in your conversations or asking a question that pertains to that topic and see who bites. Or you might suggest to others that you're seeking friends or groups who share this interest. That might be how you could get invited to a fun and interesting book or study group, concert, or class. It also may be how you meet or get introduced to that new friend who shares the same interests you do.

All you have to do is talk about it and ask!

- "Anyone here enjoy _____?"
- "Have you read any books about _____?"
- "Man, it sure would be fun to meet some fellow fans of _____."
- "I'm going to go _____ next Saturday. Interested in joining me?"

Here's another way to look at it...

It's faith: We can believe that a Higher Power or The Universe is conspiring to help us.

There's so much to be said about belief and faith in a Higher Power, whatever that is for you. There's also something to be said about the phenomenon of synchronicity, which I see as beautiful, timely, and divinely coordinated coincidences. It's been my experience that the more you believe in these, the more often they happen!

Want to hear about a beautiful coincidence that really blew my mind?

I had just purchased Priya Parker's book, *The Art of Gathering*, which I wanted to read as part of my research for this project and because I like to design and host gatherings. (It's a fantastic book, by the way.) *The very same day*, I received an invitation to attend a workshop here in Austin where Ms. Parker would be the keynote speaker. This event was not in any way affiliated with her publisher, and the sender had no idea that I just purchased her book.

I nearly fell off my office chair! Without any hesitation, I signed up to attend.

It gets better.

During Ms. Parker's terrific keynote, she asked for questions from the audience. My hand shot up like a rocket—and she called on me! What's more, she spent quite a bit of time answering my question and even set up an exercise with us to demonstrate her point. Later, as she signed my book, we had another conversation, which I found very valuable and timely. We even had our photo taken together, and she autographed my book with a personal message about THIS book.

I was still very much in "pinch me" mode.

How did this amazing coincidence happen? Who knows?! But they happen all the time. Especially when you get crystal clear on your Vision, pay attention, find your courage, and take decisive action!

Ambivalence, half-hearted dreams, and wishy-washy actions won't get you anywhere.

As motivational speaker, entrepreneur, and corporate trainer Jack Canfield notes in his book, *The Success Principles: How to Get from Where You Are to Where You Want to Be:* "If you are going to [own] your power and get what you really want out of life, you will have to stop saying, 'I don't know; I don't care; It doesn't matter to me or…whatever.' Not being clear on what you want…is simply a habit."

When you've taken the time to define and clarify your conversation Vision and keep it top of mind, don't be surprised if you find yourself experiencing more and more amazing synchronicities and coincidences that align with it.

So, let's do this! What's your Vision?

What will big-picture, long-term success look like for you? Here's an opportunity to jot down a few thoughts. Feel free to edit, update, shift, fine tune, or expand it at any time.

TRY
THIS!

Envision your ... Vision.

Imagine that—*voila!*—you are now a "successful" conversationalist who is enjoying more and better conversations. Never mind *how* you got there. You're *there!* Close your eyes for a few moments and *soak in* the amazing feelings!

Now describe what this success looks, sounds, and feels like. Supercharge this with the powerful words, "I am ..."

_____
_____
_____
_____
_____
_____

Additional specifics that may inspire you as you write: (This may be a good time to grab a journal and record your thoughts there.)

- ⁎ Where are you enjoying these great conversations?
- ⁎ What's the setting or situation?
- ⁎ Who are you talking to and how would you describe them?
- ⁎ What are you talking about?
- ⁎ How are you feeling?
- ⁎ How's your conversation partner feeling?
- ⁎ What mutual benefits are you enjoying?
- ⁎ What "emotional imprints" remain?

◂▴▸

Feeling a little stuck? Overwhelmed? Totally normal. I get it. Let's look at your Vision another way.

Try reverse-engineering or deconstructing some of your previous conversations.

Wait … what? For context, here's what I mean.

Reverse engineering: examining the construction or composition of an object, product, or experience to duplicate or recreate something identical or similar.

Deconstructing: taking something apart so its elements can be fully examined.

You can give that a try with the exercises that follow.

The anatomy of great conversations.

Think back to the really good conversations you've had in the past. How would you describe these experiences?

_____

_____

_____

_____

Or try this clever shortcut by filling in the blanks below:

I enjoy my conversations with _____ at _____ because we talk about _____ and are interested in _____ .

I enjoy my conversations with _____ at _____ because we talk about _____ and are interested in _____ .

I enjoy my conversations with _____ at _____ because we talk about _____ and are interested in _____ .

Repeat this as needed. Notice any patterns? How could you create more of these conversation scenarios?

◂▴▸

TRY
THIS!

Take the leap!

Now you may want to begin composing a draft of your Vision statement. Here's one example:

"As a successful conversationalist, I am confident and courageous enough to be myself as I engage and spark exchanges with others. I am enjoying more conversations and connections with people who are interesting, upbeat, and respectful. We are conversing in many different settings, which are pleasant and comfortable. When these conversations are over, my conversation partners and I feel energized, inspired, and refreshed. We are happy and excited to have talked, and we hope to enjoy more conversations with each other."

That sounds pretty good, right? Now it's your turn: What would your Vision statement say? (Of course, feel free to borrow some of what I wrote or discuss this with family, friends, or colleagues.)

_____

_____

_____

_____

_____

_____

◂▴▸

Need to pack your Vision into a more memorable and portable package?

Studies reveal that carefully crafted mantras, mottos, taglines, and slogans that align with what you desire can be amazingly powerful. They consist of carefully selected words or short phrases that express how we want to feel, what we intend to do, or a goal we want to achieve. These statements clarify and reinforce our values, desires, intentions, attitudes, and behaviors. And they are catchy, memorable, repeatable, and influential.

Here are two ways you can use them:

1. As a general theme or mood-setter.

- Friendly. Fun. Fascinating.
- Good conversations are a blessing.
- Every conversation matters.
- Good conversations are everywhere.

2. As a portable pep talk for a specific social setting.

- I feel great!
- I will meet someone new and interesting.
- I'm going to learn something valuable at this event.
- Whoever I meet, they will be awesome!
- Let the great conversations begin!

It's your turn for a tagline!

Create your very own conversation mantra, motto, or slogan. Play with words. Compose or collect memorable phrases that resonate with you and summarize what you want more of in your conversations. Keep a notebook and pen handy. Start a file. Feel free to break out a new pack of sticky notes and a thick marker. Create a bulletin board of your favorites. Get creative. The possibilities are endless! The only rule is to keep it short so you can remember it!

Ideas and key words for your conversation word, phrase, slogan, or mantra:

_____

_____

_____

Helpful tip: Imagine talking to your older and wiser self about what you want from conversations (or imagine talking with a wise mentor or guide who has your best interests at heart). What advice would they give you?

_____

_____

_____

◀▲▶

Now it's time to consider another essential step as you refine and solidify your Vision for conversation success.

TRY THIS!

What's your motivation ... your "why"?

Sometimes we make ourselves crazy trying to change, shift, or improve things in our lives. We work out elaborate dreams and plans. And even then ... nothing happens. Often this is because we haven't really determined why we're doing what we're doing! As you refine and solidify your Vision for conversation success, it's time to consider this essential question.

So let's hear it! What's your "why"? What compelled you to pick up this book? Why do you want to experience better conversations? What benefits do you most want to enjoy? What do you want to offer others?

_____

_____

_____

_____

◄▲►

Congratulations! This is all-powerful work! On to another step.

Take *Action* With Powerful Intentions

Vision and motivation? Check and check. Now it's time to set some powerful intentions that will get you focused and guide your actions.

But first, let's address the elephant in the room: the word *intention*. It's tossed around a lot these days. Sometimes frivolously. Everyone and their grandmother is telling us we need to be more… *intentional*. Often without really explaining what it means or how to do it.

Perhaps I'm sensing a little eye-rolling out there. I get it.

The word *intention* has indeed been overused and even abused. What's more, intentions aren't always seen in a positive light (e.g., "The road to hell is filled with good intentions.") Hell?!? Yikes!

This may lead you to think intentions are just empty words, useless ideas, or idle wishes. They certainly can be. But there's also a positive side.

Let's look at a definition that I find useful and inspiring.

Intention: a determination to act in a certain way; resolve.

Don't you love it? Determination. Certainty. Resolve. Nothing indecisive or namby-pamby there.

Or try this: Think of the word *intention* in tandem with the phrase "intent on." The only difference between the two is the letter "i."

What does "intent on" conjure up for you? Probably a lot more than empty words and idle wishes!

You can also think of intentions as mindsets, attitudes, ambitions, and decisions that support your Vision and drive your actions.

In summary, when you're truly *intent* on something—when you are *focused* and committed—you are *unstoppable*!

So, let's take this intention business for a spin.

TRY THIS!

Pay attention to your intentions

What are your intentions when it comes to having better, more meaningful conversations? What part will you play in creating your success? What actions will you take? What will you be "intent on"? You might even consider whether you have any specific and measurable goals in mind. As in, deciding how many interactions you want to spark or participate in at a certain event or on any given day. Finish the sentence below:

When it comes to striving toward better conversations, I intend to…

_____

_____

_____

The beauty of this exercise is intensified by its flexibility. As with your conversation mantra or slogan, you can create and use your intentions in two ways:

- ☀ **Big picture:** as a guide or philosophy that helps you prepare for, attract, show up for, and participate in all conversations.

- ☀ **Case by case:** as a way to get in the right frame of mind for a specific conversation or social gathering.

◄ ▲ ►

Take a breather—and a bow! If you've invested the time to consider and work on any of what you've just read, congratulations! You have created a solid foundation on your path toward enjoying better conversations.

Now, let's take a second to review:

- ☀ Can you feel yourself getting clearer on what your Vision— your definition of success—looks and feels like?

- ☀ Do you fully understand your "why"?

- ☀ What about your intentions?

Even though you are working to clarify these answers, remember they aren't set in stone. Feel free to continue updating and refining your Vision for conversation success. In fact, I recommend it!

As you move through this section and the rest of the book, the insights you gain may inspire you to come back here and do a little tweaking.

. . . .

Got your Vision and intentions ready to go on the road? Now let's get practical and look at what you can pack into your Conversation Toolkit.

Building Your
Conversation *Toolkit*

*For the record, we're not
talking about saws, wrenches,
and hammers here.*

Every task is easier with the right tools.

When it comes to practicing an art, craft, or trade, you'll often hear that high-quality work is "all about the tools." With that in mind, let's examine the fundamental tools of the art of conversation.

While some tools you can hold in your hand, these are different. They include attitudes, habits, mindsets, and practices that can work wonders as you sharpen your conversation skills.

Put another way, conversational masters offer, exude, and practice these "tools." You can, too.

Become aware of them, learn how to embody them, make the conscious choice to practice them regularly and skillfully, and they will create the basis for the conversation success you want and deserve.

Utilize
the Four Ps

While there are a number of ways to measurably boost your ability to become a sparkling conversationalist, adopting these four habits will help you get way, way ahead of the curve:

- **Be positive.**
- **Be purposeful.**
- **Be a possibilitarian.**
- **Be proactive.**

Let's find out why.

Be positive

The practice of positivity has a long history in the world of success. Believing that your conversations will be interesting and rewarding— whatever *positive* means to you—can help make them so.

Besides that, what you feed your mind—the words you say to yourself, the books you read, the shows you watch, the music you listen to, and (you guessed it!) the people you converse with—all influence your overall demeanor and self-esteem. You can control at least some of that! Focus on and seek out healthy, high-quality, positive, inspiring, and affirming input.

Related to that is the concept of *assuming positive rapport*. Here, you choose to feel optimistic about social encounters *before they even happen*. You imagine strangers as people you already know and like—and as people who know and like you. You feel confident that you'll indeed connect and find common interests quickly and easily.

But wait, isn't assuming a bad thing? As in, "Assume, and you'll make an ASS out of U and ME"?

Not necessarily.

Here's the magic of assuming positive rapport: When you go into an exchange feeling positive, confident, at ease, open, warm, and friendly, others will likely respond in kind.

It's that wonderful sensation of being in a conversation and feeling like you've known this person for years. It feels pleasant and effortless.

Note: This isn't the same as being socially aggressive. Barging in. Invading boundaries. Latching on. Taking over. Assuming you're someone's BFF.

Ewww. No!

Assuming positive rapport is a relaxed confidence. Can you see—maybe even feel—the difference?

Consider the words of Irish poet William Butler Yeats: "There are no strangers here, only friends you haven't met yet."

In contrast, heading into a conversation with hesitation, angst, or negative assumptions can adversely impact an exchange.

Would you feel comfortable talking to someone who is on edge, nervous, or uncomfortable? Someone who's already assuming the exchange will be a bust?

Probably not. It would just be … awkward, unpleasant, and draining.

In his *Wall Street Journal* column entitled, "You're More Likable Than You Think," Dan Ariely writes, "We spend so much time worrying about our own behavior and the impressions we are giving out that we miss positive signals from others, such as smiles and laughter."

This sabotages the encounter before it even gets going!

So consider the Italian phrase: *Seridi e la vita ti sorride.* ("Smile and life smiles at you.") Great advice, don't you think?

Be purposeful

Consider your Vision for what conversation success looks, sounds, and feels like. Remember your "why," your intentions, and the other discoveries you made in the previous section. Now, allow these to guide you in becoming more purposeful and prepared in conversation.

You might even sketch out a strategy as you head to a social gathering:

- Are there certain people with whom you want to meet and engage?
- Who are they, by name or by description?

- ✳ What would you like to talk about with these people?
- ✳ What would be your goal if you were to engage them in conversations?
- ✳ What topics light you up, get you energized?
- ✳ What questions or comments could you employ to get these conversations started?
- ✳ What take-away or experience are you seeking?
- ✳ What value are you offering to others?

Just remember: We don't always have *total* control over whom we converse with and what we will talk about. Forcing a topic could backfire if we push too hard. And, for goodness sakes, we don't want to be a one-trick conversation pony who can only talk about a single topic or issue ad nauseum. Boring! (And so limiting!)

But let's look at how we can exert "control" in a different way. It's all about adopting this delightful attitude.

Be a possibilitarian

Conversations can be purposeful, or they can be filled with delightful and unexpected surprises, twists, and turns.

Why not be a *possibilitarian* and allow your conversations to be a little bit purposeful *and* a little bit random, meandering, and explorative? Certainly, there are things you'd love to discuss, but what about subjects that spring up?

Choosing this dual path means you have some great topics in mind, but you're open to the unknowns and the potential in every conversation. You welcome the idea that exchanges could flow, naturally and spontaneously.

You become a conversational adventurer. Every interaction brings with it the opportunity for something new, surprising, and possibly captivating!

Doesn't that sound wonderful?

A possibilitarian also sees that there are endless opportunities to engage, converse, and connect with all kinds of people. These could be everyday encounters with friends, neighbors, and co-workers, but also bits of friendly chit-chat with service personnel, the person sitting at the next table, or other people in our midst we've never met.

Believing in possibilities is liberating, fun, and always interesting.

Someone who has successfully adopted this attitude is Brian Grazer, the movie and television producer who brought us movie hits such as "Apollo 13" (1995) and "A Beautiful Mind" (2001), as well as popular television series such as "Arrested Development" and "24."

Grazer developed a practice he calls "curiosity conversations." These are one-on-one, get-to-know-you meetings with people outside of the entertainment industry whom he has heard about and finds intriguing. He even has someone on his staff, a "cultural attaché," who sets up these meetings. (Sounds like a cool job to me!)

The secret to Grazer's curiosity conversations? No agenda, no plans. He's just fascinated by people. He's co-written a book about this called *A Curious Mind: The Secret to a Bigger Life* and written a second book called *Face to Face: The Art of Human Connection*.

This leads us to another vital component in your Conversation Toolbox.

Be proactive

This often comes as a surprise to many people. Per socialization and protocol experts, it's your responsibility (dare I say your *duty*) to be proactive about conversations.

You read that right:

It's all you, baby.
Time to stop leaning on others to get conversations going. Or expecting someone else to make them friendly, fun, and fascinating.

More specifically, when you're in a social setting, it's your duty to:

- Acknowledge the people around you (make eye contact, nod, smile).
- Offer a cordial greeting.
- Add in the other person's name if you know it.
- Introduce yourself (if appropriate).
- Engage them in dialogue (ask a question, offer a compliment).
- Make them feel comfortable in your presence.

Don't expect the party host, the bride, the conference organizer, the workshop facilitator, the social chairman, your fairy godmother, or anyone else to personally introduce you to others in the room.

You are in charge here. (And don't worry, by the time you finish this book, you will know what to do in just about any social situation!)

Think of it this way: You have the honor of acknowledging the humans around you and becoming the Instigator of Great Conversations.

(That title would look awesome on a business card, wouldn't it?)

Likewise, as you read earlier, if you're seeking certain types of conversations, it makes sense to find or create the settings and situations where these are most likely to occur.

Most importantly, be open to the possibility that any kind of conversation could happen almost anywhere!

Here are some examples of places where great conversations can begin:

- Standing in line at the grocery story, coffee shop, food truck, airport, theater, or wherever.
- When seated next to someone at a bar, on a plane, in a meeting, or in church.
- At the gym or poolside.
- In a hotel lobby.
- In a grocery store aisle.
- At the park, especially if you have a friendly dog with you!
- In a classroom.
- Wherever there are people.

What about more extended conversations? Again, the locations are plentiful:

- On a walk or hike.
- Around a fire.
- At coffee shops, cafés, pubs, or eateries with patios or decks.
- At bookstores, markets, or outdoor events.
- On back (or front) porches or wherever there is comfortable outdoor seating.
- During times of celebration or sadness.
- Wherever there are open hearts and minds, a little time, and a willingness to share and listen.

Gifted conversationalist, author, professional speaker, and corporate trainer Thom Singer notes, "Great conversations can happen in just about any situation. It's all about the enthusiasm of both parties to be in conversation and the evidence of mutual respect."

If you kick off any social interaction as a positive, purposeful, proactive possibilitarian (try saying that three times fast!), you'll gain a huge advantage.

That's a million-dollar mindset for great conversations! Speaking of words that begin with C...

CHAPTER 15

··

Consider the Four Cs

··

Regardless of your social style, skill level, or goals, the Four Cs are vital to good conversation. What are they?

- **Courage**
- **Caring**
- **Curiosity**
- **Courtesy**

Having the Four Cs in your back pocket is as close to having a conversational magic wand as you'll ever get. Let's examine each one.

Courage

Setting aside different personality types and levels of social dexterity, it takes courage to start a conversation, particularly with someone you don't know. (Okay, and sometimes even with someone you do!) It feels like there's a certain risk in sparking the exchange, "putting yourself out there," and hoping for a positive interaction.

Perfect timing for a little background on the word *courage*. It's derived from the French word *coeur*, which means "heart." Many believe having courage is being completely void of fear. Hah! Not so.

When you have courage, you may still feel unsure, nervous, anxious, or scared but, because you have *heart*, those feelings don't stop you!

You pull yourself together, dig in, carry on, and do what needs to be done. You take that leap of faith. You begin.

If a conversation goes nowhere, isn't as pleasant as you thought it would be, or the other person is a total jerk, so what? You shake it off, move on, and try again.

One thing's for sure:

You will always fail at conversation if you never find the courage (the heart) to try.

So to keep trying and learning, remind yourself there's a brilliant lesson in every perceived failure.

You can do this. Put on your super-hero cape and go for it!

Caring

I once overheard two women talking after a meeting where I gave a presentation on "The Success Secrets of The Intentional Networker." I was packing up my equipment, and they were doing the same with the registration table.

"Lisa, what do you think is the most important factor in being a good networker?"

"Well, for starters, you have to care about other people."

Bingo! I was beaming!

To have good conversations, you first have to care about other people. You also have to care about yourself.

As in, upholding your own Vision, as well as your boundaries and self-respect, which you'll read more about later on in this book.

Caring provides the ultimate foundation for high-quality connection, collaboration, and community.

You can offer that unforgettable sense of caring via warm, friendly words, a pleasant tone of voice, attentive body language, and your undivided attention.

Sounds easy, right? Well, here's the problem. We're humans. And remember those obstacles you read about earlier? They can (and do) get in the way.

So whenever possible, be the one who chooses to show up, be present, and take an interest in other people. Yes, even people who aren't just like you or who might not seem like ideal conversation partners. Ask about their days, lives, jobs, stories, experiences, interests, triumphs, and lessons. Listen attentively. This automatically puts you in the top tier of thoughtful conversationalists worldwide!

Lots more about listening in coming sections. In the meantime, focus on the caring angle. When you really care, your interactions will begin having much more meaning and—forgive the melodrama here, but it's true—your life will change dramatically for the better.

Caring is a game-changer, I promise.

Now for the third C.

Curiosity

Many people believe the key to being a world-class conversationalist is to be *interesting*. To read a lot of books, see the latest movies, visit all the cool art galleries, follow the latest trends, travel the world, and have one amazing experience after another.

Really great goals. I'm all for it! It's good to be curious and to experience new things so you can converse on many topics. But here's the twist that can make the biggest difference: The easiest way to be perceived as *interesting* is to be *interested* in others. To be curious about *them*.

Curiosity ranks right up there with courage and caring when it comes to good conversation.

No wonder self-improvement icon Dale Carnegie famously advised: It's more important to be *interested* than *interesting*. Carnegie's point is important, useful, timeless, and life changing.

Think about that for a moment. What fascinates you about people? About life? About the world? What do you want to learn or know more about? Sometimes other people hold hidden gems—stories, experiences, wisdom, expertise—just waiting to be discovered.

When you're curious, it's far more likely you'll uncover conversation treasure.

Take, for example, this possible scenario:

You're at the airport, standing in Southwest Airline's famous numbered boarding lineup. There's a guy in a suit standing next to you. You decide to be a little curious.

You: "Heading home or headed out?"

Guy in suit: "Headed out. Going to see a new client." *(You're noting his British accent.)*

You: "So, what do you do?" *(I know. What a lame question! But hang on...)*

Guy in suit: "I've been selling medical equipment since I moved here from London."

You: "London? Oh wow! What led you to make that big change?"

Guy in suit: "It was time for a more normal schedule. I used to be part of the touring crew for the Rolling Stones."

Whaaaatt?! Imagine the exchange that could go from there! Especially if you end up sitting together.

Conversations like this can and do happen every day.

Never assume other people won't be interesting and good conversation partners. With some *healthy curiosity,* you too might uncover the most intriguing tidbits about someone's life, an unusual hobby you both share, a common friend, or a source for great travel advice.

And, best-case scenario, you might make a new friend or earn a new client!

So, by all means, keep your curiosity battery fully charged at all times.

An important bit of advice regarding curiosity. Did you notice that I used the phrase "healthy curiosity" earlier? Pay close attention to the "healthy" part. In other words, make sure your curiosity doesn't begin to feel too nosey or intrusive. Like a cross examination in a courtroom or an aggressive interview for a tell-all publication. Or just plain snoopy.

> Curiosity is not a free pass to butt your nose into someone's privacy—asking about something that's highly personal and clearly not your business.

Focus on being interested without being obtrusive! And watch for signs that you've crossed the line. Curiosity with courtesy: our perfect segue to the next C.

Courtesy

We often hear people talk about their hopes and dreams for a better, kinder, and more peaceful world. Well, that begins right here, right now, with you and me. Courtesy and its twin sibling, civility, are all about manners, rules, and daily practices that make a civilized world, well, *civilized*. (This meshes nicely with caring, don't you think?)

We can begin by practicing those small but vital habits most of us learned before our first day of Kindergarten. Remembering to say:

- Hello
- Goodbye
- Please
- Thank you

These simple words are universal and show basic respect and courtesy for others. And when others feel respected by you, wonderful things can happen!

As proof, when photographer John Langford returned from a world tour of more than 38 countries, he revealed that he had a marvelous adventure, met hundreds of fascinating people, took lots of photographs, and had very few, if any, negative experiences.

His secret? Wherever John went, he generously used the four important phrases you just read. What's more, he took the time to learn how to say the phrases in each local language or dialect. From there, many conversations, lots of civility, and cordial friendships flourished. Even if another word was never spoken.

The Four Cs are, hands down, some of the most important things to pack in your conversation toolkit. But there are other attributes that can't be ignored.

Let's look next at civility's favorite great aunt: **Graciousness.**

16

. . . .

Lead with
Graciousness

. . . .

Close your eyes right now and think of someone you know who is gracious. How do you feel in that person's presence? Pretty good? Amazing?

Who doesn't relish the opportunity to spend time and converse with someone who has this rare and delightful trait?

But wait! What does it really mean to be gracious? Is it having charm and charisma? Is it that irresistible, tantalizing "it" factor?

Well, yes. And no.

A person can be *charming* (alluring, delightful, smooth, cultured, dazzling) and even *charismatic* (compelling, beguiling, fascinating, magnetic, persuasive). Charm and charisma, alone or together, can definitely make a conversation partner highly attractive, interesting, influential, and even a little intoxicating.

But don't confuse that with *graciousness,* which stands on its own.

Totally confused at this point? I get it. So let's explore this further.

While teaching a workshop on conversation and connection to a group of leaders within a financial organization, I was facilitating a discussion on graciousness. To start us off, I asked participants to think of someone they thought exhibited the characteristics of this powerful and attractive trait.

After a few moments of reflection and small group interaction, one participant raised her hand and nominated their CEO's wife (let's call her Jeanine). This prompted enthusiastic agreement and smiles from the group. Several participants even began to share memories of Jeanine that verified why they thought she was a good model of graciousness.

"When Jeanine hosts parties for the staff, she always makes us feel welcomed and at ease. You can tell she has put a lot of thought and work into making it special for us."

"When she comes by the office, she takes the time to chat with us at our desks or in the hallways. She's interested in how we're doing and what's going on in our lives. She wants to get to know us."

"When I'm in conversation with Jeanine, I feel safe and like I've known her forever. She listens attentively and respectfully—she never makes me feel like she's superior to me."

"Jeanine usually remembers names. She makes you feel like the most important person in the room, even though we only see her a few times a year."

"She's fun, interesting, and energizing. She listens, she's respectful, and she doesn't judge."

By the time this discussion wrapped up, I wanted to meet and get to know this incredible woman! Wouldn't you? She had warmed up the room—and she wasn't even present!

How powerful is that?

> If you want to bring your "A" game to a conversation, it's time to get to know, practice, and show up with an abundance of graciousness.

Ready to learn more about what it is and how to do it?

Let's begin by examining its root word, *grace*.

Grace

At its heart, grace is about love, kindness, generosity, and forgiveness. Someone grants or offers you something special, welcomed, and precious. And, the truth is, you didn't expect it, earn it, or deserve it. But the person gave it to you anyway.

Or perhaps you offered grace to someone else. And you did it because you chose to, not because you *had* to. You adopted the intention to be gracious.

Here are a few more specific ways grace can be defined and experienced, all of which can be applied to conversation and how we treat each other:

* Free and unmerited favor, pardon, or assistance.
* Decency, kindness, courtesy, or goodwill.
* Simple beauty or loveliness.
* Elegance, class, and refinement.
* Quiet strength.

Amazing grace!

What words or phrases would you add to the list of definitions for grace?

_____

_____

_____

Ever experienced a gracious or grace-filled conversation? Can you describe it? How did it make you feel?

_____

_____

_____

◂▲▸

Anne Lamott, one of my favorite writers and a keen observer of life, once wrote, "I do not understand the mystery of grace—only that it meets us where we are and does not leave us where it found us."

Boy, howdy. When someone offers you grace, you never forget it.

And here's another handy tip: Understanding what it means to offer grace and being open to experiencing it can be so powerful. This changes almost everything for the better.

Our world could use a lot more grace, that's for sure. Why not be someone who offers it freely?

Along those lines, here's a topic I get asked about a lot: the challenge of remembering and using others' names. This one requires showing a little grace, with others and with ourselves.

There is no doubt about it. We love hearing our names! Many say it's our favorite word. Yet remembering others' names can be universally challenging. Yep, it happens to me, too. During introductions, names often go in one ear and out the other.

Even so, we can do our best to share, ask for, pay attention to, use, and remember names whenever possible. (But not so much so that it comes across as affected and unnatural—or like Lesson #46 in a corny sales training handbook.)

What to do if you forget someone's name? *Graciously* ask again. ("Gosh. I'm so sorry. Could you please remind me of your name...one more time?")

If others don't remember your name? Please, please, please! Don't make a big stink or get offended. *Graciously* remind them. You might even add in a funny line like: "Hey, no worries! You can ask my name as often as you need to. I'll always remember it!"

Practice offering this small but important gift of grace, and you'll find that other attractive virtues will naturally follow!

Kindness

A vital component found in the gift of graciousness is kindness. Frank Lipman, M.D., a pioneer in functional medicine, notes that, "Kindness is a universal language that crosses perceived boundaries. It's one of the easiest things to exchange."

When we offer the gift of kindness, it often comes back to us in many ways, including an increase in our own happiness.

You could argue that happy people tend to be kinder, meaning it's hard to be kind if you're not happy. Fair enough. But think back to how doing something kind for another person made you feel. Maybe it made you smile. Maybe you felt warm inside or satisfied in some way. Perhaps that feeling lasted for more than a few moments or... forever!

Kindness has the power to create joy for all involved.

Imagine infusing all your conversations with kindness. Talk about making a memorable impact!

"Everyone is looking for an edge," writes Arthur C. Brooks in his *Wall Street Journal* article, "Nice People Really Do Have More Fun." Brooks is a Harvard Professor, social scientist, best-selling author, columnist, and enthusiastic teacher on the art and science of living a better life. Citing numerous studies and "the best available research," Brooks sums up by saying, "That edge is being pleasant and friendly."

Sounds so simple, but how do we do this?

Is kindness the same thing as "being nice?" Not really. Nice can be cordial, agreeable, pleasant, and cheery. It has its merits. We all know people who are nice. But are they also kind? Not always.

Kindness is more active than nice. It involves more caring, generosity, and action. A kind person might be nice, but a nice person doesn't necessarily offer kindness.

It's compare-and-contrast time again!

Analyze the traits of people you know who are nice versus those of the people you see as kind. Grab some paper and populate your own Venn diagram with the characteristics that come to mind, and note the similarities and differences.

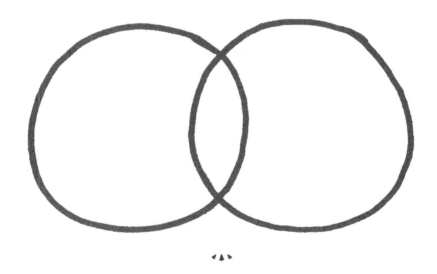

◄ ▲ ▶

Perhaps an example of intentional and active kindness will be helpful. When author Deborahann Smith began doing temp work to help pay the bills early on in her freelance writing career, she brought with her and displayed a sign in her workspace that read, "Be excellent to each other." (Yes, if you must know, the inspiration came from the 1989 movie, "Bill & Ted's Excellent Adventure.")

Smith says the sign started out as a reminder to herself to do excellent work and to do her best to be friendly, kind, and gracious to even the most unpleasant co-workers.

The sign helped keep Smith on task and upbeat during a lot of boring work. But it had an unexpected and positive impact on the culture of the organization, too. Many colleagues began responding to or were inspired by Smith's many examples of kindness—compliments, words of thanks, overall friendliness, even defending someone from malicious gossip. They also responded to the message of her sign.

Overall, most employees and managers began treating each other with more respect, appreciation, and thoughtfulness. They began standing up for each other and pointing out when someone wasn't "being excellent." Smith also admits there were people who never noticed or cared about the sign. And even a few who were so miserable and mean that no amount of excellence or kindness could change them. She had to give up on those folks.

Despite that, Smith reports that she toted her little sign with her to dozens of workplaces where it frequently made a positive impact. The catalysts here were Smith's own intentions and determinations:

- To adopt an attitude and standard of excellence in all she did.
- To treat others kindly.
- To share these philosophies in a subtle way.

For the most part, the rest took care of itself. "Now instead of a sign, I carry excellence within me as a mantra, as a presence," says Smith.

She also adds an important footnote: "Excellence has the most impact when I first focus on my own peace and happiness, then send it out into the world."

Fantastic advice, in so many ways.

When I think about the nice-versus-kind distinction, another story comes to mind that might help you visualize the nuances.

On a cloudy September morning in San Diego, California, I was aboard the hotel shuttle heading back to the airport after presenting at a conference. The only other person on board was a woman neatly dressed in comfortable attire: yoga pants, T-shirt, pink hoodie, and sneakers. She was holding tightly to a pink rolling suitcase and a black tote bag bedazzled with the words "Dance Mom."

The driver hopped in energetically, asked us which airlines we were on, nodded his head as we told him, and threw the van into drive.

I knew the trip would be short, as you can practically walk from downtown San Diego to the airport ticketing terminals. I was happy to have my presentation behind me and to be heading home.

Meanwhile, my van companion didn't seem happy at all. In fact, she looked stressed and anxious. She nervously shuffled through her tote bag, triple-checking its contents. Then she shifted in her seat restlessly as she looked out the van window.

I wondered: Should I strike up a conversation? Or just continue the ride in silence?

Hoping I might be able to distract her from her worries, I asked the usual question: "Where are you headed?"

"To see my aunt back home in Kansas," she replied, still looking distractedly out the window.

After a short pause, she looked at me and added, "To be honest, I'm a little nervous."

"Oh no!" I replied sympathetically. "What are you nervous about?"

"I don't fly very much," she confessed. "And I have to change planes in Dallas. I know it's a really big airport, and I'm afraid I won't know where to go. What if I miss my flight?"

I felt for her, remembering when I was younger and learning the ropes of traveling solo. Plus, I knew firsthand that travel is often full of unexpected…adventures. I wondered what I could say to make her feel better.

Then it hit me. I thought of *The Wizard of Oz* and that magical moment when Dorothy finally discovers the power of those jazzy, glorious ruby slippers—the ones she's been wearing all along!

The woman's "Dance Mom" tote bag told me all I needed to know about her. Those two words translate into "woman on a mission who can do *anything*, on time, on budget, and with a high degree of style and sparkle."

While I wasn't a Dance Mom, I had once been a Soccer Mom. (Same concept, less sparkle.) I could quickly deduce her capabilities, as well as her anxieties. I had driven my son (and sometimes his teammates) to endless tournaments, both in metropolitan areas and at some of the most obscure and well-hidden soccer fields. And all before smart phones and GPS devices were in the hands of mere mortals.

I could relate to this woman. I wanted to help.

"Looks like you have a child who dances," I said, glancing at her bag.

The woman brightened. "Yes," she said proudly. "I actually have two daughters who dance. And they're really good."

"You do much traveling for that?"

"Oh yes! I drive them all over. Pretty much every weekend."

"I bet you have to travel to a lot of places you've never been to before."

"All the time. And, oh, the traffic!"

"Well, trust me," I said, "if you can do that, you can certainly navigate around any airport. In many ways, it's actually easier. Just follow the signs and ask for help if you need it."

And then I added (for style points): "Dance moms are some of the most courageous and resourceful women I know. You've got this!"

As we neared my drop-off spot at the terminal, the woman smiled at me and let out a breath of relief. She glanced at her boarding passes and proudly reconsidered the sparkly writing on her tote bag. I could see the anxiety and tension melting out of her shoulders.

"Have a great trip," I said, as I gathered my things and stepped out of the van.

"I will. Same to you," she said. "And thank you. I appreciate your words of encouragement."

See how easy that was? I had three basic choices. I could have:

1. **Ignored my van mate.** (I don't know her. I'll never see her again. What's the point in engaging? *This is indifference.*)

2. **Offered a friendly greeting.** ("Good morning." Far better than ignoring her. *This is being nice.*)

3. **Noted her distress, engaged, and then said or done something supportive, uplifting, and helpful.** ("You've got this!" *This is being kind.*)

I chose #3. Even though we spoke for less than five minutes, we both left the conversation feeling better.

When you have the opportunity to offer even a tiny nugget of kindness, don't hesitate to offer it. It can change everything! And, trust me, it will make you feel good, too!

Generosity

You can't really discuss graciousness and kindness without adding in a discussion about generosity. They are all intertwined.

Generosity means offering and sharing your best and in gracious abundance, whatever that looks like for you. Your generosity might be a listening ear, a compliment, a word of encouragement, or a sincere apology. The whole point is to make another person feel special and cared for.

Take, for example, my friend Sue Sturrock. For many years, she and her husband ran a popular, small-town café in Rosebud, Texas. An expert in hospitality (an important form of graciousness and generosity), she came up with a metaphor that beautifully sums up generosity and grace.

"Imagine taking the time to bake delicious homemade cookies from your most treasured family recipe. You shop for and use the best and freshest ingredients available. You bake the cookies with care, put them on your best platter, and share them with guests, neighbors, colleagues, or even strangers."

This simple example demonstrates that generosity is intentional, sincere, and *active*.

It's choosing to help or give something to someone without expecting anything in return. It's going the extra mile, even when it's not convenient. It's using your unique gifts to delight others.

Who wouldn't love that? And again, that warm feeling inside will likely be shared by the giver and the receiver.

In conversations, generosity can mean any number of things:

- Giving someone your focused time and attention.
- Asking open-ended questions that encourage conversation.
- Listening more than you talk.
- Using kind, supportive, positive, encouraging words.
- Seeking to understand.
- Being open to hearing other ideas and viewpoints.
- Apologizing to someone you've wronged.
- Giving people the benefit of the doubt.
- Being flexible and open to where the conversation goes.
- Offering a sincere compliment.
- Remembering someone.
- Inquiring about someone's day, family, work, or something of similar interest or importance.
- Expressing genuine happiness about someone's good news or success in their lives (called "supportive joy").
- Releasing the need to enter into a debate or be right.
- Following up on a previous conversation or inquiry.
- Introducing someone to your friends or others in the room.

Generosity has many faces. It isn't always easy or convenient, but it's worth it!

Presence

There's another powerful element to this graciousness business. And, really, it's not that hard. It's the practice of having presence and, by this, I mean:

1. Choosing to be fully present with others in the moment.

2. Carrying yourself with dignity and composure.

3. Exuding an open, approachable warmth.

Presence is highly attractive! In many ways, presence is a form of the three types of intelligence you read about in Chapter 11.

TRY THIS!

People with presence.

Think about someone you know who always shows up with the traits just listed. That person enters a room, and it's suddenly a better place. What do they do or say that gives them that sense of presence?

_____

_____

◂▴▸

Respect

When it comes to graciousness, respect is a pivotal component. But even if you know most of the words to the famous song by Aretha Franklin, how would you actually define *respect*?

Here are a few ways to describe it:

- Simple acknowledgement and consideration of others.
- Treating others with care and dignity.
- A sincere effort to understand.
- Positive feelings, perhaps appreciation or admiration.
- Making others feel welcomed, included, valued, and safe.

Can you feel the graciousness just oozing through all of those? Yep, they are close cousins!

One thing we know for sure about respect is that we all want it. Some people are even so bold and brazen as to *demand* it, as if others owe it to them. (That in itself seems a little ungracious and disrespectful, doesn't it?)

And yet:

- How often do we offer the level of respect to others that we would like for ourselves?
- Why is respect so frequently a one-way street and in such short supply?
- Where has respect gone?
- Where do we find it?
- How can we add it back into our daily repertoire?

Respect is something we all have the power to revive with our words and actions in conversations. We just have to commit to practicing and offering it more often.

Beginning today.

Go back to the previous list. Review what respect is all about. How, where, and with whom can you exude these traits more often?

One thing's for sure: When you increase the level of respect you give to others in your conversations, they are more likely to perceive you as gracious and kind. You might also get more respect in return.

Genshai

All these facets of graciousness remind me of a favorite term that can be used as a little mantra whenever you are socializing: *genshai* (pronounced GEN-shy).

I was first introduced to this word while reading the wonderful book, *Aspire*, by business consultant, speaker, and coach Kevin Hall.

What exactly is genshai? It's a Japanese term that means "the practice of never treating others in a manner that makes them feel small or less than."

Not sure what I mean? Here's a story that illustrates a situation where genshai was not practiced.

While working my way through a happy hour buffet line on the first day of an association conference, I found myself standing next to a woman I had met at the previous year's conference. I remembered her quite well, but it quickly became clear she didn't remember me. At all.

Me: "Hello, Angela! So great to see you again! I don't know if you remember me, but we sat together last year during the breakout session on Creativity." *(See what I did there? I gave her a clue to help jog her memory.)*

Angela: "Oh?... And you are…?" *(She never made eye contact, but instead offered a cursory glance at my name tag. Then she proceeded to fill her plate.)*

Me: "Patti DeNucci. From Austin. I write and speak about networking, conversation, and connection. We did one of the creativity exercises together in that session."

Angela: "Oh, okay..." *(She continued working her way diligently through the buffet, adding an array of appetizers to her plate. Never looked at me. Never said a word. Walked off and joined her pals across the room.)*

Alrighty then.

I can tell you this: I felt pretty insignificant and small after that. And it didn't feel particularly good.

Has this ever happened to you? Have you ever done this to someone else?

This, my friends, was a fitting example of someone practicing neither genshai nor graciousness. And, honestly, I've never forgotten it. (Maybe a little ungracious of me, I'll admit.)

Olivia Fox Cabane, author of *The Charisma Myth: How Anyone Can Master the Art and Science of Personal Magnetism*, notes, "You might not remember the exact content of a conversation…but you probably do remember how it felt. It's not the words, but the emotional imprint that remains."

In the meantime, what might Angela have done to be more gracious?

A few options:

- She could have said, "Hey, great to see you!" (*Even if she had no recollection of who I was.*)

- She could have been totally transparent and said, "Gosh, I'm so sorry. I'm drawing a complete blank. But hey, it's great to 'meet' you again!"

- She could have tacked on: "You'll have to excuse me. My friends are waiting over there for me. Maybe we'll get to talk later?"

- Even better: "Say, when you're done filling your plate, come on over and meet my friends. Maybe join us if you don't have other plans?"

Wow, any of that would have been very gracious! And it wouldn't have been difficult.

The more we practice the art of being gracious, the more successful we'll become at life—personally and professionally. We'll also become infinitely more likable, which is an attribute highly interconnected with graciousness. They definitely overlap if we start playing with the Venn diagram again.

Want to guess what the next chapter is about?

Ramp Up
Your Likability

. . . .

Funny thing. People who exude graciousness, respect, and all the traits you've read about so far tend to be very... *likable*. So, thankfully, you already know many of the attributes that can enhance your likability.

And, as you might guess, there are a few more!

But first... this question may come up: Why bother to be likable? Who cares?

There are certainly people who are not one bit concerned about whether they are likable or not. (You can probably think of a few right now! Maybe you're one of them.)

In contrast, it's certainly not wise to dwell on making sure everyone likes you. Especially if you want to be liked *at all costs*. (You may know a few of these people as well. And perhaps this is you.)

Likability is powerful, but not synonymous with being a supplicating doormat.

In its true form, likability does have its advantages. Generally speaking, most of us:

- Enjoy knowing and spending time with people we like.
- Work better, harder, and longer for (and with) people we like.
- Prefer doing business with people we like.
- Tend to support and be generous with people we like.

In short, likability is a good thing.

Here's another way to think about it. You know how sugar, salt, and pepper improve the flavor of so many foods? In conversations, likable people are the "flavor enhancers." They bring "that special something."

Want to know some powerful characteristics that are also very likable? Let's explore more of the traits and habits that give us that "likability edge."

Integrity

What does integrity have to do with likability? As it turns out, quite a bit. People with integrity have character and a moral compass. They are trustworthy. You can count on them. I think you can agree that it's easier to like someone you can trust over someone you can't.

Here's some proof. While facilitating a discussion with a group of Houston business professionals, I put the participants into small groups and asked them to come up with three traits they most valued and appreciated in their colleagues.

After the initial discussion, the list of potential traits was much longer than just three! We next merged the small groups into larger groups with continuing encouragement to keep paring down the list until they arrived at only three traits.

This was a challenge, and the room was filled with lively discussion and debate!

As a final step, I had the entire group vote on their favorite top three. The winners?

- ☀ Integrity (Top of the list!)
- ☀ Caring (No surprise.)
- ☀ Consistency (Steadiness, reliability, trustworthiness.)

Others that were semifinalists? Read on.

Optimism

Optimism (a sibling to positivity) is a wonderful trait. Not only are optimists cheerful, hopeful, energizing, and enthusiastic, they also rank high in likability. They have the power to lighten up just about any mood, room, scene, or discussion. They also score high in happiness and satisfaction with life and work.

Now there's some "emotional contagion" we could all use!

Some say optimists aren't realists. Sorry. There are already too many realists and negative people in the world. I'd rather have an upbeat optimist as a conversation partner any day. How about you?

Sense of humor

Speaking of upbeat people, a person with a wry sense of humor is such a gift! The combination of intelligent wit, lightheartedness, and fun is endlessly entertaining, likable, and appealing.

I'm referring to someone with the ability to see the irony, silliness, and even the absurdity in any situation. Even better, someone who can comment on what's happening with near-perfect comic timing. They know how to add an unexpected and clever phrase that surprises, delights, tickles, and evokes authentic smiles.

Keep in mind, this is far different from the attention-hungry clown who has to spew a constant stream of wise-guy quips. Or the person who inserts a bad joke *at the wrong time* or *at the expense of another*. Or even the flitty, silly person who is really just immature, nervous, or insecure. Or has clearly had too much caffeine or alcohol. These types of "humor" have the opposite effect and are generally not appealing.

You may think humor and laughter aren't important. Maybe even a waste of time. Guess again. Studies reveal that humor is a powerful medicine that can soothe many social interactions, lighten a heavy mood, and make the day brighter. Even better? Laughter and humor have the power to:

- Strengthen and oxygenate the cardiovascular system.
- Increase the flow of oxygen to the brain.
- Enhance brain connectivity.
- Release endorphins and serotonin.
- Reduce inflammation, pain, and blood sugar levels.
- Increase job performance.
- Bond people emotionally.

Pretty strong reasons to lighten up
and enjoy a chuckle regularly!

While we're on the topic of humor, the following trio is worth a mention.

Wit, irony, and sarcasm. Many of us assume these facets of humor can add zest to a conversation. They can! Each one has its own personality and impact, but they also come with the potential to be confused and, in some cases, misused. This quick road map may be helpful.

Wit is defined as "mental sharpness, keen intelligence, and a natural aptitude for using words and ideas in a quick and inventive way to create humor" or, more briefly, "the ability to say or write things that are clever and usually funny."

Benjamin Errett, author of *Elements of Wit: Mastering the Art of Being Interesting,* calls wit "the ability to be creative on the fly, to combine ideas in conversation, to make connections quickly and with joy, and in doing so make life worth living. To create delight…"

Well, that sounds fun! I do enjoy spending time conversing with and listening to someone who is witty. Maybe you do, too.

Irony is about "using language that normally signifies the opposite, typically for humorous or emphatic effect."

This can be amusing and fun as well. But keep in mind, not everyone will understand what you're really trying to say or the intent behind your use of irony. My suggestion? Proceed with caution here.

Sarcasm is a tricky one. It's defined as "the use of irony to mock or convey contempt;" "a mocking or ironic remark;" and "caustic use of words, often in an ironic way." In other words, it is irony's evil twin.

Whoa! This doesn't sound appealing or friendly at all! And yet many of us use sarcasm in conversation. We're just trying to be funny, right? Has it gotten us in trouble now and then? Probably.

P. Valerie Dauphin, certified life coach and author of *Feel Good Kick Ass Confidence: Using Your Body to Rock Your Life*, explored the use and the effects of sarcasm as a student at the University of Pennsylvania. In her research paper titled, "Sarcasm in Relationships," she draws the following conclusion:

"[We] must be careful with how [we] use sarcasm...The thing with sarcasm is that there is too much room for misinterpretation...One can never be 100% sure what the sarcastic person means by his or her statement... [We] can and should think about the implications and consequences of what [we] are about to say before [we] say it."

The takeaway from this discussion? When it comes to humor in conversations, a large serving of wit is always a fan favorite. Go easy on the irony. And skip the sarcasm.

Humility

Also on the likability list: humility, a word which is often misunderstood. The definition that typically comes to mind is something like this:

"A modest or low view of one's importance."

We are sometimes led to believe that humility equates to being meek, less than, low on the totem pole, or cowering in the corner.

But that's not it.

Consider these definitions:

- Freedom from pride or arrogance.
- Being no more, but also no less than, who you are meant to be.

Humility isn't about being weak.
It's really about balance.

People who are humble and likable can acknowledge their areas of ignorance, human fallibility, and mistakes, *yet also* appreciate and share their knowledge, talents, gifts, and blessings. They neither disappear into the woodwork nor suck up all the oxygen in the room.

These are the folks who can engage in genuine conversations because of their willingness to embrace both their vulnerabilities *and* their strengths.

I want to be around people with those qualities!

This seems like a perfect time to mention the unfortunate phenomenon of "humblebragging." So many of us are guilty of it these days!

Humblebragging shows up in conversations and is also common on social media. It's the act of trying to *seem* humble when, in fact, your true motive is to show off or impress.

See if these examples sound familiar:

- "Well, I will say this: Running that marathon wasn't as easy as I made it look."
- "I nearly forgot my opening line while giving my Pulitzer Prize acceptance speech the other evening."
- "This week I'm going to have to settle for driving my wife's Cadillac; my Jaguar is in the shop."

Or there's always the timeless classic: "I'm truly humbled to be chosen for this award."

What's your true reaction to people who do this?

Enough already with the humblebragging. When we do it, we aren't fooling anyone. My advice? Stick with genuine humility and balance.

"The most important life lesson I've learned is the importance of humility," says Pharrell Williams, the American rapper, record producer, singer, songwriter, and entrepreneur who is known for his quiet yet dignified and highly creative image. "You want to shine, but not so bright that you burn everything in the room. As long as you've got your light, people will see you, and it's all good."

Open-mindedness

Speaking of humility, do any of us really enjoy conversing with those who are so opinionated, so locked into their own singular, set-in-concrete perspectives, that they can't take a moment—not even one—to hear or consider the slightest possibility of another view? Or they mistakenly believe that conversation is about converting others to their side?

Gotta be honest: Being highly opinionated is a total conversation killer!

Bill Bullard, Former Dean of Faculty at San Francisco University High School, prepared a commencement speech to share with the class of 2007. Bullard was sidelined with food poisoning and didn't actually present the speech, but it was published and this wisdom within it is still often quoted: "Opinion is really the lowest form of human knowledge. It requires no accountability, no understanding."

How absolutely true!

In delicious contrast, it can be so invigorating to have a civilized, thought-provoking, lively, and expansive discussion with those who have other opinions and ideas and can share them with tact and grace. Or with those who are willing to examine and even re-think their views!

Isaac Asimov, science fiction writer and professor of biochemistry at Boston University, made that point elegantly, noting, "Your assumptions are your windows on the world. Scrub them off everyone once in a while or the light won't come in."

Speaking of light, think of the stimulating and collaborative energy—and innovation and insight—that can emerge in discussions when many perspectives and possibilities are brought to the table. And imagine what happens when open minds take it all in!

Related to this…

Trust and safety

Are you someone with whom others can comfortably share sensitive or personal information during a conversation? Can you be trusted to keep that information private rather than spreading it around?

And what about your reactions? Do others feel safe revealing their thoughts, fears, unpopular opinions, and vulnerabilities with you? Can you remain calm and neutral? Or do you jump to judgment? Do you pounce on, attack, scoff at, or belittle what they say, making them *really sorry* they ever spoke up?

I think, if we're honest with ourselves, we can all work on this one!

Let's pause for a moment and think about that. We live in extremely tender, sensitive, and uncertain yet highly contentious times. Trust and safety matter more than ever, but these traits are often hard to find. And hard to embody.

Offering, earning, and preserving trust and becoming a "safe" conversation partner can dramatically transform and improve the tone and depth of our interactions and our relationships.

If we regularly and consistently demonstrate trust and safety in our discussions with others, we can create a unique space for interesting and meaningful conversations that go well below the surface.

What happens when you add that to your integrity, optimism, humor, humility, and open-minded thinking? Your sense of likability will get a giant boost.

Be *Authentic*

Authenticity. Such a lovable trait. Yet many situations aren't conducive to bringing out the "real" that can make conversations interesting and endearing. By way of example, see if you've ever heard (or said) any of these:

- ❋ "I hate networking events. Everyone is fake and out to impress."

- ❋ "The conversations at that party felt so awkward and forced."

- ❋ "I'm afraid to be myself. What if no one likes the 'real' me?"

- ❋ "Oh man. She's such a phony."

Geez, none of that sounds pleasant at all!

In contrast, people who are comfortable being authentic are so refreshing. They are real and delightfully imperfect. You don't have to waste precious time or mental energy wondering who they are or whether they're putting on an act—hiding how they really feel, pretending to be your fake friend, or just trying to impress.

Being brave enough to take the lead in dropping the pretense and working at being more genuine is a courageous step. Interestingly and ironically, it's a mindset that can make you a lot more likable and bring you other positive results as well.

As you strive to become a world-class conversationalist, make sure working on your "authenticity quotient" is front and center in your toolkit.

Because really... Why be a bad copy of someone else when you can be a really good version of you?

There's no shortage of wisdom singing the praises of authenticity.

"Our job in this lifetime is not to shape ourselves into some idea we imagine we ought to be, but to find out who we already are and become it," notes Steven Pressfield, author of numerous books including *The War of Art*.

American author, philosopher, theologian, educator, and civil rights leader Howard Thurman said it this way: "Follow the grain in your own wood."

John Jantsch, "the world's most practical marketing consultant," provides this wisdom in his daily reader, *The Self-Reliant Entrepreneur*: "Your force lies in the incredible lightness of being yourself."

And finally, the profound and prolific American writer Joseph Campbell wrote in one of his many books, *Reflections on the Art of Living*: "The privilege of a lifetime is being who you are."

Did you read that? *The privilege of a lifetime.*

How can we do this? Oddly enough, it takes courage, exploration, honesty, perspective, and practice! You did some of the work earlier in this book in the Preparing to Succeed section. Now let's take a look at what *not* to do.

Choose fresh, not canned

Ever been in a conversation with someone when it felt like they were reciting scripted lines from a speech, movie, or book? (Or most of their words literally were from a speech, movie, or book?) It not only sounds canned and unnatural, but it can also be downright annoying and off-putting!

The following story illustrates the negative impact canned or contrived conversation can have.

I once was part of a leadership committee within a national association. We were recruiting members for the following year's training team and were considering a list of nominees. We only had a few spots to fill, so we scheduled phone interviews to screen and get to know each candidate individually. Two or three of us from the current committee would be on the calls with each prospective member.

On one of the calls with a nominee, my colleagues and I noticed a pattern that emerged almost immediately. For each question posed, the candidate offered a "sound bite" or pearl of wisdom he had pulled from a reliable source. A speech he had heard. A book. A movie.

Interesting, yes, but definitely not genuine or original.

In addition, when we asked him questions, he frequently offered answers that made no sense. It was as if he hadn't heard the questions correctly. Or he was answering entirely different ones!

In general, this man's words sounded overly crafted—like he had planned the interview before knowing what the questions were. It was a lot like some of the political debates, press conferences, or television news interviews I've watched over the years. "Gotta control the narrative! Stick to the talking points. Add the spin."

Talk about conversation dissonance!

Not surprisingly, this candidate didn't impress us in the way we (or he) had hoped. We never really got a feel for who *he* was. No stories, no original thoughts, no lessons learned, no personal philosophies. Just a parade of prepackaged answers he thought we wanted to hear.

You guessed right. He was not invited to join the leadership team.

What was behind this? Fear? Insecurity? A desire to impress? Who knows? It begs the question, why are we afraid to be ourselves? What does that even look like?

Let's explore that.

Authentic people are typically:

- Self-aware.
- Comfortable being themselves, human, and imperfect.
- Not attention-seekers.
- Unconcerned with being liked by everyone.
- Honest, reliable, and consistent.
- Not focused on or impressed by material goods.
- Thick-skinned and appreciative of truth and candor.
- Humble.
- At ease with a little self-deprecation.

- ❊ Known for practicing what they preach.
- ❊ Open and transparent without going overboard.
- ❊ Can tell when others are dishonest or less than truthful.

How about that last one? Apparently, you can't trick anyone who's authentic! They'll see right through any attempt to be someone you're not.

If we want to spend more time conversing with people who are authentic, it looks like we'd better show up that way ourselves!

Authenticity in action.

Your turn. What does authenticity look, sound, and feel like to you?

_____

_____

How would you describe people who are authentic?

_____

_____

What do you think is most refreshing and enjoyable about conversations with them?

_____

_____

◂ ▴ ▸

"Conversation can move to the next level of connection when both people are speaking from their hearts," says Jan Goss, founder of Show Up Well and Civility Consulting. "From there you can find common interests, passions, and beliefs. Even fears and flaws. Once you're attached by your mutual truths, the positive vibrations and trust level go way up."

TRY THIS!

Will the real YOU please stand up?

Think about who you are, what you love, stand for, and believe in. As you go about your days and have exchanges with others, ask yourself:

- ☀ Am I being true to who I am, what I believe in, and what's most important to me?
- ☀ Am I showing up as the real me, flaws and all, while speaking my truth graciously?

◂ ▴ ▸

As you're thinking about these things, here's something you'll want to consider.

Be honest, but not inconsiderate

Authenticity is about being real, but it's never a free pass to carelessly blurt out whatever is on your mind and ignore, hurt, or trample on others' feelings. Nowhere under the definition of "authentic" will you find words like abrasive, brash, blunt, brutal, careless, crude, crass, inconsiderate, mean, pompous, unkind, unfiltered, or even vulgar. I'm not even a fan of the term "brutal honesty."

That's not being authentic; that's being a bully. Furthermore, unhinged emotional attacks or outbursts will definitely not help you build your reputation as authentic and likable.

In these times when speaking our minds, expressing our outrage, and using social media to blast every passing thought or emotion seem to be all the rage (and often out of control), we may need to dial back the drama a few notches.

We can all work on expressing our authentic, sincere, and honest thoughts and feelings with a generous helping of graciousness, respect, tact, and diplomacy.

When you can use this proven yet often forgotten formula, you will create some powerful conversations! You can get your point across without being disrespectful.

The great mathematician, astronomer, physicist, alchemist, theologian, and author Sir Isaac Newton once said, "Tact is the art of making a point without making an enemy."

British statesman, soldier, and writer Sir Winston Churchill went one step further, noting, "Tact is the ability to tell someone to go to hell in such a way that they look forward to the trip."

Brilliant!

TRY THIS!

What's your authenticity quotient?

How do you show your authentic self in dialogue with others? How would your conversation partners answer that question about you?

_____

_____

What do you think prevents you from being more graciously authentic in your conversations?

_____

_____

Are there opportunities for improvement? What steps could you take?

_____

_____

◂ ▴ ▸

CHAPTER

19

Show Some
Vulnerability

If authenticity and humility had a precious love child, the result would be vulnerability.

Great conversationalists have this trait in spades. They go beyond merely being authentic to show that they are *human*, flawed, and susceptible. Yet, they are confident and secure enough to know that imperfections are normal. This can create emotional connections with others.

What makes this possible?

Being vulnerable is a bit like a mini confession. It's revealing and intimate. We can show that we trust someone enough to share our imperfections and missteps. (Perhaps they will reciprocate?) We also are proving we have acceptance and compassion for ourselves.

Showing a little vulnerability will not be the end of the world. In fact, it can open new worlds and levels of connection.

Think about the brave guy at the party who isn't afraid to share a funny, self-effacing anecdote. It could be a silly story of how he accidentally locked himself out of his hotel room, clumsily dropped his brand-new smart phone in the lake, unknowingly walked around the office all day with spit-up on the back of his shirt after dropping his son off at daycare, or inadvertently burned the carrot cake he was trying to bake (from scratch) for his daughter's birthday.

Once the "real" is out there, you can feel a collective wave of relief. We may laugh, sigh, or shake our heads and admit, "Oh, I've SO done that!" or "That could have been me!"

From that point forward, nearly everyone feels safer showing their own vulnerabilities as the dialogue progresses.

In his book, *The Seven Levels of Intimacy: The Art of Loving and the Joy of Being Loved,* Matthew Kelly offers this advice: "If we are willing to take the risk and reveal ourselves for who we are, we discover that most people are relieved to know that we are human."

It all starts with giving ourselves (and others) permission to be the flawed humans we are.

Robert Bernard Reich—American professor, author, lawyer, political commentator, and former Secretary of Labor—adds, "I have found over the years that the most important way of getting people to relax is self-deprecating humor."

Hey, nobody's perfect!

Do you find it difficult to be vulnerable when talking to others? Why or why not?

_____

_____

_____

What do you think prevents you from showing more of your human side and the silly mistakes you've made as you navigate work and life?

_____

_____

_____

Vulnerability can lead to meaningful and memorable conversations, but it can't happen without honesty and sharing.

◄▲►

Share openly

The only way to truly get to know one another and be a real contributor to a conversation is to disclose something about ourselves, share a story, or describe an experience we've had.

And what if we don't? Well, that's like going to a potluck dinner party without bringing a dish to share.

Scan your memory, and see if you can recall a conversation when it felt like you were doing all the sharing. The other person offered nothing. Zip. Nada. Or maybe you were hesitant to share, and the other person opened the floodgates and revealed *way too much*.

In either case, it can feel very uncomfortable.

Mutual, balanced, and *tactful* sharing gives a conversation direction, momentum, life, color, and fuel.

You share a tidbit with me, and that gives me something to respond to, comment on, or ask more about. I may share a similar thought, story, personal truth, or even a challenge or weakness.

Bam! We are connecting!

Without sharing, a conversation quickly becomes the dreaded *non-versation*. No vulnerability. No give-and-take. Just a boring dead end.

The exception, of course, is when you are there to be a really good listener, a topic unto itself which you'll read more about up ahead.

So, feel free to share those stories and memories. Reveal those amusing quirks, fears, lessons, and imperfections. Make it an entertaining, interesting, relieving, and human exchange.

Sharpen your storytelling skills

If you're going to beef up your conversations by sharing and telling great stories (we all have them!), make sure you follow some basic guidelines:

- Share authentically, but judiciously.
- This sounds so basic, *but have a point.*
- Frame what you share in terms the receiver can understand:
  - Translate or explain jargon, technical terms, or acronyms
  - Don't go into excruciating detail (especially details that don't enhance or pertain to the point of the story)
  - Simplify language when possible
- Include the basics of good storytelling:
  - The setting
  - The characters / people involved
  - The mission or quest
  - What was supposed to happen
  - What actually happened (this is often the best part)
  - The quest / adventure / tragedy / hilarity that ensued
  - How things were resolved
  - How you dealt with the results
  - The Big Lesson
- Omit what's not relevant unless it's an amusing or pertinent side note.

Take the lead

It's often easier to share your story after your conversation partner has already gone down the vulnerability path. But sometimes, we have to be the ones who set the example. Like in this story, which first appeared in author and speaker Jan Phillips' Museletter, but can also be found in her book *Marry Your Muse: Making a Lasting Commitment to Your Creativity.*

When she was a young journalist, Jan set out from upstate New York on a cross-country trip through the small towns of America. Her plan was to interview ordinary people about their social and spiritual values. She had a notebook filled with questions she hoped to ask. And yet, Phillips found herself losing her confidence in her project. She admits she drove through several states without asking anyone anything.

Then, at a Waffle House in Virginia, things shifted. She approached a young man who agreed to be interviewed.

Her first question to him was: "Where did you get your values?"

To which the young man offered "a deep, vacuous look" followed by a very Southern, two-syllable, "Wha-ut?"

Phillips confesses she panicked for a second, but then heard a little voice in her head whisper, "Go first."

She proceeded to tell the young man a story about how her mother always told her to look people right in the eyes, give them a friendly smile, and say "Hi." She added that this was initially difficult for her since she was very shy as a child. But it got easier.

"Now I do it all the time. So being friendly is one of my values. And I got it from my Mom."

The young man listened, then asked, "Is it like this?" From there he told a story about his abusive, alcoholic father and how his grandfather advised him to work out all his troubled feelings by writing.

"So, I did. I wrote a lot of poems," he said.

The young man even recited a poem by heart and then wrote it down in Phillips' journal.

It was a profound moment of vulnerability and sharing. But it had needed a little help to begin.

"We sat in that plastic booth for another hour and a half while he told stories he had never told to another person about his own anger, his big dreams, his pickup truck and double-wide, his drinking problem, his fear of being in love and messing it up like his dad," recalls Phillips.

"And every story he told me illuminated my own darkness, taught me something I never knew, and opened my heart to bigger love and deeper courage. He found parts of himself that had been long lost, simply because I was there to hear and receive them. And the same was true for me. When we left that restaurant, we were two different people from the ones who had walked in, alone, and afraid."

That day Phillips says she learned the importance of "going first." Leading. In fact, the word *leadership* comes from an Old English word that means "go first."

Phillips notes, "I now know, from that one experience, that I can be the cause of a profound conversation, if I dare to go first, if I share something personal and meaningful, if I ask of another a question that matters, and listen like our lives depend on the answer." In some ways, they do.

The truth behind the curtain.

Can you recall a conversation where one person—maybe you—had the courage to reveal something vulnerable, and it led to a more meaningful and truer level of conversation and connection? What did the person share and what impact did it have?

Describe one or two of these situations and pinpoint how the moment of vulnerability shifted the substance and tone of the discussion. How did it change the relationship with your conversation partner?

_____

_____

_____

_____

_____

_____

_____

_____

_____

_____

_____

_____

_____

◄▲►

Stock Up on *Patience*

Occasionally, despite our best efforts, conversations may not go as planned or meet our expectations. They go nowhere, take bizarre twists, or run completely off the rails.

It happens.

That's real life—and it's okay! In these cases, we have to practice patience, which is a form of generosity and grace. Here are several ways you can extend that grace in the process of becoming a better conversationalist.

Be patient with yourself

There will be moments and situations where you just aren't in the mood to chat. You know there are solid benefits. You know it's what you should do. *But you're just not feelin' it.* Before you metaphorically kick yourself for missed opportunities, give yourself a break.

We all have moments where we just don't want to engage with others. We're tired, in a bad mood, in the wrong setting, or… (Fill in the blank with one of the obstacles you read about earlier.) A big scoop of patience with ourselves is certainly in order.

However, if "not feelin' it" becomes your standard internal response to any and every potential social interaction, you may also need to give yourself a little tough love. Existing on an antisocial island is no way to live.

Another area where we need to be patient with ourselves is in the aftermath of a conversation. The dreaded postmortem review.

- What in the world possessed me to say *that?*
- Why did I have to bring up *that* subject?
- I just stumbled all over myself! How embarrassing!
- Was that an awkward silence or a natural pause?
- Ugh! I said the wrong thing and totally offended him.
- Oh no! That didn't go well at all!
- She must think I just fell off the turnip truck—or was driving it!

Whoa! Easy there!

Life isn't scripted or rehearsed. We are imperfect humans, and we can't control every nuance of our interactions.

It's perfectly normal to think about what we might have done differently. That's how we learn and improve. But don't allow yourself to churn endlessly over the would-haves, should-haves, and could-haves. That most definitely is *not* helpful. It's over.

Forgive yourself. Do an honest recap. Inventory the lessons. Strive for improvement. Move forward.

Be patient with others

Even if you summon the courage and interest to engage and do everything right, you may find that your potential conversation partner is about as friendly as a prickly pear cactus, limp as a wet noodle, or simply not on the same conversation planet as you are. Time to read the signals, give yourself (yet) another break, and practice some social compassion for others.

Need some examples of what I mean?

The prickly pear cactus.

Let's say you offer a co-worker a chipper, "Hey, how's it going?" And all you get in return is a semi-irate or full-on cranky, "Eh, it's going." Don't take it personally. You probably caught him at a bad moment.

Still, short exchanges do matter. If you are so moved, you could add a quick, "Well, I hope things get better soon!" A word of encouragement never hurts.

Bravo! You did your bit. Next up?

The wet noodle.

Not unpleasant, just not interested. Let's say you're taking your seat on an airplane and observing the cues and clues emanating from the people around you. It's always appropriate to offer a polite greeting to your seatmates. Share your name if you like.

"Hello, good morning. I'm Maria."

Now, let's say your seatmate is less than responsive, isn't making eye contact, has her earbuds plugged in, seems engrossed in a book or her phone or laptop. Maybe she leans back with eyes closed. Or has given you The Glare.

Hello! Clear and universal signals she wants and needs some time all to herself.

Honor that and save the sunny dialogue for a willing participant. In other words, don't be that person who becomes the in-flight pest!

Cultural norms also come into play here. Riding the commuter train in a large metropolitan area is a fitting example. There's an unwritten rule that you should NOT under any circumstances start chatting with the person sitting next to you. It's practically forbidden! People are jam-packed in a crowded and noisy space, facing a hectic day—or trying to recover from one. It's not a relaxed cocktail party or *kaffee klatsch* ripe for witty banter. No one speaks. That's just how it is.

No need to get your knickers in a knot. Just recognize this is the norm and follow the conversation rules. Trying to be a rule-breaker might not go well.

We can also make permanent peace with the notion that some folks will never want to engage. Now, later, with anyone, or ever. This, my friends, is not about you.

Finally, the one that even makes expert conversationalists shake their heads.

The people on a different conversation planet.

Let's say you find yourself chatting with someone who has an entirely different conversation pace, vibe, or skillset. The person talks verrrry slowly or yammers on at warp speed. He's oddly sentimental, incredibly wound up, or uncomfortably gruff. She moseys extensively into technical topics that don't interest you one bit. He launches into an unprovoked political lecture, sermon, or rant.

These folks will likely provide the ultimate test for your patience. I recommend a deep breath, a splash of compassion, and a giant wave of "benefit of the doubt." No, you don't have to stand there and listen to endless amounts of dull or crazy. But sometimes it helps to think about the words of the classic Greek philosopher Plato:

"Be kind, for everyone you meet is fighting a hard battle."

As you plot your quick exit from the conversation, just briefly consider the possibility that this person may be struggling with physical, mental, or emotional challenges. They could be dealing with the fallout from a terminal cancer diagnosis or an unexpected layoff at work or the shocking news that the person they've been dating for two years is actually married. Whatever it is.

When life gets messy (and it does), people may not bring their best selves to their conversations. Or good conversation may not be their strong suit, and they haven't read this book yet (wink). Using that thought to reframe the situation may help you muster up enough patience to graciously wrap up the interaction before moving on. A lot more on that up ahead.

Be patient with the process

As you work toward becoming a skilled conversationalist, don't expect perfection. That's rarely a realistic goal! Some of what you learn here and start to test drive will feel weird, awkward, or even scary. You will experience the delights, frustrations, trials, and errors. Don't give up or be too hard on yourself.

The quest to create, manage, and enjoy higher-quality conversations is an ongoing journey rather than a final destination.

Small, steady shifts and even microscopic adjustments over time will lead to big improvements, greater ease, confidence, and even excellence and enjoyment.

21

....

Be *Sure* to Practice

....

If you want things to improve in your conversation world, you have to get started and then stick with it. Practice is the key. Beginning today, utilize what you've learned about becoming a better conversationalist and then continue on a daily basis.

Pick out a few strategies and tips you've read so far. (You'll have a lot more to choose from as you continue reading.)

- Try them out in various settings and situations.
- Test drive a new tip or idea each day.
- Note what works for you and what doesn't.
- Strive for incremental progress.
- Keep tweaking and customizing your approach.
- Go for increasingly challenging strategies.

It's this dedication to creating and sticking to positive habits, even if you take tiny steps, that will make all the difference in the long run.

Trust me, even as you move through the initial stages of improvement, you'll be light years ahead of most people in your conversation savviness.

. . . .

Whew! That's a lot of gear to pack into your conversation toolkit. But as I always say when I'm packing: "Better to have it and not need it than to need it and not have it."

The next section gets into even more practical, try-today techniques, tools, tips, and tricks. In fact, you'll start to sketch out a plan that will make conversing easier, more pleasant for all, and something you look forward to and enjoy with greater frequency.

Creating Your Conversation *Action Plan*

Great conversations can happen almost anywhere. That's right, anywhere. Grab your trusty toolkit, get out there, and find them. Better yet, instigate them.

You're just about ready.

If you've read everything up to this point, you've done some important prep work that will create a strong and useful foundation for conversation success. Now it's time to map out a quick action plan for your next social event or potential conversation and utilize some practical techniques.

Some of what you learn here may seem like a refresher. As in, "Seriously? That's it?? I already knew that."

Not so fast!!

Good ideas and best practices are always worth reviewing with an open mind and fresh consideration. There's always a chance that, even if we think we already know things, we may not be actively *practicing* them. Trust me, even as someone who has studied and taught this material extensively, I am a mere mortal like you. I still need reminders and refreshers, and I have to work at practicing what I preach *every single* day!

Here's the fun and exciting part:

As you read this section, you might learn some surprising new techniques and strategies or have a total conversation epiphany that could shift your views on social interaction forever.

Intrigued? Then let's go!

The *Pregame* Warm-Up

You've done a lot of preparation. Now it's "go" time. You have a social situation coming up. Perhaps moments away. Here are four basic things you'll want to do before you head into any social scenario.

Set a few quick intentions

Back in Chapter 12, you established a Vision and set some broader intentions for improving your conversations. Now let's get specific.

- Identify your Vision for success at this social event.
- Imagine the great conversations you'll have.
- Define the strategies you'll use to make this success real.
- Write or think out your plan: "I intend to..."

For inspiration, here are a few of the intentions I often set. Feel free to borrow these or come up with your own.

In my conversations today or at this event, I intend to:

- ☼ Enjoy myself.
- ☼ Meet interesting people.
- ☼ Pace myself.
- ☼ Listen more than I talk.
- ☼ Ask interesting questions.
- ☼ Be open to other viewpoints.
- ☼ Manage my energy.
- ☼ Exit while I'm still having fun.
- ☼ Commit to reconnecting with those I enjoyed and found interesting.

What else would you add?

_____

_____

_____

_____

Get your head in the game

Consider this your attitude check and a time to review the attributes commonly found among great conversationalists. In other words, revisit all the good tools we covered in the previous section. Go back and do a quick review or check out the list below.

A good conversationalist is:

※ Positive	※ Respectful
※ Purposeful	※ Likeable
※ Open to possibilities	※ Known for integrity
※ Proactive	※ Optimistic
※ Courageous	※ Ready with a sense of humor
※ Caring	※ Humble
※ Curious	※ Open-minded
※ Courteous	※ Trustworthy
※ Gracious	※ Authentic
※ Kind	※ Vulnerable
※ Generous	※ Willing to share
※ Present	※ Patient

It's a tall order, but a solid one. A good visual is to imagine "weaving" these attributes together and putting them on like an amazingly comfortable, custom-made outfit that makes you look and feel great!

If you're feeling overwhelmed, drop those tense shoulders, take a few deep breaths, and relax. You're going to be awesome!

Also, have your custom conversation mantra handy. This would be a great time to trot that out. Or put it in your purse or pocket.

※ This is going to be great / fun / interesting / life-changing!

※ I'm going to talk to some friendly and fascinating people today!

※ Calm. Confident. Caring. Curious.

※ Today I will feel comfortable conversing.

Whatever it is. Do you need a special mantra for this particular occasion? Write it down! Always a great idea to customize for the event.

Now, what should you do with your mantra?

- ❋ Say it out loud (preferably when you're alone).
- ❋ Write it on a piece of paper and keep it with you.
- ❋ Repeat it silently to yourself as you walk into the setting.
- ❋ Embroider it on a pretty handkerchief if you're the crafty type.

Knowing it, saying it, and keeping it close will boost your confidence.

Seriously. Try it. You're welcome.

Think through your strategy

If you're attending a small dinner party with three acquaintances, this step may not apply. You'll head from the front door to one of the stools around the island in the kitchen where everyone is congregating. Let the conversation roll. Easy peasy.

But what happens if your social gathering is significantly larger and filled with complete strangers? That can be overwhelming and intimidating. It helps to go in with a plan for how you'll move throughout the venue rather than stepping inside and freezing in place. I guarantee you might initially be tempted to take a seat, pull out your smart phone, and look engrossed in an important email.

(Remember? That's called "phubbing." Lots of people do this. But not you. Nope. Not an option.)

Instead, you're going to mingle around and look for someone standing alone. You'll casually approach that person, smile, say hello, extend your hand, and introduce yourself.

At a minimum, you'll have a brief exchange and build your confidence.

You might even try this tactic, courtesy of the late writer and magazine editor Julie Tereshchuk, who was respected and beloved by all who knew her. You say, as brightly as you can, "Am I the only one who doesn't know anyone here?"

If indeed you are the only one who doesn't know a soul and the person you're talking to knows others in the room, perhaps she will be gracious enough to introduce you to a few people. You can always ask. (But remember: It's not her responsibility!)

If that person doesn't know anyone either, then—*eureka!*—you will instantly have something in common! A conversation can begin.

Try the 10/5 Rule.

As you gain momentum and begin to move around the room, you may want to employ the handy trick known as the 10/5 Rule. Ever heard of it?

Here's how it works:

- Within 10 feet of another person? Acknowledge her by making eye contact and smiling. Add a nod, friendly wave, or gesture if you wish.

- Within 5 feet? Add in a greeting and, if possible, use the person's name. "Hello! Good morning, Keiko!"

The 10/5 Rule is also known as the Rule of Hospitality, the Zone of Hospitality, or the Friendliness Rule. It's taught and used in the retail and hospitality industries, as well as in corporations and other organizations.

But it's not just a great strategy reserved for the business world. It's actually basic social courtesy that should apply to every one of us on the planet. Acknowledging others is important, and it matters in virtually every setting.

Simple as it is, the 10/5 Rule has single-handedly created friendlier, more welcoming, and respectful customer experiences and company cultures. It can change your conversation life for the better as well.

I follow this rule every morning when I'm out walking. It may not be practical in a crowded urban setting, but it works well where I live. It's how I've prompted easy, upbeat conversations that helped me get to know dozens of interesting neighbors.

Friendly acknowledgment can lead to positive things, including goodwill and respect.

(And trust me, I also remember the people who can't be bothered to say hello or even make eye contact. Yet again, there's that emotional imprint.)

See? You have options! It's going to be a piece of cake! But please don't forget this next step... and I'm not even kidding.

Complete a mandatory hygiene check

While this can be a rather personal and awkward topic, it really does matter. I'm probably not alone in noting that little details can be very important when engaging in conversation, especially at close range.

And when I say, "little details," what I really mean is oral hygiene. And when I say, "oral hygiene," what I really mean is the quality of our breath. There, I said it.

Bad breath can be one of the biggest obstacles to good conversations— or any conversations, for that matter.

I don't think I'm alone when I reveal that I find it extremely distracting, off-putting, and gross to converse with someone who has—how can I put this?—*dragon breath*. I can think of people I know right now, people I do actually enjoy talking to, who have had breath that has been so bad, so foul, it about knocked me off my feet. When that happens, it's hard not to grimace! Or find a speedy way to make an exit.

Please *don't* do this to your fellow conversationalists.

Take "The Sniff Test."

Again, I'm not joking. This trick was developed courtesy of the folks at Colgate to help you evaluate the freshness of your own breath.

1. Go somewhere where no one can watch you do this.

2. Lick your wrist. That's right. Lick it. Then let it dry for a few seconds.

3. Take a whiff. Unless you've lost your sense of smell, this should give you an idea as to whether your breath is ready for prime time—or needs some remedial help. A good brush, a swirl of mouthwash, a strong breath mint. Please, for the sake of your upcoming conversation partners, do it.

◂▴▸

Let's all commit to visit the dentist regularly, tend to our daily brush-and-floss regimens, keep a breath mint or two handy, and limit our ingestion of noxious foods and beverages that can negatively impact our conversations.

While we're on the delicate subject of hygiene...

This should probably go without saying, but why should I stop now? If you want to make a positive impression during your interactions, pay close attention to your overall hygiene and appearance. You know what I'm saying here. Shower, trim, comb, shave, pluck. Whatever it is you do to "show up well," just do it before you get up close and personal for a conversation!

Right-o!

The moment has arrived. Your Vision and intentions are set. Your attitude is primed for success. You're silently repeating your inspiring mantra, and it's got you totally jazzed up. You have a strategy for the moment you walk in the door. And your breath is minty-fresh.

Nice work! You are ready! Make your entrance...

TRY THIS!

The rules of engagement.

Check out these tips for friendly, gracious, memorable engagement:

- **Make eye contact and smile.** Eye contact shows acknowledgement. Smiling shows warmth and friendliness.

- **Consider that you have 3 to 7 seconds to make a great impression.** (Yup, that's how fast it happens.)

- **Step up your greeting game.** Sorry, but the casual greetings of "Hi" and "Hey" land in the "eh" category. Definitely an improvement over no greeting at all. But you can do better, especially in professional settings. Here's how:

  - Say "Hello." For extra bonus points, add in a secondary greeting such as "Good morning" or "Good afternoon" or "Good evening." A whole new level of warmth and class, right? Even better...

  - Say the person's name if you know it. "Hello! Good morning, Robert..." (Admit it. That sounds pretty darn good!)

  - Say your name clearly when introducing yourself, especially if you have an unusual name or one that's hard to pronounce or remember.

- Repeat your name as often as necessary. Spell it if that helps. Tell a little story about it if that might assist others with remembering it, or toss in an easy nickname.

- Show some patience if others don't hear your name or say it correctly right away. Graciously repeat it as often as necessary. We all have a lot we are trying to remember these days!

◂▴▸

Two more quick notes about maneuvering around a group event.

First, it's not considered good form to walk up and interrupt two people who are already engaged in conversation. Especially if they appear to be discussing something important, private, or personal. Observe their body language. Are they leaning in? Looking serious? It's their conversation. Let them finish it.

Second, if you want to work your way into a group of people conversing, approach the circle, try to make eye contact with someone in the group, and pray they are friendly and gracious enough to welcome you in.

I find this tricky. So my go-to method is to look for a group that appears to be having a good time. They are smiling, perhaps even laughing.

I make my approach with as much courage as I can muster. I assume positive rapport. Then, with my biggest smile and best possible comedic timing, I say something like, "Whatever the punchline was, I just missed it." If someone in the group responds, I introduce myself, and I'm in.

If they look at me like I have two heads, I move on. *Whatever.*
Not my people.

(And, trust me, you will find that some folks just aren't yours either.)

Before this chapter ends, I want to toss out some tips on how to nail your self-introductions: They should be short and sweet. Your name, what you do, where you're from, how you know the host, and so on. Include the information that may be relevant to the situation. There's no need to unload your entire life story accompanied by several random side bars. (Or, God forbid, some kind of sales pitch.) If you have time to visit, additional details will surface during the conversation.

What to do next? Read on.

The Big *Advantages* of Small Talk

"Small talk? Oh no, please! Are you kidding me?"

I can sense some of you wincing, rolling your eyes, groaning, and maybe even considering slapping this book shut or tossing it aside at this point.

Don't do it! Stay with me!

I know, I know. Small talk tends to get a bad rap. Many people are quick to reveal that they *absolutely and totally despise it*. They find it awkward, predictable, repetitive, shallow, forced, inauthentic, simple-minded, boring, draining, a waste of time and breath, and ... insert any number of negative descriptors here.

Totally understandable.

I've been in some really grinding and exhausting small talk situations myself. One of the many reasons this book was my pet project for nearly a decade.

To borrow the words from author Steve Hockensmith in his book *Dawn of the Dreadfuls,* an unimaginative small-talky exchange can feel like this: "The conversation limped along...lifeless...mindless and making jelly of whatever healthy brains were within its reach."

Yep, it can certainly feel that way.

But love it or hate it, small talk is a necessity when it comes to conversations.

It is a social grace. It's a warmup. And guess what? We have the power—and the responsibility—to manage, change, shift, or exit a tedious conversation if we aren't enjoying it.

Think of it like this. Small talk is how the conversation dance begins. It's where we have a light, easy exchange, and a chance to warm up and get acquainted. It's where we can establish a positive and cordial foundation for whatever comes next. There's just no getting around it.

Imagine meeting someone for the very first time, doing the usual introductions, and then following that immediately with an unexpectedly intense question such as: "What do you think is preventing you from being the person you want to be?" or "What's your biggest regret?"

That would be weird, right?

While some people can pull this off, that discussion right out of the chute would likely be far more awkward than a brief discussion about last night's crazy thunderstorms, how the day is going, or where we grew up or went to school.

The point is, you've got to start somewhere. And small talk is your ticket! Just don't get stuck there. Grab the wheel, navigate a path, nudge the gas pedal gingerly, and steer the exchange in a direction you want to go. Options on how to do that up ahead. But first, a little reflection...

TRY THIS!

Where do you stand with small talk—right now?

Use the following questions as journaling prompts or discussion topics:

How do you currently feel about small talk?

_____

_____

What do you like about it?

_____

_____

What do you dislike about it?

_____

_____

How could you improve your small talk experiences?

_____

_____

What are your preferred go-to topics for small talk when you need to use it as a conversation tool?

_____

_____

◄▲►

Your insights here may prove useful as you learn how to make small talk scenarios surprisingly enjoyable and interesting. (Yes, even with people you assume will be dreadfully boring.)

Small talk really does add value

If you're still unsure about this concept, here are a few ways you can benefit from mastering the art of small talk (rather than avoiding it).

It can boost your professional success.

Unless you're in a job or business where you will never ever encounter another human being, small talk matters. People who can engage in small talk confidently and comfortably on a variety of both work and non-work-related topics are highly prized in any environment. But being able to exchange a few pleasantries before talking business can help build rapport and relationships and, in the long run, enhance your professional reputation and career.

In his book, *How to Get a Job on Wall Street,* Scott Hoover, the A. Stevens Miles Professor of Banking and Finance at Washington and Lee University, writes that, while getting down to business is critical to success, the "simple, innocuous conversations" are just as important. Small talk is like the glue that holds the bigger stuff together. He emphasizes, "Success in the business world depends as much on networking and relationship-building as it does anything else."

The obvious exceptions? If you're a professional who works with urgent, life-threatening situations (say, a surgeon, emergency medical technician, or a firefighter responding to a crisis), please save the chit-chat for later!

It can enhance your personal life.

Whether you are on a date, at a family reunion, or enjoying a dinner party, strategic small talk can make you a personality magnet. Being someone who can engage in warm, pleasant small talk easily and confidently puts others at ease and is often perceived as more intelligent and attractive.

Who wouldn't want that?

"Excelling at small talk will make you popular and justifiably so," says Ruth Graham, author and daughter of the late Reverend Billy Graham. "Mastering it can make you a pleasure to be around. Someone who can carry on a conversation with anyone; someone who is sparkling and witty on simple topics; someone who puts everyone at ease—that's the definition of the perfect guest, perfect host, and perfect co-worker."

It can help you vet your conversation partners.

While small talk can quickly establish connection, it can also help you determine that *(ahem)* you really don't want to spend much time with this particular person. As you engage in basic dialogue, you might wonder:

- Is this person likable, interesting, and pleasant?
- Is the conversation flowing easily?
- Do we share similar energy and interests?
- Are we both enjoying this exchange? Or not?

❊ Is this a conversation that can be lightened up, switched up, or made more enjoyable in some way? Or is it a lost cause?

❊ Is it time to make a gracious escape?

No one said you would enjoy every conversation you enter into. And if the answers to those questions indicate that you are not, in fact, enjoying a particular exchange, you also don't have to endure it.

Thanks to small talk, you have a slick way to vet your conversation partners and weed out the duds.

Stay tuned for some highly useful—okay, *life-changing*—advice on how to manage, shift, and even exit conversations you're not enjoying. That's up ahead in the section called Drainers and Downers.

But for now, back to the priceless value of small talk and how to do it well…

It's worth learning how to do it well.

Susan RoAne, author of *How to Create Your Own Luck,* offers some encouraging advice about the beauty and power of small talk, everyday exchanges, and getting conversations going.

"Make small talk," RoAne says. "People who create their own luck don't wait for a great opening line, nor do they initiate conversation with big talk… They tend to talk about little things: weather, traffic, movies, and the like. They might start by saying, 'Hello, how are you?' Then they listen to the response, build on it, and create a connection. By seeking out serendipity, they make things happen in their lives."

Great opening lines can get conversations going

Sure, saying hello and introducing yourself launches an exchange. But if that feels too direct, here are some other, more spontaneous options to get the ball rolling.

Make a remark about something in the vicinity.

It might be the room, the weather, the scenery, the food on your plate, or something happening nearby. Don't gripe or complain—unless you can make it *funny*. I like to imagine what someone witty and charming like Hugh Grant (or my father) would say.

For instance, at a networking luncheon or banquet, Hugh might flash his signature smile and say, "What a lovely job they did of dressing up these rubber chickens!"

Or I can imagine my Dad arriving at a meeting, drenched from a spring storm, and kicking off the conversation with a little self-deprecating humor. "Well, the label says this raincoat is water repellent, but I guess actual results may vary."

If you can make others around you chuckle, you are already a hit. And if you're around people with no sense of humor whatsoever, you can decide whether this is the optimal conversation group for you. Or whether it's neither the time nor the place for humor.

Offer a compliment.

Within the boundaries of being respectful and appropriate, of course, try offering a sincere compliment. Maybe pertaining to something the person is wearing, their smile, or something they do well.

"Those are beautiful earrings. Is there a story about where you got them?" (Once when I used this line, I ended up having a delightful conversation with Sarah Butler, one of Austin's most respected philanthropists. I didn't know who she was until she introduced herself toward the end of our visit. You never know!)

Or use an unexpected, witty, and even flattering opening line. A notable example is what speaker, author, and humorist Christine Cashen says when she gets on a plane, has found her seat, and meets her seatmate: "Just so you know, I have a superpower. I always sit next to the most interesting person on this plane—and that must be you!"

Of course, Cashen says this with her signature smile, charm, dash of humor, and twinkling eyes. The person can either engage at that point (and they often do), or they can just accept the unexpected compliment and get back to their book, game, work, or nap.

What if you're the recipient of a compliment? To clarify, a compliment isn't just a compliment. It's a gift and an opportunity or invitation to connect. (Unless, of course, the giver is giving you the creeps. Then you can ignore it and move on.) But, if you do respond, keep these things in mind:

- ❋ Don't downplay or reject it. ("What? This old thing?")
- ❋ Don't neutralize or deflect it. ("Oh… It was no big deal.")
- ❋ Don't agree too enthusiastically. ("I know! Aren't these boots just soooo fabulous? Don't they look amazing on me?")

When in doubt, simply respond to a compliment with two easy, sincere, and always appreciated words: "Thank you."

That's it! If you have an amusing story to share or more conversation flows from the exchange, great!

Share one of your experiences from the day.

This might include telling someone about a great, off-the-grid spot you found for breakfast, something funny that happened on the way to the event, or an interesting person you just met. Again, keep it positive.

- "Man, I had the coolest thing happen to me today."
- "Wow, have you seen the amazing artwork in the lobby?"
- "Have you tried the bagels over at Angie's Bakery?"

Those comments can kick things off. Then ask how the other person's day has gone so far or what's new with them.

Start with the weather. (Seriously.)

Irish poet and playwright Oscar Wilde once noted that "conversation about the weather is the last refuge of the unimaginative." On the other hand, the American cartoonist, humorist, and journalist Frank McKinney "Kin" Hubbard saw it differently, writing, "Don't knock the weather; nine-tenths of the people couldn't start a conversation if it didn't change once in a while."

Fair enough.

The weather is, indeed, something we're all experiencing. What's more, if you've ever lived in or visited an area where the main industry depends on the weather (say, because of agriculture, tourism, or sports), the weather—past, present, and future—isn't just important. It's critical! This means the weather is discussed daily, fervently, and in great detail.

Do we need to spend every spare moment discussing it or going on and on about it? No. Should it always be the main topic of discussion? Heck, no! But it is a safe, easy place to begin. Everyone is likely aware of the weather. Unless they are in a submarine or in outer space. (Which could prompt an entirely different type of conversation!)

Small talk is the bridge to something better

Any of these approaches could help you get started—or inspire you to produce a few of your own.

As you work to improve your conversation skills, you'll be grateful to find yourself paired with a small talk wizard. It's like having a dance partner who makes you look good, even if your dance skills are slim to none. Why not be that small talk wizard for someone else?

Ruth Graham adds to her earlier thoughts: "Small talk is not wasted talk. It's a social lubricant as essential as wine and laughter that allows strangers to make crucial first connections across demographic lines. And it's far from meaningless. People are rebelling against it today in a misguided dismissal of social graces that seem old-fashioned, boring, or wasteful. In fact, we've never needed such graces more…"

Beth Beulow, author of *The Introvert Entrepreneur: Amplify Your Strengths and Create Success on Your Own Terms,* observes that most "powerful conversations don't typically start out that way. There's just chit-chat that takes a turn and goes deeper organically. It's not forced or contrived. It just evolves."

Beulow adds that this is especially true when we can create a safe space for deeper conversations and when "a question is posed that takes us into territory that's personal" or gets beneath the surface of a topic.

Getting stuck in a small-talk rut can derail your Vision

Hopefully, I'm starting to convince you that small talk is a big deal. Just don't get stuck in it.

For example, ever been in conversations that dance around the minutiae of the day, covering all manner of trivial and unmemorable topics while somehow never getting to what's most important, meaningful, and memorable?

This happens a lot. Even with people we know really well. Perhaps especially with people we know really well! We get stuck in ho-hum, predictable, conversational shorthand mode, and it's hard to break out.

Psychologist Laurie Helgoe, author of *Introvert Power: Why Your Inner Life Is Your Hidden Strength*, has found that small talk can frequently *block* true interaction. It offers a barrier we can hide behind.

American writer, comedian and commentator Baratunde R. Thurston once quipped, "Every ten minutes of office small talk takes one year off your life."

It can indeed feel that way. And when we get stuck there, we miss out on so much!

I often regret that I didn't ask my parents more important and interesting questions before they passed. I would have enjoyed hearing their answers to questions like these:

- What did they do for fun as kids?
- Who was their favorite teacher in school?
- When did they first meet and "like" each other?
- What attracted them to each other?
- Where and when was their first kiss?
- What was their early dating life like?
- What was it like when Dad was away serving in World War II?
- How did they each get through that?

We had so many conversations about homework and new shoes and our pets. But why did we just stay with "safe" and easy topics? Why didn't I ask them more weighty questions about their early lives, hopes, dreams, experiences? Aaaaah, to go back and change the conversation... Do you ever feel that way?

TRY THIS!

Connection builders.

Think of someone you know, love, admire, and find interesting or want to get to know better: a family member, friend, neighbor, teacher, mentor, or colleague. Get curious and creative as you come up with 5 to 10 questions you'd like to ask them.

What questions come to mind?

_____

_____

_____

_____

Interview that person and write down the answers so you can remember their words. Could these questions become part of conversations you have with others you know or want to get to know?

◄ ▲ ▶

If you want to feel greater connection with your conversation partner, don't allow small talk to stay small or create a barrier to true connection. Nobody wants to be subjected to a tedious round of chit-chat!

Small talk is just a way to open the door to a conversation. It's your responsibility, metaphorically speaking, to walk through that door.

How do you make that happen? I'm glad you asked!

The key to shifting into discussions that are more substantial than the everyday, predictable, and mundane is to ask questions that spark deeper, more meaningful conversations. Up next are some ideas on how to do that. You can also take a look in the Appendix at the back of this book for more ideas!

The *Genius* Behind Smart Questions

Ask any writer or journalist who wants to capture an interesting story. Ask any professor or facilitator who wants to get people thinking and cultivate a rich discussion. Ask a coach or therapist who wants to help a client or patient work through an issue.

These people will tell you that *good questions* are invaluable tools.

Conversationalists know this, too.

According to one of my favorite conversation partners, Dr. Donald Christian, President and CEO of Concordia University Texas, asking interesting and well-thought-out questions can:

- Help others become more present.
- Create engagement.

- ❋ Challenge others and make them think.
- ❋ Get them talking.
- ❋ Get them to ask more (and more interesting) questions.

Smart and interesting questions really can pack a conversational punch. So how can you become a world-class question-asker?

Dig for the story

There's a simple truth about most of us: We love to talk about ourselves, our lives, our thoughts, and what interests us most. Further, we have stories to tell, experiences to share, perspectives that others may find interesting or useful. We are all little treasure troves.

When we take the time and make the effort to ask questions that draw out these stories from others, we can easily become the most likable and memorable person in the room. (Even if all we did was ask the questions!)

My good friend and former client Debbie Herrington notes that her dad often advised her as a teenager to "show a little human interest." Wise words, which she has never forgotten.

The other benefits of asking smart questions? You can strengthen bonds more quickly. Good questions lead you to:

- ❋ More interesting and unforgettable interactions.
- ❋ Shared wisdom and expanded knowledge.
- ❋ Inspiring ideas.
- ❋ More understanding and compassion.
- ❋ Broader perspectives.

A long list of delightful benefits to be shared and enjoyed! Just by asking questions that aren't the same predictable inquiries.

So, what would the process of developing your conversation questions look like? Here are some clues:

- Consider what you are most interested in knowing about other people.

- Evaluate which questions would be interesting but also appropriate, given the setting and situation.

- Think like a journalist: Who? What? Where? When? Why? How?

- Stick with open-ended questions—the kind that require an answer other than a simple *yes* or *no*.

- Offer follow-up questions after commenting thoughtfully on the answers the person gives.

- Keep the focus on the other person but share occasionally to keep things flowing and friendly.

- Explore potential commonalities by asking targeted questions.

- Use questions to help you shift smoothly into new topics for discussion.

- Ask the questions you wish others would ask you—and watch what happens.

In certain cases, inquiries aren't actually phrased as questions. Some socialization experts believe that "Tell me..." are two of the most powerful words in conversation!

- "Tell me about how you came up with that million-dollar idea."

- "Tell me what it was like to meet Elton John."

- "Tell me how it felt to be in the middle of a tornado."

Technically, those aren't questions, but the results are the same. And how often do we use "Tell me" phrases? Probably not often enough!

TRY THIS!

The magic words ...

As you just read, "Tell me" is a powerful conversation enhancer. You can also go a step further and say, "Tell me something interesting about...":

- Yourself.

- Your job.

- Where you live.

- Where you grew up.

- Your family / grandparents / ancestors.

- Your recent (or favorite) vacation.

- The book you're currently reading.

- What you do for fun / leisure / relaxation.

- Your typical day / week.

The options are endless!

Now go ahead. Imagine yourself as a journalist searching for a good story or a gracious talk show host trying to uncover some interesting facts about your guest's work, life, and interests. What would be fun to know? Dig in to find that gem of a story.

◄ ▲ ►

Watch for the light-bulb effect.

In your conversations, watch for clues as to what makes others smile or light up: a child, pet, project, upcoming trip, hobby, book, movie. Ask follow-up questions since you've just struck conversation gold.

When you next see that person, ask for an update.

- ⚘ "Hey, how's that grandbaby doing?"
- ⚘ "How's work going on the book?"
- ⚘ "Isn't your trip coming up soon?"

Doing this shows you not only listened the first time, but you're still interested.

Big takeaway: They'll feel good, and they'll feel good about you.

◄ ▲ ►

But what if your conversation partner starts talking about something you don't understand or a topic you know nothing about. Strategic comments and questions to the rescue!

Let's say she begins talking about a technical topic, and you have no idea what it all means. You might, with a touch of humor, say something like:

- ※ "That's not familiar to me. Could you explain that?"
- ※ "Hmmm. I don't know much about that. Could you enlighten me in terms I can understand?"
- ※ "Whoa! / I'm sorry! / Easy there! / Excuse me, I'm afraid you're going way over my head and pay grade on this! Would it be possible to give me a more digestible version?"

Fear not. This won't make you look less intelligent. If anything, you will look *interested*. Which, as you read earlier, makes you *interesting*.

Spice things up

In certain situations, it can be fun to follow up a few easy questions with something completely unexpected.

- ※ "What was one of your most profound childhood experiences?"
- ※ "Who is (or was) the love of your life?"
- ※ "What three values are most important to you?"
- ※ "What would you do if you discovered you had a year off and a million dollars you had to spend?"

It might seem jarring at first, but asking an unexpected question can be an effective way to quickly get you off the potentially mind-numbing small talk merry-go-round.

Check out this example: I was preparing to present at an evening meeting for a group of project managers, and I was dining with some of the participants before setting up my AV equipment. I had never met any of them.

"Do you all know each other?" I asked of my tablemates.

"No," they all replied, looking around at each other.

Discovering this, it made perfect sense for each of us to offer a quick introduction: who we are, what we do, and a favorite interest, hobby, or passion.

I tossed out that idea for consideration. Everyone agreed and the process began. (The big blessing here was that people followed the prompt, spoke efficiently, and didn't launch into rambling tangents that would have wasted valuable time or pulled us off track.)

The last person to share was a woman who worked for a local school district and had a Ph.D. in history. A follow-up question posed by the man sitting next to her was priceless and unexpected.

"Are you a good storyteller?" he asked. At first, the woman looked puzzled. This was clearly not the question she expected.

He explained. "History is full of so many good stories. I just wondered if you like stories and enjoy telling them."

"Well, actually, yes. I do," the woman said.

From there, the conversation around the table blossomed. The woman shared a story about why she was so interested in history—an anecdote about her ancestors, where they came from, and what they did. That prompted the rest of us to take turns sharing stories about our ancestors, as well as our favorite history teachers, books, podcasts, and documentaries.

It was unlike any "networking" discussion I'd ever experienced. And it's because we connected as *people*, not just as professionals.

I have no idea where the time went, but suddenly I was being summoned to go set up my slides and do a microphone check. I was sorry to walk away from such a lively and stimulating discussion.

All it took was one thoughtful and unanticipated question!

"Questions are interpersonal relationship magnets, compelling us to reveal personal information that builds mutual trust," says Elizabeth Weingarten, journalist and applied behavioral scientist.

Did you read that? Questions are *magnetic!*

Speaking of which, let's look at someone who can pull off the curious (okay, and the oddball) question, primarily because it's his job: author and humorist David Sedaris. Maybe you're a fan of his books like I am.

In his MasterClass on writing, Sedaris shares that, since he's always looking for a funny or unusual story and despises ho-hum small talk, he asks quirky questions of the people he encounters while traveling: airline personnel, taxi drivers, hotel clerks, and such.

Once, quite randomly, Sedaris asked a woman, "When was the last time you touched a monkey?" Turns out, *quite by coincidence,* that the woman *had* recently touched a monkey!

"You can smell him on me, can't you?" she replied.

What were the chances?

Had she not touched a monkey recently, she could have answered in other ways.

- ❋ "Mmmm, noooo. I've never actually touched one before."
- ❋ "Nope. Never. Not gonna happen. Not in my lifetime. Gross!"
- ❋ "I would love to! Sign me up!"
- ❋ "What? You have one with you?"

Any of us can do this and push the conversation boundaries to some degree. But remember, Sedaris is a skilled professional and successful humor writer. He can get away with a lot! (Then again, some conversations just need that extra push to the edge!)

How about another question that can spice things up and help you get to know others?

This one was in a feature article by Sam Anderson in the *New York Times Magazine.*

"Who's on your Mount Rushmore?"

In other words, who are the top four people you most admire?

If that's too general (and it usually is), you can get more specific and ask something like:

- ❋ "Who's on your 'Favorite Fiction Author' Mount Rushmore?"
- ❋ "Who's on your 'Favorite Actor' Mount Rushmore?"
- ❋ "Who's on your 'Favorite Historical Figure' Mount Rushmore?"
- ❋ "Who's on your 'Friendliest People at this Company' Mount Rushmore?"

When you use this question in conversation, you might think first about how you want the conversation to go and what you'd like to learn about the other person.

A little caveat: Remember that posing a quirky or unexpected question may catch others off guard. Give them plenty of time to ponder the question and formulate an answer! If you have to go first to provide an example, do so. But do it quickly and then revert to your conversation partners for their thoughts.

Other comparable questions:

- ❋ "Who are your top three choices for best _____?"
- ❋ "You're hosting a dinner with six celebrities or historical figures: Who will you invite?"
- ❋ "Who would you want to play the leading role in a movie about your life?"
- ❋ "If your dog or cat had the voice of a celebrity, who would it be?"

Capture the power of "beautiful questions"

Beautiful questions can be described as powerful, wonderfully thought-provoking, and endlessly discussable. These can be questions we ask others or even those we pose to ourselves (like the ones you answered in Section Three: Preparing to Succeed).

The poet David Whyte often speaks and writes on this subject.

While on Krista Tippet's *On Being* podcast, Whyte revealed: "The ability to ask beautiful questions, often in very unbeautiful moments, is one of the great disciplines of a human life. A beautiful question starts to shape your identity as much by asking it, as it does by having it answered. You just have to keep asking. And before you know it, you will find yourself actually shaping a different life, meeting different people, finding conversations that are leading you in those directions that you wouldn't even have seen before."

American journalist and author Warren Berger observes that beautiful questions have the power to shift current thinking, open up new possibilities, and lead to breakthroughs.

"Questions show interest, create understanding, and build rapport," Berger explains in *The Book of Beautiful Questions*. "Those are three strong legs upon which a relationship can be built and supported."

A few of Berger's tips for generating beautiful questions include:

- Be willing to be seen as naïve.
- Become comfortable asking questions with no immediate answers.
- Be willing to move away from what you think you know.
- Be willing to slow down and consider.
- Be open to being wrong.

Plant the seeds for beautiful questions to bloom!

Start a list of beautiful questions you'd like to ask in conversation.

_____

_____

_____

_____

What's the most beautiful question you've ever been asked?

_____

_____

_____

_____

◄ ▲ ►

"I would rather have questions that can't be answered than answers that can't be questioned," said the brilliant Richard Feynman, theoretical physicist, and co-winner of the Nobel Prize in Physics (1965).

Rachel Naomi Remen, M.D.—author and professor at the Osher Center of Integrative Medicine at the University of California, San Francisco—adds her twist on this: "Perhaps the secret of living well is not in having all the answers, but in pursuing unanswerable questions in good company."

That sounds like Conversation Paradise to me! How about you?

With time and practice, you will develop your own portfolio of go-to questions that make you a memorable and enjoyable conversation partner (and allow you to enjoy yourself more, too).

Want a full list of conversation-starting questions and additional resources?

That's right, I've got a treasure trove of conversation kick-starters, organized by the type of event you might be attending. Handy and concise! Check the Appendix in the back of the book. And if you'd like to download a PDF version of this tool, please visit my website at **www.PattiDeNucci.com**.

Now let's look at ways to use all these questions to go broader and deeper in our conversations. That's up next!

....

The Art of *Expanding* the Conversation

....

As your conversations (and conversation skills) progress, you may decide it's time to not only move past the small talk, but also practice the art of using questions to expand the conversation. There are two basic routes you can take as you do this. One path is to go broader. The other is to dive deeper. Both options can be pleasant and interesting.

Broadening. This path is explorative and expansive. You begin with one topic, then remain open to taking a delightfully meandering journey across several other topics as well. Broadening is an excellent route to take when you're with someone new and are searching for common interests. Or when you're catching up with someone you haven't seen in a while.

Deepening. This route is focused and reductive as you explore more details on a single topic. These discussions often happen when you find a mutual interest and begin comparing notes. Or when there's a challenge to be discussed and solved.

Either way, you can help do the steering.

Here are a few sample dialogues to illustrate these paths.

Broadening

"Do you like to travel?"

> "Yes, we just got back from Italy."

"Nice! Did you visit any other countries while you were across the pond?"

> "We made stops in Ireland and France, as well."

"That's a great itinerary! Do you have family or ancestors from any of those countries?"

> "Yes, my mother's family is Irish, and my husband's family is French. We visited Italy because we love wine and food."

From there, you could ask about any of the countries visited, the ancestors, immigration stories, history, culture, art, architecture, wine, food, cooking, and more. Or meander ("bird walk") across a wider range of topics. As long as there is mutual interest, flow, and enjoyment in the discussion, it's a win!

When you land on a subject that's especially interesting, you can always go deeper! Here's an example of that.

Deepening

"Do you like to travel?"

> "Yes, we just got back from Italy."

"Nice! Venice is one of my favorite places in the world. Was that one of your stops?"

"Absolutely. We loved it."

"When we are there, we eat gelato three times a day. What did you enjoy most about your time in Venice?"

Here, the conversation stays primarily on Venice.

At any point, you could pull out that magic phrase and say: "Tell me more about…" This allows others to share what they want.

Or you could continue to ask specific questions:

- "What museums or galleries did you visit?"
- "Which were your favorites?"
- "Where did you stay?"
- "How did you get around?"
- "What was your favorite meal on your vacation?"
- "What about this trip would you recommend to others?"
- "Anything you missed that's a must-see for next time?"

The choice to go broader or deeper might be clear. You touch on a subject, and you've hit the motherlode with a mutual interest you can chat about for hours. Deeper it is!

Or, in stark contrast, the topic has lost steam or doesn't really resonate with your conversation partner. In that case, revert to the broader route and wander through other topics that could be of mutual interest.

Easy as 1-2-3!

When possible, try to go at least "three deep" with your questions on a single topic. Ask your first question. Listen. Ask your second question. Listen again. Then ask your third. If you want to continue beyond the third question, by all means do it! Committing to ask at least three questions helps give a conversation focus and enough time to gain traction.

Once again, you don't want your questions to start feeling like a stilted inquisition or interrogation. So, keep the pace leisurely and make sure you occasionally share your thoughts, too.

‹▲›

NOTES:

_____
_____
_____
_____
_____
_____
_____
_____

And the answer is ... more than one.

Want your conversations to go broader or deeper? When another person asks you a question, respond with more than a one-word answer.

A one-word response can be a signal that you might not want to engage. It takes the exchange absolutely nowhere!

For instance, let's say your co-worker Rachel asks you how your day is going. Don't be the person who says, "Good" or "Fine" or "Okay." Give her something to work with! A few sample options to inspire you:

- **"Going well, thanks.** It was a fantastic morning for a walk with my dogs."

  (*Now she can ask you more about your walk or your dogs.*)

- **"Pretty good,** but it will be better when I get my work project done. I'm going to celebrate after that!"

  (*Now she can ask about the project or how you plan to celebrate.*)

- **"Great!** The caffeine is kicking in! By the way, have you seen the new coffee machine in the break room?"

  (*Now you can discuss the merits of the new coffee machine. Maybe delve into favorite coffee shops, coffee drinks, or coffee varieties.*)

Or...you can always ask Rachel how her day is going. But if she initiates the conversation, please give her more than one word!

Courtesy note: If you are truly pressed for time, use a friendly tone and then quickly explain why you can't visit.

◂▴▸

Remember, it all starts with small talk. With dual participation, a friendly exchange can flow from there—going broader, deeper, or any direction you decide to take it.

Want more ideas for taking charge of managing and shifting the conversation or wrapping things up? **Please, keep reading!**

The *Wisdom* of Managing and Shifting

Sometimes you're just ready for a change. Whether you want to shift to another topic with the same conversation partner or are more than ready to move along to visit with someone else (or make an exit), let these tips guide you:

Shifting conversation topics

This can be as easy as asking a question on a new topic or saying something like:

- "I know this is shifting gears…"
- "My apologies for changing the subject…"
- "This is totally off topic, but…"
- "You know, I've been meaning to ask you…"
- "Would you mind if we talked about something else?"

Making graceful exits

When a pleasant conversation ends, it's nice to have a warm sense of closure and leave a positive impression. Obviously, it makes sense to adjust your goodbye to the situation.

If you've had a great conversation, you might wrap things up by saying something like this:

- ⁂ "This has been so enjoyable. But I really have to go."
- ⁂ "Our talk has been very helpful. I'll let you get back to work."
- ⁂ "This has been great. I enjoyed talking to you, but I do need to run." *(Double bonus points if you can tack on:* "Hope we can do this again."*)*

Running for your life

We've all been there. Sometimes a conversation is less than enjoyable and a faster, more abrupt exit is needed. I am immediately reminded of several examples I'm happy to share.

In one case, I had an interaction with a woman while we were waiting to be called in for jury duty. I didn't even know her name, but she went off on random tangents, scurried down irrelevant rabbit holes, and had sketchy boundaries. Like… she revealed to me that she always carries spare panties in her purse. (Whaaaat? Why did I need to know that???)

Another time, the man sitting next to me on a turbulent, nausea-inducing flight insisted on sharing the gory details of the challenges he was facing with his cat's litter box. (Again, why??)

The point here? Some conversations can't end fast enough.

And yet, if you're feeling up to it, you can view potentially challenging conversations as stimulating exercises.

You can choose—and it is a choice—to practice your gracious conversation skills, continue to participate, and attempt to find the entertainment value (or pearls of wisdom) in the situation. At the very least, you could gain a bit of experience in listening under difficult circumstances. There could be a silver lining in there somewhere. A person can dream, right?

As my friend and the CEO/Managing Partner of Truckee Gaming Ferenc "Z" Szony quips, "People can be endlessly entertaining."

They sure can!

Then there are conversations that need to be nipped in the bud as fast as humanly possible.

For example, suppose your conversation partner crosses the line and starts asking questions that feel too invasive.

Step one is to pause and take a breath. This can stop you from reacting or soften the reaction.

Next, you can try one of these go-to replies:

- "Why do you want to know?" (*This classic is straight from Dear Abby!*)
- "Sorry. That's private / something I prefer to keep to myself."
- "My apologies, I don't feel comfortable talking about that."
- "I'd rather not discuss that here." (*Perhaps look around the room, as if there could be undercover spies in your midst.*)
- "Mmmm, I can't / would rather not talk about that."
- "I'm not at liberty to reveal that information."

Think those clever phrases will transform this overly inquisitive out-law into a boundary-respecting citizen? Right, I admit that could be a stretch. And we all have our limits! So if you've hit yours and suddenly have the sinking sensation that you are being held hostage, you do have some acceptable options.

When it's time for a non-bridge-burning yet swift exit, try these three very gracious words: "Please forgive me…" (followed by whatever reason you wish to use).

Please forgive me…

- "I really have to go."
- "I have to be on my way."
- "I just realized it's time for me to leave."
- "I really need to close my eyes and have a nap." *(Great in-flight choice!)*
- "I have a meeting / call I must attend to."
- "I need to refresh my drink."
- "I see one of my friends over there and need to say hello."
- "I need to visit the restroom."
- "I think that's Halley's Comet over there…"

You get the idea. Liberating, isn't it? And so easy, not to mention *polite*.

As always, balance and boundaries are your friends.

Keeping these trusty pals close and extracting yourself from draining conversation scenarios will go a long way toward helping you be at your best when good conversations present themselves.

One last comment to be filed under "Worst-Case Scenario." What happens when your conversation partner appears to have little or no concern for common courtesy or basic manners? I'm referring to those rare but toxic conversations that become uncomfortable, downright unpleasant, overly heated, or potentially volatile.

My advice is clear: Just walk away. (Repeat: Walk away!) No need to say "please forgive me" or provide any reasons. Why waste another breath (or your brilliant conversation skills) on someone who is apparently unable or unwilling to engage in a civilized, productive discussion?

The exit strategy is ... just exit!

. . . .

Alrighty then! Your basic conversation action plan is in place. Now it's time to move on to some important conversation secrets, advanced skills and, shall we say, *finesse*. One of those secrets is the art of listening. It's so important that I've dedicated an entire section to it.

Expanding and *Polishing* Your Listening Skills

There comes a time in every conversation when closing our mouths and opening our ears will make us the most fascinating and memorable person in the room.

Pro tip: Less talking, more listening.

Many believe the secret to being a good conversationalist is knowing precisely what to say, when to say it, and how to say it. We want to sound smart and interesting and make a *dazzling* impression.

Truth is, one of the most powerful secrets to good conversation—that allure and super-power that makes you exceptionally memorable and interesting—is *listening*.

Expanding, polishing, and practicing your listening skills can be a conversation game-changer.

Unfortunately, few people understand that or know how to do this well, making good listeners rare and highly prized.

How rare is rare? And how highly prized? **Read on to find out!**

The Rarity *and Value* of Good Listeners

Consider this: How often do people listen *intently* and *completely* to what you have to say? How often do they do it without interrupting or shifting the conversation back to them? How often do you do the same for others?

Right. I thought so.

Graham D. Bodie, Ph.D., a listening educator and consultant who has studied listening for more than 20 years, reveals that listening is "the least trained 'soft skill.'" His research suggests that most of us are emotionally attuned to what a speaker is saying less than *five percent* of the time.

Surprised?

Reflect on the conversations you've had recently. Did you or your partner ever lose focus, interrupt, or just keep talking, talking, *talking*... when you should have been listening? It happens all the time.

Some experts believe only 10% of us are consistently attentive and generous listeners, which means 90% of us could improve!

"But I'm smart and successful," you say. "And I do really well in social situations. People seem to like me. So that must mean I'm a good listener, right?"

Maybe. Maybe not.

Don't assume that being intelligent, educated, successful, and social make you a great listener.

Jim Karrh, Ph.D., author of *The Science of Customer Connections: Manage Your Message to Grow Your Business,* notes, "Many high-performing professionals name listening as one of their top skills. And yet they can be the worst offenders."

Karrh adds that this is likely because, "they are problem solvers with fine-tuned radar to locate patterns. They know (or think they know) the path that will be best, and they want to get right to it."

Impatience takes over when listening, courtesy, and curiosity should prevail.

Does that resonate? *Even just a little?*

Also, don't assume that, as you've gotten older (and supposedly wiser and more experienced), you've become a more attentive listener. Quite the opposite might be true.

A study done by Ralph Nichols, a professor at the University of Minnesota, revealed that bubbly, bouncy first-graders are less distractable, more interested, and more tuned in—in short, better listeners—than older students and adults. In fact, most of us get worse at listening as we age, and we don't even realize it!

If all this doesn't have your attention, consider the feelings associated with being heard—or not. That's up next.

CHAPTER

The *Power* of Feeling Heard

The need to be heard and given attention is firmly ingrained in us as humans. We want to be cared for, to belong, and to be acknowledged and validated. It's in our DNA!

The innate need for expression

Our very first cries as newborns indicate we are alive and want attention. "I'm here! I exist! I have needs!" we wail metaphorically as we stretch our little lungs. "Pay attention to me! Love me! Listen to me!"

From that point on, if all goes well, we continue to communicate via cries, giggles, gurgles, coos, and other sounds that eventually develop into words, phrases, and sentences. It's the way we let others know how we feel, what we need, what we see and experience, what is delightful and comforting, and what is disagreeable and distressing.

~ 269 ~

Studies reveal that babies who are ignored, who aren't cuddled and fussed over and listened to, don't thrive. They are often stunted for the remainder of their lives. Some die.

Attention from others—for starters, being heard—is absolutely critical to our good health, development, and well-being.

While we adults are (supposedly) more sophisticated and self-sufficient than tiny babies, most of us still yearn to be acknowledged, listened to, and supported. We have feelings and thoughts we want and need to express and process. We have ideas, stories, and experiences to share.

"The most basic of all human needs is to be understood. The best way to understand is to listen," notes B. Joseph Pine II, author of *The Experience Economy*. Maybe that's why he says, "the experience of being heard is so compelling you can charge admission." And it's probably why counselors, clergy, therapists, and other "professional listeners" stay so busy.

The frustration of feeling unheard

So, what happens when we try to share news or personal revelations and our conversation partner isn't listening? Or what happens if no one ever asks us:

- "How are you doing?"
- "What's new?"
- "What are you working on?"
- "What do you think?"
- "How are you feeling?"

I'll tell you what happens: We feel ignored, unvalued, insignificant, and lonely.

Oh sure. Sometimes someone asks how we are or what we think. Then, as we begin speaking, we're blown off, interrupted, derailed, one-upped, judged, or even chided. Maybe the other person hijacks the situation and puts the focus back on himself, leaving us in the conversational dust.

How does that feel? Like crap, that's how.

More specifically, people who responded to a survey reported strong feelings associated with *being unheard:*

Angry	Exasperated	Irritated
Annoyed	Exhausted	Lessened
Dejected	Frustrated	Puzzled
Demeaned	Humiliated	Put down
Devalued	Hurt	Resentful
Diminished	Ignored	Sad
Disrespected	Insignificant	Small
Drained	Invalidated	Tossed aside
Embarrassed	Invisible	Unimportant

Ouch! It really hurts not to be heard!

What other feelings come up for you?

_____

_____

_____

_____

Now...

Think of all the times *we've been guilty* of not listening to others and how that probably made them feel.

Did we do this on purpose to make the other person feel bad? Probably not. But it's also a great reminder that we don't want to feel those emotions—nor be the reason someone else does.

The joy of being heard

What about the flip side? What is it like when someone does listen to us? It feels pretty good, right?

According to my research, when people sense that someone is listening to them, they feel:

Accepted	Good	Respected
Accomplished	Grateful	Satisfied
Acknowledged	Happy	Seen
Actualized	Honored	Smart
Affirmed	Inspired	Special
Amazed	Intelligent	Strengthened
Appreciated	Joyful	Supported
Calmed	Kinder	Touched
Confident	Loved	Transformed
Connected	Motivated	Uplifted
Delighted	Moved	Validated
Embraced	Pleased	Valued
Gifted	Relieved	

Scientists at Harvard found that talking about ourselves (or topics we enjoy) and having someone genuinely listen to us (and let us finish our thoughts before they jump in) feels not just pretty good, but *really good*. So good, in fact, that it triggers the same pleasure points in the brain as *eating*. Eating! We find it, literally, *delicious*.

Imagine feeling this good a little more often. Even better, imagine making *others* feel this good more often. Just by listening!

That's powerful.

"At its most basic level, good conversation addresses our deep human need to be heard and understood," says Carla McDonald, nationally recognized entertaining and conversation expert and founder of The Salonniere. "As a result, it's a wonderful and immediate way to learn something and to form a meaningful connection with someone. In an instant, someone who had been feeling marginalized in a social situation can feel content, included, and important."

Is it any wonder that good listeners are highly prized and that listening more can vastly improve your conversations and relationships?

Coming up are many more reasons why becoming a better listener is so important. We'll cover different types of listening and a boatload of other helpful information to help you do it better.

The Benefits of Becoming a *Better Listener*

Beyond what you just read, there are many compelling arguments as to why better listening is part of any good conversation toolkit. Let's take a look at the reasons behind that.

Listening well creates connections

Imagine this: You've gone to a social event or networking function so you can meet and get to know people. But when the event is over, you realize that in each interaction, *you* did most of the talking. Or you were so concerned about what to say that your listening was distracted and disjointed. Which means you didn't learn all that much about the people you met.

I've so done this. Maybe you have as well.

It's easy to forget that, while engaging, asking questions, and knowing what to say are important conversation basics, *listening* is what helps you learn about others:

- Who they are.
- Where they're from.
- What keeps them busy.
- Where they've been.
- Where they are now.
- Where they're headed.
- What's important to them.

When we listen, we learn about lives, careers, families, feelings, experiences, interests, perspectives, priorities, stories, successes, challenges, and more. Hopefully, we are also getting a chance to share a little. (Balance is a good thing!) But we generously keep the focus on the other person.

This is the fertile ground for connection.

Dutch Catholic priest and professor Henri Nouwen put it so beautifully: "Listening is a form of spiritual hospitality by which you invite strangers to become friends."

Listening well takes the pressure off

For some of us, knowing what to say next can be tricky. In this case, doing more listening can be a welcome relief. What's more, when we listen well, we hear clues that can make it so much easier to respond with pertinent comments, questions, or similar stories that can take the conversation further.

It's much like improvisational ("improv") theater, which is totally un-scripted and spontaneous. Improv performers listen closely to each other for clues and inspiration on what to say, ask, or do next.

But don't worry! A conversation isn't a performance, and it doesn't have to move as quickly or be as zany as improv. But you get the idea. You follow along, listen, then ask or say what seems like the next logi-cal or interesting step.

Listening well uncovers hidden treasure

Almost everyone—yes, even those we are certain will be boring—has an entertaining story, a poignant memory, or a precious bit of wisdom to share. You just have to be patient, open, and willing to search for it. But don't expect to be handed a map with a big "X" telling you where the gold is. Challenge yourself to listen, ask questions, and listen some more to uncover the hidden treasure.

Listening well guides you in finding solutions

Speaking of hidden treasure, listening well can vastly accelerate your learning curve, problem solving, and creativity. As others share their thoughts and ideas, you might catch a valuable tidbit, hear a new idea or perspective, or receive a timely reminder of something you'd completely forgotten. You may even gather up seemingly disparate bits of knowledge that, when combined, form the perfect solution to a troublesome challenge or a tricky project on which you've been working.

Eureka!

The Dalai Lama taught this exact concept, noting, "When you talk, you are only repeating what you already know. But if you listen, you may learn something new."

Listening well benefits your conversation partners

When we listen to others, we are offering them our attention and a chance to share, but we may be doing so much more. Those who are speaking have an opportunity to:

- Process and work through their issues aloud.
- Hear and learn about themselves.
- Potentially enjoy big breakthroughs and shifts.

"When I have been listened to and when I have been heard, I am able to perceive my world in a new way," writes American psychologist Carl Rogers. "It is astonishing how elements which seem insoluble become soluble when someone listens."

Listening well breaks down barriers

Listening to others' stories, experiences, feelings, and perspectives provides us with golden moments to view and understand the world from a new and different angle. This has the power to change us for the better. We may soften and experience new levels of awareness, compassion, understanding, and respect.

The more you know…

A Danish nonprofit called The Human Library Organization offers you the opportunity to "check out" a fellow human ("teacher," "refugee," "artist," "inventor," "CEO") at one of their locations within libraries in more than 80 countries. You sit with your chosen person, face-to-face, in a cozy setting for 30 minutes and listen to their life story.

The mantra of this organization? Unjudge someone.

In a similar vein, Margaret Wheatley—an author, teacher, consultant, and community leader—owns a T-shirt from a conference that expresses the power of listening very well: "You can't hate someone whose story you know."

Listening well strengthens your patience and compassion

Listening well can be a challenge for those of us who are energetic, love to talk, and like fast-paced banter. Slower-paced conversations can feel unnatural, frustrating, or nearly impossible. Yet listening to someone unlike us and at a pace that's different from our own teaches us patience, courtesy, and compassion.

As a patient listener, all you have to do is relax, be present, hear what's being said, and offer a comment or a question here and there.

Listening increases your influence

It may seem counterintuitive, but when you control your need to talk and thoughtfully listen, something amazing happens. Others become far more likely to listen to you and respect what you have to say when it's your turn to speak. Your responses, observations, summations, suggestions, and ideas will likely hold more weight, making you all the more influential, persuasive, and memorable.

Imagine if someone took the time to listen to you and then said, "I've listened carefully to everything you've said, and here are my thoughts…" As opposed to the person who interrupts often, stops you before you're finished, and then produces a knee-jerk response.

Whose thoughts would hold more weight for you?

Listening well brings out the best in others

Some people know how to inject life, fun, good vibes, and positive feelings into any setting. They get conversations going. Then they listen attentively to what's said by others. They ask good questions to keep things headed in productive and positive directions. They listen to the responses. They draw out the best in the people around them and build conversation momentum. Everyone present benefits.

Know someone like this? Good listening is part of their secret recipe.

According to Jack Zenger and Joseph Folkman in their article, "What Great Listeners Actually Do" in *Harvard Business Review*, "...good listeners are like trampolines. They are people you can bounce ideas off of—and rather than absorbing your ideas and energy, they amplify, energize, and clarify your thinking. They make you feel better not merely by passively absorbing, but by actively supporting."

All this listening can culminate in yet another mega-benefit...

Listening well makes you magnetic and memorable

At its core, being a good listener is courteous, generous, and gracious. It makes others feel good—*really good*—in your presence.

Since good listeners are so rare and delightful, listening well can give you that special edge.

"The true spirit of conversation consists more in bringing out the cleverness of others than in showing a great deal of it yourself," said the French philosopher Jean de La Brùyere. "He who goes away pleased with himself is also greatly pleased with you."

But don't worry! No one is saying you have to listen ALL the time. Again, balance and boundaries are important. (Have I mentioned that before?) The truth is, listening can be challenging for many reasons. Seems like the perfect time to run through the big barriers that stop us from listening well.

Barriers to Good Listening

Considering all the benefits of good listening, why aren't we scrambling to become master listeners? I'll tell you why: We have some serious challenges and hurdles to overcome.

We struggle to be "present"

Listening can be difficult for our overloaded, very busy, highly distractible brains. And for most of us, listening (which is a *sensory function*) is a lot harder than talking. It requires conscious focus, patience, and self-control. On most days, we can only listen for a brief 20 seconds. Then, something happens...

We love the release and satisfaction of talking

Talking is an *expressive motor function*. This means our pressing thoughts are yearning to escape and the impulse to talk (and be heard) can get the best of us. We want to offer our own news, ideas, feelings, commentary, opinions, advice, solutions, or a similar story (about us) in response to what others say.

We may even impulsively interrupt or blurt out something random and irrelevant that just popped into our heads. Who cares if it changes the subject or hijacks the conversation abruptly? It's a glorious release that gives us immediate gratification.

And yet, our need to talk, talk, TALK can prevent or destroy the possibility of enjoyable conversation and connection. It can also diminish others' respect for us.

Let's examine the stages that often lead to overtalking.

1. You begin sharing something you want to say. You are focused and on task. So far, so good.

2. Subconsciously, you discover that the more you talk, the more relief you experience. It feels soooo good to keep... talking! (At least for you...)

3. Within a few moments, you may have *totally lost track* of what you initially wanted to say. Or you've said it and are now on to another topic.

4. You are hesitant to let the other person back in because, again, talking feels soooo good.

5. You sense a need to keep the others engaged and entertained.

6. You try *even harder* to captivate the attention of the person to whom you are speaking.

7. Yes. You are now talking too much.

I can freely admit that I have done this. How about you?

In my research, I had no trouble finding friends, colleagues, and experts weighing in on the phenomenon of overtalking. Taken to the extreme, done chronically, and exercised without regard to others, overtalking is not only disrespectful and annoying, but it's also sometimes referred to as "conversation narcissism."

Ouch!

Pardon the pun, but that really says something!

We just don't see our failings

Some of you may be saying to yourself, "Sure, I like to talk. But I think I'm also a pretty good listener."

Despite how we may see ourselves, all of us have "areas for growth" that we just can't see. Based on the research, improving our listening skills could likely be one of those areas.

It's time to ramp up our self-awareness, remember our humanity, and go after the truth.

We talked about getting feedback on our conversation skills from people we trust in Chapter 11, but it's also a critical exercise when it comes to our listening.

We can ask: "Do you experience me as a good listener?"

If you get anything less than a five-star rating, don't worry! You're in good company. And even if you get high ratings as a good listener, it doesn't hurt to polish your talents even further.

At this point, you may be thinking: "Ugh! Listening sounds like hard work! I can't possibly do this. I'm not even sure I want to!"

Before you give up, remember this: There's a high price to pay for having weak listening muscles. Poor listening (and overtalking) negatively impact your:

- Communication
- Relationships
- Learning
- Career
- Reputation
- Happiness

With this in mind, let's move on to the different types of listening we use (or could try) every day.

Types of *Listening*

Listening is more than simply hearing, which is a *physiological* act. True listening requires *conscious attention*. We have to focus on and consider the meaning of the words being said, as well as the emotions and intent behind them. We have to be alert to subtle nuances. And we have to manage and contain our own urges, emotions, inner dialogue, judgment, and so much more. Not going to say this is easy, but it's worth it.

Here it's helpful to explore the diverse forms of listening that show up in personal and professional settings. Maybe some of these will sound familiar. I've listed them from least focused and interested to most focused and interested.

Eager-to-talk listening

Honestly, I'm not even sure this can be classified as listening. But it's so pervasive it has to be at the top of the list. Here, we listen (for about half a second), then swoop in, steal the spotlight, seize control, and add our own comments and very important thoughts that must be expressed *right now*.

> # Despite how often this happens, eager-to-talk listening is a total conversation killer and wreaks havoc on relationships, reputations, and much more.

(Remember all the negative feelings associated with not being heard?)

For some, the thought of having a conversation with someone whose regular mode is eager-to-talk listening can totally shut down all desire to socialize. With that person or anyone else.

Can we all please vow to work on this?

Thoughtful-reply listening

In this case, you're fully engaged, but simultaneously processing what's being said. This allows you to offer an appropriate response or comment that keeps the flow of the conversation going.

You're working at knowing how and when to speak and what to ask next. You're thoughtfully preparing to lob the "conversation ball" back to the other person, perhaps with a follow-up question or an encouraging comment. The focus stays on the other person.

Doesn't that sound great? It is!

Except when we let eager-to-talk listening creep back in. Suddenly, we can't hold back an instant opinion, quick retort, unsolicited advice, or dismissive comment.

Oh no, here we go again!

(Consider that excited atmospheres—as well as caffeine and alcohol—can play a role here. And don't ask me how I know this.)

Along those lines… There are ways to break in if it's done thoughtfully and with finesse.

That's right. Sometimes it's semi-okay to interrupt.

Let's say you're in a conversation and the other person is talking—maybe even on a roll. You suddenly have a question, need clarification, or want to offer a quick comment. You could interject with something like, "I'm so sorry to interrupt, Ahmed, but I have to ask…" or "Please forgive me, Amy, but I wanted to interject one thought…"

Then say what you have to say (*very briefly*) and encourage the person to continue on. Because you've interrupted the flow of the conversation, you may have to help them figure out where they were and allow them time to regroup, elaborate, and complete their thought.

TRY THIS!

Hold your horses, Buckaroo!

Desperate to take the reins of the conversation? Yearning to chime in? Practice waiting. Then follow up. The other person is talking. You're listening. Something she says triggers a response you want to share or a question you want to ask *right at that moment*. It's going to be tough, but hold that thought and try to remain engaged.

When the other person has completed what they have to say, offer your thought or ask your question. A few ideas on how to gently backtrack:

- "I'd love to go back to an interesting point you made earlier…"
- "I have a few thoughts about what you said a while back…"
- "When you were talking about _____, it made me think about _____."
- "I'd like to circle back to something you mentioned a few minutes ago…"
- "Before we get too far off topic, can we return to what you said about _____?"
- "I have a question based on what you just shared…"

If you can pull this off, trust me, you'll sound thoughtful and brilliant! Bonus points for great listening.

◂▲▸

Multitasked listening

We think we are so clever and efficient! We genuinely believe we can concentrate on a complex or all-absorbing task (answering emails, reading the paper, watching an intense movie, performing physics calculations, painting a replica of the Mona Lisa) while also "listening" to others: our kids, significant other, co-worker, neighbor, mother-in-law.

We may even enhance our little performance by interjecting random "uh-huhs" and "hmmms."

Come on! Who are we fooling? Mostly just ourselves.

Think of all the households and work settings where this is likely happening right now—with dismal results.

Here's the caveat.

Multitasking and listening *can* work (and be rather pleasant) if you're involved with a less intense activity such as washing the dishes, pulling weeds, folding laundry, fishing, doing basic carpentry (no power tools, please), enjoying a walk-and-talk, putting together a jigsaw puzzle, or even driving (say, on a low-traffic road).

Doing an activity *together* while conversing can take the pressure off, allow us to relax, and give us a chance to *really* talk and listen. In those situations, multitasked listening is an appropriate option.

Selective listening

This kind of listening involves tuning in only for whom and what we consider to be "important." This can be influenced by several factors, filters, and biases. Among these:

- Our relationship with the person talking.
- Past experiences.
- Future expectations.
- Culture and language.
- Values and beliefs.
- Attitudes and intentions.

Subconsciously or consciously, we tend to listen for information we:

- Are intentionally seeking out.
- Find appealing.
- Feel may impact us positively or negatively.

We also tend to listen more closely to:

- ❋ People we know, like, and respect.
- ❋ People we believe may have some kind of influence over our lives or careers.

Our brain's filter is at work again! It's far harder to listen to people we think we'll never see again or who are talking about things that don't interest us.

Selective listening can be annoying to others. ("I specifically told you to take out the trash!") Or it can negatively impact us. ("What? The deadline for that project is *today*?")

Sometimes selective listening works well.

Certainly, there are situations in which we must listen closely to all that's being said. However, when done purposefully and skillfully, selective listening can be effective in situations where we have to do a lot of listening and must discern what's most important. Greg McKeown, author of *Essentialism: The Disciplined Pursuit of Less,* calls this technique "filtering for the fascinating."

When we are utilizing what McKeown refers to as "essentialist listening," we are filtering as well as listening more multidimensionally and less literally. You might think of it as "listening between the lines."

"We know instinctively that we cannot explore every single piece of information we encounter in our lives," McKeown says. "Discerning what is essential to explore requires us to be disciplined in how we scan and filter all the competing and conflicting facts, options, and opinions constantly vying for our attention."

Notice McKeown uses the word *disciplined*.

As with other types of listening, this is one that requires practice. Here's a quick sampling of how he differentiates between essential and nonessential listeners:

Nonessentialist

- ☀ Pays attention to the loudest voice.
- ☀ Hears everything being said.
- ☀ Is overwhelmed by all the information.

Essentialist

- ☀ Pays attention to the signal in the noise.
- ☀ Hears what is *not* being said.
- ☀ Scans to find the essence of the information.

Explorative listening

The name of this one says it all. With this technique, you incorporate targeted questions to *explore* the angles, possibilities, and emotions within the speaker's words and message. You help the other person expand and evaluate the topic of discussion. Or you use questions to help her think beyond her current view. Despite your involvement, you stay *completely neutral* on any desire to influence or control the outcome. You're purely *exploring*.

Supportive listening

With supportive listening, you listen carefully, demonstrating empathy and allowing the other person to set the pace of the conversation. You're fully invested in *supporting* them as they express themselves and consider solutions to a tough problem or creative challenge. *You are not, however, telling the other person what to do or offering advice.*

And since I've mentioned that...

The painful irony of advice-giving.

Many of us can barely control our desire to offer our ideas, advice, wisdom, or commentary. In fact, some of us positively *thrive* on it. Because, well, we want to help. And *we know best.*

> News flash! In day-to-day social discourse, most people are not interested in our advice, suggestions, or solutions, particularly if they haven't asked for them.

Why? Sometimes we just want to vent. What's more, we are tired of others (parents, teachers, bosses, spouses, well-meaning friends and family members, the media, the government, and any other "authority") telling us what to do! We'd really prefer to figure things out for ourselves! We want to try doing things our way, learn our own lessons, and (yes!) even make our own mistakes.

Back to explorative and supportive listening...

These kinds of listening can be quite valuable to practice and master. By all means, explore and support, but also find out if the other person actually wants input or advice. You might clarify by asking something like:

- ※ "Do you just want me to listen? Or do you want to hear my thoughts?"
- ※ "What specifically do you want from me—to just listen or to comment?"
- ※ "What would be most helpful to you right now?"

And don't forget: If your advice is not requested, listening is still helping.

Starting today, let's drop our urge to be Chief Advice-Giving Officer and instead don the cap of Chief Listening & Support Officer.

Another quick note. When you're listening to someone vent and you realize you have a similar story to share, ask first if he'd like to hear it. Sometimes we dive headfirst into our similar story before we've even let the other person finish theirs! Or worse, we try to one-up what they are saying. That's not supportive listening. That's putting the spotlight back on us.

Active listening

Break out your most regal curtsy or bow, because this one's the Queen Mother of Good Listening.

Ironically, active listening sounds like an oxymoron, doesn't it? As in, we're doing jumping jacks or playing tennis while we listen. Nope, that's not it. We're not even doing the dishes here.

With active listening, we are 100% tuned in. We are attentive, focused, and listening at a deep and soulful level to learn and to show interest, respect, or support. We're hearing the other person's words, but we are also paying close attention to their facial expressions, tone of voice, speaking pace, gestures, and body language.

We're trying to understand what's really going on beyond the words— what the other person is feeling and sensing. We're even listening for what's not being said. (Again, listening between the lines!)

We maintain appropriate eye contact (a soft gaze, not an intense stare) and may offer our own facial expressions and open body language (such as leaning in or a nod). We might make a very brief comment that ensures the speaker that we are listening. We encourage them to go on.

We don't fidget, put our hands in our pockets, jiggle our feet, or gaze around the room. (And please! Ignore or even put away your phone!)

We may occasionally paraphrase back to the other person what we are hearing. We might ask for clarification. We encourage the speaker to continue or elaborate. (Perfect time to try those powerful words: "Tell me…" or "Tell me more…" There's also this gem: "Please continue…")

You might also share what you're hearing, as in:

- ☀ "I'm hearing _____ in what you're saying."
- ☀ "It sounds like you might be feeling _____."
- ☀ "You sound rather _____ about this."
- ☀ "It sounds like what you're saying is _____."
- ☀ "Am I right in hearing that you _____?"

> ## To the person speaking, the experience of being heard at this level feels so good and is so effective at building trust that some refer to it as "charismatic listening."

In fact, it's so powerful that it has been known to radically shift relationships and reputations. It can even enhance productivity, cooperation, and collaboration.

Active listening is a go-to strategy used by successful leaders. It works well in one-on-one conversations, as well as in meetings and other group settings. It's not easy and takes practice. But it's worth the effort.

The full spectrum of listening

A quick recap for you:

- An *eager-to-talk listener* is listening (sort of) but wants to talk.

- A *thoughtful-reply listener* is engaged, but also considering an appropriate answer to keep the conversation flowing.

- A *multitasked listener* might be:

  - Distracted by doing several (or too many) other things at the same time; OR

  - Is able to listen well while involved with an easy or collaborative task.

- A *selective listener* filters the information heard, either:

  - Paying attention to only what matters to them; OR

  - Identifying the most essential messages in a cluttered environment.

- An *explorative listener* broadens the conversation by asking strategic questions without being invested in a particular outcome.

- A *supportive listener* is sensitive and empathetic but doesn't feel the need to provide advice or make suggestions.

- An *active listener* is fully attentive, focused, and searching for the true meaning behind the person's words; also called "charismatic listening."

Get strategic about listening!

Before a conversation or meeting: Consider what type of listener you intend to be. What would be most useful and appropriate for the situation?

_____

_____

_____

After a conversation or meeting: What kind of listener were you? Was it right for the circumstances? Or would another method have been better? Where could you continue to practice and improve?

_____

_____

_____

What's your current default listening style and what needs to shift or change? Do you have a style you tend to use out of habit? Could you be more intentional and mindful? Try other styles?

_____

_____

_____

◂▴▸

Observe and learn from others.

As you engage in discussions over the next few days or weeks, see if you can identify which types of listening styles your conversation partners use. How do they make you feel? How do they impact your interaction?

_____

_____

_____

_____

_____

_____

◂▴▸

NOTES:

_____

_____

_____

_____

_____

_____

_____

CHAPTER

32

The *Attributes* of Great Listeners

Now that we know about the diverse types of listening, let's look at the common characteristics of outstanding listeners—the rock stars with whom we love to converse! What attributes, mindsets, and practices set them apart?

If you recall the traits of good conversationalists, which you read about in Section Four (Building Your Conversation Toolkit), these are also the characteristics of good listeners. For reference, here's that list:

❋ Positive	❋ Curious
❋ Purposeful	❋ Courteous
❋ Open to possibilities	❋ Gracious
❋ Proactive	❋ Kind
❋ Courageous	❋ Generous
❋ Caring	❋ Present

- Respectful
- Likeable
- Known for integrity
- Optimistic
- Ready with a sense of humor
- Humble

- Open-minded
- Trustworthy
- Authentic
- Vulnerable
- Willing to share
- Patient

For good measure, here are some additional traits to consider. Good listeners are known for having:

- Compassion
- Focus
- Self-control
- Adaptability
- Discretion
- Objectivity
- Appreciation (for other good listeners)
- Forgiveness (for those who aren't)

What else would you add to this list? Isn't it fascinating that the traits of good listeners are eerily similar to those of good conversationalists? Coincidence?

_____   _____
_____   _____
_____   _____
_____   _____
_____   _____

Listen up!

Who are the good listeners in your life? Perhaps you have friends, neighbors, family members, colleagues, mentors, or even "professional listeners" such as clergy, counselors, and coaches. What makes them such good listeners?

_____

_____

_____

There is no greater way to honor these great listeners than by following their good example, working at becoming a better listener, and telling them now what positive influences they have been on you!

◄▲►

As we expand our ability to listen, we can also show patience and compassion for ourselves and others.

As A.A. Milne's sweet, lovable bear Winnie the Pooh once noted, "If the person you are talking to doesn't appear to be listening, be patient. It may simply be that he has a small piece of fluff in his ear."

Whatever that fluff is, maybe it will be gone tomorrow. And we should check our own ears for extraneous fluff as well!

CHAPTER

33

....

Key Steps to Becoming a Better Listener

....

You've learned a lot about listening so far! Now it's time to offer a gentle reminder that becoming a better listener starts with choosing and committing to improvement. After that, it's time for action!

Here are some steps you can take to kickstart the process.

Pay attention to how well you listen—and how you could improve

As you've read, most of us overestimate how often and how well we listen to our conversation partners. Now that you're aware of this, put yourself to the test.

TRY THIS!

Honest evaluation time!

For the next several days, pay attention to what's happening when you're in conversation with others:

- How much are you talking?
- How much (and how well) are you listening?
- How long can you sustain that listening?
- What kinds of listening are you employing?
- Which one is your default or "go-to" style?
- What impact is this having on the quality of your conversations?
- How can you strengthen, expand, and diversify your listening habits?

Use that information to help you identify areas for improvement.

◂▴▸

Tap into the power of a mantra or slogan

In Chapter 12, we talked about the power of mantras and slogans. Since listening is often the hardest part of being a great conversationalist, a targeted mantra could be a catalyst for elevating your listening skills.

Create your listening slogan.

Write it on a notecard and put it where you can see it daily.

_____

_____

_____

Need some inspiration? Here are a handful of ideas:

- Simply listen.
- Today I choose to listen more, talk less.
- My goal is to show interest in others.
- When I listen, I learn.
- What are others here to teach me?

◂▴▸

Give your inner judge and critic a vacation

The best listeners try to be objective, but it's so easy to respond (internally, as well as externally) with snap reactions, criticism, and judgment. It might make us feel good or superior in the moment to offer our immediate and expert analyses of what others are doing or expressing. But it helps neither the conversation nor the connection.

What's behind our need to judge or criticize? American author, teacher, and Buddhist monk Jack Kornfield notes, "The judging mind often represents all the critical, disappointed voices from our childhood. If we fight it…we only add more judging."

What to do about this? Per Kornfield, "When the judging mind appears, we can simply acknowledge it with an inward bow and say, 'Ah, yes, the judging mind.' As soon as we do, the judging mind often loses its power over us."

Matthew Kelly, author of *The Seven Levels of Intimacy,* offers another great idea: Swap out judgment and plug in *fascination.*

"Too often we prejudge people because of an idea someone expresses," Kelly says. "The secret is to look beyond the idea itself and discover what has caused a person to believe that such an idea is good, true, noble, just, or beautiful. What is most fascinating is not what people think or believe, but why they think and believe what they do."

Strive for excellence, not perfection

No one, and I mean *no one,* is a perfect listener all the time. Frankly, most people don't even come close. (After reading this chapter, you'll definitely notice this!)

> As you work to enhance your listening skills, remind yourself that being perfect is not the goal. Being better, more often, is.

Take steps to become keenly aware of the quality of your listening. Strive to make small improvements every day. Just by getting through this section, I'm pretty sure you'll be better simply because you have new awareness!

CHAPTER 34

Listening Techniques You Can Try Today

Whether you tend to be a lively talker or quiet and reserved, check out these practical rules that prove it's possible to be a great listener—without having to become an *exhausted* listener. Again, enjoyable conversation is all about balance and mutual interest!

The 60:40 Rule

When in conversation, practice doing at least 60% of the listening and 40% of the talking. (Some experts argue that the ratio should be closer to 70:30.) You may even be thinking, "Hey! Wait! If both people are good listeners, how can they each listen more than half the time? That doesn't add up."

Okay, smarty pants. You are technically correct. The point is, when in doubt, do more listening than talking.

The Equal-Pie-Slice Rule

What if you're in a conversation circle with a group of participants? Here, you often see one or two people dominating the conversation (a.k.a. "holding court" as in, "Oh, there's Professor Lindberg over there, holding court with some of his freshman students.")

Just because this happens frequently doesn't make it right. A far more courteous practice is to "divide the conversation pie" as equitably as possible.

Four people in the group? Everyone gets to talk around 25% of the time, which means they are listening 75% of the time. More people? Divvy up the talking time evenly. Less talking, more listening.

The 40-Second Rule

Forty seconds—yes, a mere *40 seconds*—is an appropriate length of time to share a few thoughts. After that, pause, take a breath, and let others chime in.

TRY THIS!

Start your timer!

Try playing the 40-second game. This is a great exercise in seeing how long (or short) 40 seconds really is. In a group setting or with a partner, designate someone who will set a timer for 40 seconds.

Choose a topic or question to discuss or weigh in on. Each person in the group gets 40 seconds to talk. Pay close attention to how quickly 40 seconds goes by and how much (or how little) information you share in that time span.

Ask yourself: Did you use your 40 seconds wisely? Could you "tighten up" your speaking style? Keep practicing!

◀▲▶

The Read-the-Room Rule

Here (and everywhere), it's worth repeating: "Read the room" as best you can. Watch for little clues that others are losing interest in what you are talking about: fidgeting, glazed-over stares, glancing around the room, peeking at phones and watches, attempts to comment (a raised hand or open mouth), pain-filled grimaces, and even exiting the vicinity. If you see any of these, it's time pick up the pace, wrap it up, and give someone else a chance to talk!

The W.A.I.T. Rule

W.A.I.T. stands for *Why Am I Talking?* In other words, pause, think before you speak, and have a purpose. Likewise, check in with yourself to see why you're still speaking. It could be time to listen. And listen a little more.

No-Partner-Left-Behind Rule

Not everyone is outgoing and talkative. Or clever. Or assertive at inserting their thoughts. So, here's a lovely and generous thing to do when you notice that a quieter person in the group hasn't had a chance to speak.

Say something like, "We haven't heard from Michelle on this topic…" or "Excuse me. Can we take a quick pause and see what Darius has to say on this matter?" or even "Anya, let's hear your thoughts…"

Still waters can run deep.

The Mirror Rule

If you want to be known as a great listener, pay attention to the other person's energy and pace. When you can mirror (or in some cases, balance) their conversational demeanor, it could help them feel more comfortable and set the stage for a higher quality discussion. What are you seeing?

- Is the conversation lively and animated? Or thoughtful and quiet?
- Is this a serious, all-business discussion? Or is there a bit of humor in the air?
- Does the other person seem troubled or stressed? Or relaxed and at ease?

Maybe it's even time to be silent. (Yes! Knowing when to say nothing at all so the silence can fall for a few moments is golden!)

I know that's tough if you're an extrovert. It's your job to carry the conversation, right? Nope, not always. There are times when sitting quietly next to someone is infinitely more powerful than stringing together a lengthy parade of the most eloquent sentences.

While we can never assume or truly know how another person is feeling or what's on her mind, it pays to note both the obvious and not-so-obvious emotions and undercurrents within a conversation. This takes both skill and practice.

One final listening tip that may come in handy... Don't let your body language undermine your efforts.

Even if it feels to *you* like you're offering your conversation partner world-class listening skills, your facial expression and body language may betray you. You might inadvertently be showing signs of disinterest or lack of focus, as mentioned earlier.

We think others don't notice, but they do. And the impact is disastrous. It takes time to gain someone's trust, but just a few seconds to lose it.

Walking to Listen:
A *True Story*

Need proof that good listening can make a difference in your conversations—and your life? Check out this real-world story of a young man who really wanted to become an expert at listening.

Speaker, peace activist, and author Andrew Forsthoefel discovered what he calls "the transformative power of real listening" shortly after graduating from college. He was just 23 and had no idea what to do next with his life, so he decided to walk 4,000 miles across the United States with a sign on his backpack that read, "Walking to Listen."

His mission was simple:
He wanted to gather wisdom and guidance from everyone he met.

"It wasn't in the classroom, but on the road, on foot, with thousands of different Americans, that I received my unofficial training in [listening], this most rare and necessary skill," says Forsthoefel. "I wanted to see each [person as someone] worthy of my attention, each one with a unique wellspring of experience that I could learn from if they were willing to share."

Some of the incredible lessons Forsthoefel acquired on this journey include:

- Listening and learning begin with humility.
- Upon asking a question, never assume you know the answer.
- Listening requires authentic respect for the struggles, complexities, perspective, and value of the other person's life.
- Listening involves a choice to love or at least try to understand someone, even when they give you a reason not to.

One day Forsthoefel found himself walking through New Orleans. He had what began as a negative and perhaps even frightening encounter with a local resident. A man sitting out on his front porch began yelling a steady stream of expletives and insults at Forsthoefel as he walked by. When Forsthoefel calmly explained what he was doing, the angry man softened substantially.

And then he invited Forsthoefel into his home for a beer.

Sitting at the man's kitchen table, Forsthoefel listened attentively to the man's stories, memories, heartaches, tragedies, and regrets.

"When people entrust me with their stories—their brokenness, their frailties, and fallibilities—it becomes impossible for me to hate them, even if I was deeply disturbed by some of the things they believed or had done," Forsthoefel explains. "And when I…asked them questions without malice, they could remain open. It is in this openness that transformation becomes possible…"

Forsthoefel adds in a few more lessons worth noting: "Listening is about forgetting yourself for a moment, letting go of your agenda, abandoning the need to prove anything or dominate the conversation or convert someone to your cause by showing them how wrong they are.

"It is, instead, simply—and challengingly—about witnessing someone… It's a commitment to exploring and building connection with others based on our shared humanity, even when that kind of connection seems impossible."

Isn't that delightful? In so many ways, it warms my heart.

Before we conclude this section, I want to share one more thing: a poem by speaker and author B.J. Gallagher that beautifully captures the magic of listening.

The Gift of Listening

Listening is the gift we give to others.

Listening tells the other person that they are important.

Listening shows others that we genuinely care.

Listening says, "I value you, your thoughts, ideas, and feelings."

Listening is love.

Listening is a gift we give ourselves as well.

Listening gives us the opportunity to grow wise by learning from others' experience.

Listening gives us a chance to see the world through others' eyes and discover something new.

Listening enables us to feel another person's pain and sadness, as well as their joy and delight. We connect to others through our shared feelings.

Listening provides us with the opportunity to hear God speaking to us through others.

It's clear that effective listening is multidimensional and more challenging than talking. But it's worth learning how to do well, and it can make such a difference in the quality of your conversations and relationships. Put this awareness and what you've just read to work. Then observe and enjoy the benefits.

. . . .

As we wrap up this topic, I suspect there may be a question you're asking yourself right now: "Listening is powerful, but do I have to listen to *everyone?* What about the people who are chronically negative or unpleasant on a regular and relentless basis?"

The short answer is: No. We do not have to waste our time or energy listening to those who are…shall we say…draining the life and light from our souls.

Without a doubt, these people are out there. You need to be prepared to recognize them and respond accordingly. Ready to find out more?

Dealing with *Drainers* and *Downers*

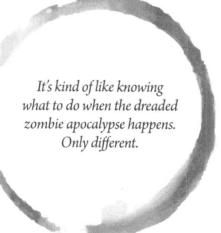

*It's kind of like knowing
what to do when the dreaded
zombie apocalypse happens.
Only different.*

Help!! Save me!

A great conversation partner is a beautiful thing. But, let's face it, life is eventually going to put us on a collision course for an interaction with someone who is a chronically negative and endlessly irritating time-waster.

You know exactly who I'm talking about: the person who regularly dampens our otherwise-sunny moods and drains our batteries with their daily gripes or drama. Or the egomaniac who hogs every conversation, makes us feel less-than, and has perfected the art of driving us stark-raving mad. I'm not referring to someone merely having a bad day. I'm talking about the repeat offenders who sabotage most conversations.

I call these characters Drainers and Downers. D&Ds, for short.

It probably won't surprise you that D&Ds take a serious, significant, and wide-ranging toll on us. Which is why I devoted an entire section to identifying, dealing with, and minimizing your exposure to these pesky folks.

Look at it this way. The point of this book is to help all of us enjoy better conversations. With that in mind, if we want to have the time, energy, and focus to be present in the important and pleasant conversations and relationships—the ones we DO want to enjoy—we will need guidance and strategies for what to do when a conversation partner serves no other purpose but to bring us down.

So here we are. And, trust me, you're not going to want to miss one page. Get comfortable and settle in! This section could offer you some fascinating, if not surprising, answers on how to handle the people and situations that are just such … Drainers and Downers.

....

Spotting D&Ds

....

You're at a social gathering or networking event and have the great misfortune to be cornered by *That Person*. The one who doesn't realize that his sour and gloomy mood, negative energy, and off-putting (if not offensive) socializing habits are having a not-so-positive impact on everyone he encounters.

Right now, his target is you.

I'm sure you can think of someone like this. If not, then lucky you!

This person gripes about how long it took him to get to the venue—because traffic was terrible, someone gave him bad directions, and there's no convenient parking anywhere nearby. Even worse, the lot down the street charges $10 an hour, and the parking spaces are made for those silly "smart cars."

But wait. *That Person* is not finished.

He notes that the coffee is awful, and he's sure the food will be second rate. (He has already made it clear he's a food snob, has digestive issues, and/or is on a *very strict* diet.)

Then he shares a droning and pointless tale about the latest unspeakable experience he's had at the job he despises. He finishes that off with a less-than-complimentary comment about a person standing across the room (who happens to be one of your friends).

Even after just a few minutes in this person's presence, you already feel like every ounce of positive energy and good cheer are draining from your body. You almost want to take a shower. Or bolt for the nearest exit.

It's safe to say we've all had bad days where nothing goes our way. And everyone experiences annoyances, disappointment, challenges, hardships, and tragedies. When we do, it feels so good to share and discuss our worries, heartaches, complaints, bad news, and problems with a friend, loved one, co-worker, neighbor, or a kind-hearted bartender.

Once again, it's that delicious (if not intoxicating) feeling of being heard.

There are even times when a story of unfortunate circumstances, told well and with a sense of irony and humility over drinks or coffee, can be highly entertaining and amusing. Or the basis for a hit country song. Or a story that enriches a book and makes a point. This can feel cathartic and actually creates a positive from a negative.

Ahhh, but then...

Then there are people who turn venting, complaining, grousing, criticizing, chiding, and spreading all forms of negativity and ugliness into an extreme sport. Nothing and no one are ever quite right or nearly good enough. They see themselves as "special" or as perpetual victims, always getting an unfair deal and finding drama in pretty much…everything. What's more, they feel compelled to share all the gory details (and how they feel about them) with anyone who will listen.

And their stamina in doing this is unmatched.

These people are also seasoned pros at seeking out and sharing the latest controversial or fear-inducing news and doom-and-gloom du jour. They freak out, hop on the soap box, clutch their pearls, purse their lips, and express judgment, resentment, or outrage accordingly. Some also offer up a steady stream of unsolicited criticism, self-righteous opinions, and malicious gossip.

These folks are the negativity ninjas who have made it their mission to introduce, foster, and spread pessimism and bitterness at every possible opportunity.

And it seems like their goal is to make sure any joy, fun, hope, or positive energy in their vicinity is completely obliterated.

In short, they are experts at spreading depressing and destructive vibes wherever they go. It's their primary objective, even if subconsciously. We've all experienced them in one form or another.

You can certainly try, but it's nearly impossible to have a good or productive discussion with Drainers and Downers. These D&Ds are the conversational wet blankets nobody wants to encounter—but we all know them when we experience them.

Here are some of the emotionally irksome traits that embody classic D&Ds. You'll know you've likely spotted a D&D when someone is chronically:

❋ Angry	❋ Irritable
❋ Annoying	❋ Judgmental
❋ Anxious	❋ Lecturing
❋ Attention-seeking	❋ Malicious
❋ Badgering	❋ Mean
❋ Belittling	❋ Needy
❋ Bitter	❋ Negative
❋ Blaming	❋ Obnoxious
❋ Bullying	❋ Outrageous
❋ Caustic	❋ Overly dramatic
❋ Chiding	❋ Pessimistic
❋ Complaining	❋ Petty
❋ Critical	❋ Playing the victim
❋ Defensive	❋ Pontificating
❋ Full of excuses	❋ Prone to outbursts
❋ Gloomy	❋ Resentful
❋ Gossipy	❋ Rude
❋ Grumbling	❋ Self-righteous
❋ Guilt-generating	❋ Snippy
❋ Harassing	❋ Toxic
❋ In denial	❋ Whining

Go ahead. Visualize the culprit.

You probably have a D&D in mind right now. If so, what other D&D traits would you add to this list?

_____

_____

_____

◂▴▸

Whew! Highly unpleasant, to say the least. Are you ready to learn more about what makes D&Ds tick and what to do about them? Onward!

Understanding D&Ds

As flawed humans with imperfect and sometimes challenging lives, jobs, and relationships, we all have moments when we can't help but drift into less-than-cheery topics in our conversations. We have problems, and we need to vent about them now and then. Having someone who will listen is a blessing.

D&Ds are different. Negativity is habitual for them. They thrive on it. It's their daily M.O. They take it to new heights—and depths.

In his article entitled, "The Secret to Dealing with Chronic Complainers," Guy Winch, Ph.D., clinical psychologist and author of the book *Emotional First Aid,* contrasts cheery optimists with two types of D&Ds.

Optimists believe the glass is half full. *Pessimists* believe the glass is half empty.

Chronic complainers believe the water is tepid, the glass has a smudge, and—wait—is that a streak on the side? Because I just got new dishwashing detergent that isn't supposed to leave streaks, so…great, what a waste of money! It's just so unfair! Why do these things keep happening to me?

This description made me laugh out loud. And yet…it's not funny when you're caught in the grasp of a D&D.

Unfortunately, D&Ds lurk everywhere: in your family, neighborhood, workplace, social circle, book club, volunteer committee, classroom, or gym; at your favorite coffee shop or grocery store; on your flight or on your building's elevator. You may even have D&Ds as clients or customers.

We've all encountered them. They are an unfortunate reality of life. Which begs the question, what's up with those people? Why do they seem to be…everywhere? What makes them the way they are?

Why would anyone want to be so darn negative?

There are plenty of reasons why D&Ds exist. For one, the human brain is wired to focus on the negative. This is called our *negativity bias*. It's a survival feature that's kept us alive since the dawn of humankind.

For example, if you discovered that a plant was poisonous and would hurt you if you ate it or touched it, you wouldn't want to forget that and make the same mistake again. You'd also share what you learned with your family or tribe. The other plants aren't nearly as memorable. (And most people already recognize the delicious ones!)

The same thing applies to modern life. Let's say you just delivered a big presentation to your sales team. Everyone gave you a big "thumbs up." Except for that one grumbly colleague who openly criticized your slides. Which input are you going to obsess over and talk about with a friend while drinking a fish-bowl-sized margarita?

Uh-huh. We all do it.

And then there's the media, which makes its living sharing constant negativity and drama with readers and viewers 24/7. They know we can't look away. The old journalism adage is quite telling: "If it bleeds, it leads."

In short, we tend to focus on and remember the negative.

Our brains can't help it! But most of us have the good sense to turn it off and at least try to look on the bright side.

Not D&Ds. Here are more reasons why they are so doomy and gloomy.

They are born irritable.

Beyond a normal degree of negativity bias, some people are just wired to have pricklier personalities. They are cranky and fussy the moment they exit the womb. Maybe the moment they are conceived.

They are unhappy.

They feel disrespected, unloved, disappointed, or dissatisfied. They firmly believe that life has given them a raw deal. And maybe it has. Injustices of all kinds—sometimes real, sometimes imagined, sometimes circumstantial, sometimes self-generated—have left them in a constantly negative state. They can't seem to pull themselves out of the negativity vortex.

They have had more than their fair share of challenges, sadness, trauma, and loss in their lives.

Many people suffer from the pain of horrible experiences, abuse, grief, relationship struggles, health problems, depression, mental illness, addiction, accidents, injuries, financial woes, and career challenges. Poor choices may be to blame. Or maybe it's just an endless string of bad luck. The metaphorical grey cloud just seems to hover over them wherever they go. They can't seem to shake it. The emotional wounds are painful and real. They are tired and worn out.

They have acquired negativity as a habit.

They've learned this trait from parents, family members, friends, or co-workers. Being negative is "normal"—practically a cultural requirement. What's more, negativity is contagious and tends to beget even more negativity!

They have learned to use negativity to their advantage.

In their lives or their careers, D&Ds have learned to use chronic complaining and drama to get attention and the results they crave, to earn good deals or freebies, to play the victim, or even to feel superior.

They find being negative energizing.

Wait!! What?? Yes! When D&Ds can blame anyone but themselves for their woes or whatever is "wrong" in the world, it helps them settle into the victim role, take the moral high ground, and feel better about themselves. Plus, venting is expressive and can be pressure-relieving. For a D&D, it can feel great to grouse.

They are complete mysteries.

Meaning, we have no idea why they are the way they are!

Some D&Ds might even consider themselves happy, upbeat people.

They don't even realize they are spewing doom and gloom. No one has ever called them on it.

The problem is, when we encounter them as conversation partners—invited or not—we run the risk of becoming the collateral damage. Negativity takes its toll, sooner or later. And wait until you read how serious that toll is. It's a little unnerving.

Recognizing the *Devastating Impact* of D&Ds

If someone were to ask me to describe what it's like to be with a D&D, someone who is chronically negative, I would use words such as unpleasant, annoying, exhausting, exasperating, stressful and, in some cases, even frightening.

What words would you use, by the way?

_____

_____

_____

Sadly, that's just the tip of the iceberg. Did you know that D&Ds do far more damage than just causing us frustration, ruining our moods, and being painful or upsetting to associate with?

Studies reveal that they can negatively impact our lives in significant ways. D&Ds have the unfortunate power to:

- Hijack our attention, focus, and productivity.
- Waste our time (a resource we can never get back).
- Drain our energy.
- Erode or destroy our self-esteem and motivation.
- Test our goodwill.
- Make us question our own sanity.
- Spread toxic emotional contagion.
- Ruin otherwise-pleasant events and gatherings.
- Poison the individual and collective attitudes and culture of an entire group, family, office, team, or airplane full of people.
- Damage and destroy relationships, communities, and other groups.

And here's the kicker… D&Ds also have the power to:

- Create stress responses that rewire our brains, which damages our short- and long-term health—and can take years off our lives!

Yes, you read that correctly: *years* off our lives.

In short, D&Ds aren't just nuisances; they are venomous, damaging, destructive, and deadly.

In his book, *Social Intelligence: The Revolutionary New Science of Human Relationships,* author and Pulitzer Prize nominee Daniel Goleman notes that "nourishing relationships have a beneficial impact on our health, while toxic ones can act like slow poison in our bodies."

Wow. Slow poison. I'm feeling that one right now. You?

And what if D&Ds have found their way into your staff or organization? (What? Someone let them in? What were they thinking?) Now the impact isn't just annoying and deadly; it's also taking a toll on the bottom line.

Negativity is contagious, so D&Ds can do a real number on your team morale and productivity.

Collaboration breaks down. Tempers may flare. Engagement could hit rock bottom. Sooner or later, that one bad apple will begin to poison the whole team's ability to achieve goals and perform at an optimal level.

The message for leaders and HR managers? Your D&D radar needs to be fully active. If you're in charge of screening new hires, pay close attention to a candidate's overall attitude and outlook on life. And what happens if a D&D slips through the cracks? Deal with them quickly before they taint the rest of the group. Their impact can be devastating.

Why do we put up with that?

Despite the damage that D&Ds do, we often let them get away with it. We may feel helpless, trapped, taken aback, and even paralyzed in their presence.

What? That's crazy, right? Why would we do it?

Somewhere along the line, we were led to believe we had to be kind, understanding, patient, polite, and respectful to *everyone*. Even to people who are upsetting us, making us sick, and *slowly killing us.*

Whoa, Nellie! That's not right.

No, it's not. And experts in relationships, communication, etiquette, and protocol will assure us that we do NOT have to fall prey to a D&D's endless negativity. If it sucks away our energy and good mood, stresses us out, ruins our parties, keeps our teams from working together peacefully, or undermines anyone's performance, ruins our health, or generates dysfunction or co-dependency, we have the right to end this madness and say, "Enough!!"

Why do we need to manage the D&Ds in our lives?

First, we'll have less negativity and drama in our world, which means we can enjoy a happier, more peaceful state of mind. Our stomachs will unclench. The throbbing headaches will recede. We can go about our days and live our lives in peace with restored productivity. We will probably sleep better, too.

That already sounds good, right?

As an added bonus, when we create and uphold our boundaries, the D&Ds will soon understand we are no longer willing to be easy targets for or tolerate their rantings. They will leave us alone and move on to someone else (who has not read this book).

The big bonus: When we learn how to avoid and manage the D&Ds in our midst, we will have more time and energy for what's good in our worlds.

I'm all in for that! How about you?

So, what techniques do we use to manage and deflect D&Ds? Great question!

Coming up, I'll describe **four strategies** you can use with the D&Ds who repeatedly try to rain on your conversation parade (and life). Within each strategy are several techniques and tips. These ideas come from a range of sources and experts, and some may even seem contradictory. That's because different D&Ds (and different situations and scenarios) will require different strategies.

Also, take note: These ideas aren't presented as no-fail formulas guaranteed to work 100% of the time with every D&D you encounter. Like most things in life, nothing is a given. Trial and error will be involved. You may have to blend techniques or create your own unique style. My goal is simply to give you some inspiration.

Ready?

D&D Strategy #1: Setting *Boundaries* and Limits

It's one thing to be a caring and compassionate listener for someone who is truly hurting, sad, or under stress and strain. It's also a kindness to patiently hear what's on someone's mind and to let them share without dismissing, interrupting, or offering an instant solution.

As you read earlier, at its easiest, this type of social generosity can be a challenge for our tired, overloaded, and easily distracted minds. But we are willing to do it and hope someone will someday be there for us. However, when it comes to unrelenting complaints and negativity, it can send us right over the edge.

Also, think of it this way: When we indulge the D&Ds in our lives, we are actually communicating that it's acceptable to be chronically negative. We may even be *rewarding* them by regularly attending their performances!

Feel the drain ...

You likely have some D&Ds in your life. They have your number and love dialing it, literally and figuratively. How does it feel to be around them and listen to them constantly? What impact does it have on your mood, energy, focus, and productivity?

_____

_____

_____   _____

_____

Yep, it's no fun at all and can completely ruin your day—and more!

◂▴▸

It's time to develop, enforce, and communicate clear and consistent policies and boundaries for defending yourself against the D&Ds in your world. Here's a big one.

Stop being a doormat

Strange as it might sound, some of us are just too approachable, kind, compassionate, and "polite." Put another way, we are suckers, easy targets, and total pushovers. Our sweet, kind, generous, comported, don't-rock-the-boat personalities mean we end up becoming the overly receptive targets and emotional dumping grounds for D&Ds.

And many times, we don't even see that a speeding, heavily loaded 18-wheeler of negativity is upon us…until it's too late!

Worth repeating: Etiquette experts, business protocol professionals, and psychologists will enthusiastically insist that we have the *right and duty* to protect ourselves from someone who is chronically negative, in whatever form that takes.

Repeat after me: I am NOT a doormat.

Now let's look at how to stop opening the floodgates for potential D&Ds.

Vow to start every conversation on a positive note

The mood of a conversation often starts with us. Alrighty then. Let's make it our personal policy, dare I say our *mission*, to enter every conversation or meeting with a smile and an impenetrable positive attitude. Greet everyone with a cheerful "Good morning" or "Good afternoon." Bring up positive topics whenever possible. Better to light a candle than curse the darkness.

Wait! Won't that continue to make us easy targets for D&Ds? Not necessarily. It's possible to be upbeat and positive without making ourselves vulnerable.

Vowing to protect our positivity is a smart, proactive defense. There's an ultra-slim chance it could bring out the D&D's more positive side. Certainly worth giving it a try, right?

Tim Sanders, best-selling author and former Yahoo Chief Solutions Officer, regularly uses the following greeting to infuse an air of positive expectation into a conversation:

"What's the good word?"

This shows friendliness, warmth, and interest. He wants to start the conversation on a positive note and is really not interested in hearing something negative.

Bert Jacobs, Chief Economic Optimist for the Life is Good Co., recalls that his mom had a similar philosophy. At the family dinner table, she'd say: "Tell me something good that happened today." As a busy single mom raising Bert and his brother, she needed some good news to keep her going! (Don't we all?)

This ritual of purposeful positivity taught the boys that you can nearly always "change the energy of a situation" and take action to "turn obstacles into opportunities."

Bert and his brother even leveraged that upbeat attitude and made it the theme for their highly successful business! To this day, they believe and teach that "optimism is pragmatic and logical."

Here's another simple way to prime a positive conversation. Try saying something like:

- "Good morning, Gloria! Hope you're having a nice day!"
- "Hello, Al. Would love to hear what's good in your world!"
- "Tell me what's new and exciting!"

Come up with your own variations on this theme of greeting others, saying hello, wishing them well, and asking for the positive side of life.

Just saying...

With known D&Ds, please be careful with these greetings:

- ☀ "How are you?"
- ☀ "What's new?"
- ☀ "How's your day going?"

You just might hear ALL about it. And not in a good way.

What if things go sideways, despite your best efforts? That's next.

Graciously request a shift

Let's say an exchange takes a negative turn into D&D territory. After a few minutes of their negativity or complaining, especially if there is no sign of a shift, you are well within the bounds of courtesy, civility, and self-preservation to request a change in subject.

It's time to say something like, "Man. That really stinks." Then quickly move on to another topic. Any topic.

I was once at a cocktail gathering in a beautiful home with a number of friends, old and new. The food and wine were delicious, the company captivating, and the atmosphere lively and fun. I was chatting with a friend and, somehow, we became fixated on a recent news story that was both tragic and perplexing.

After a few moments, we caught ourselves slipping down the sullen slope of becoming D&Ds. My friend beat me to the punch. "Wow, what are we doing talking about something so depressing when we're at this cool party?" We quickly snapped out of the negativity and found something better to talk about. Complete mood shift—for the better!

Help put things in perspective

Sometimes in talking with a D&D, you might have an opportunity to change the playing field: attempt to create a solutions-oriented conversation, reframe the situation, or see the sunny side.

- ❊ "What have you tried in response to that problem?"
- ❊ "Have you looked at that from a different perspective?"
- ❊ "On the upside…"
- ❊ "Sounds like there are some valuable lessons in here…"
- ❊ "Certainly, you'll figure this out…"

With statements like these, you may be able to help D&Ds find a solution or the positive angle they've been missing. More importantly, you're demonstrating that you're not going to jump on the negative bandwagon with them.

My friend Carla Smith shares this story of a woman who graciously provided her with some much-needed positivity and perspective on a really difficult day.

Carla was flying to Albuquerque to attend the annual International Balloon Fiesta held every October. The first leg of her flight was behind schedule, so she barely made her connection. She was the last person to board the plane before they shut the doors. The flight attendant directed her to the very back of the plane for the one remaining seat. (Yep, you know the one. Last row. Center seat.)

Carla made her way down the aisle, completely out of breath from running through the airport. She was tired, frustrated, and flat-out angry about her bad luck. She was also prepared to hate the people seated on either side of her who were already invading her space.

The man to her left kept his earbuds in the entire flight, but the woman on her right was actually quite friendly and struck up a conversation—a risky choice, given Carla's demeanor. Sure enough, Carla launched into a full-fledged, world-class venting spree.

Carla: "Everything is going wrong today! It's been one thing after another. Then I missed early boarding."

Perspective-Providing Woman: "But you made the flight!"

Carla: "I always check a bag when I fly. The one time I decide to just do a carry-on and put everything I need in there, they tell me at the gate that I have to check it because there's no more space in the overhead bins. Why didn't I just check it like I usually do?"

Perspective-Providing Woman: "But if you'd stopped to check your bag, you probably wouldn't have made it here on time!"

The exchange went on like this for the next two hours. No matter how many complaints Carla had, this woman remained kind, supportive, and positive. Never scolding or judgmental.

By the time the pilot announced they were preparing to land, Carla was in a completely different frame of mind. She was incredibly grateful to be "stuck" in that middle seat with someone who gently helped her find the silver linings in every dark cloud.

Carla said she'll never forget the gift of conversation with that woman. More importantly, she told me she's committed to emulating her when she's given the chance. You never know when you can totally shift someone's perspective.

With that said...

Recognize that a cheerful spirit won't always be welcomed

More specifically, it could indeed be totally ignored, challenged, and resented.

Carla's story is probably the exception rather than the rule. In many cases, misery loves company and despises cheery optimism.

As hard as you might try to infuse some sunshine into a D&D's day, they may go through elaborate maneuvers to hold tight to their sticky web of negativity. They may even try crafty and elaborate methods to suck you in to join them. Some may even get angry with you for resisting or for ruining their pity party.

That's their issue. Ignore it. Resist it. Move along and find a more positive conversation partner. Drop any guilt. Even the tiniest bit. Escape with your life.

Address the problem head on

Some people may not realize how much negativity they are spewing forth and the impact it has. One solution may be to directly point it out to them in a respectful way.

Fair warning: This is risky and may or may not be well-received. However, if someone's constant gloom and criticism are making you or others in your presence uncomfortable or upset, you have the right to call them on it.

You might say:

- ☀ "Wow, this conversation is really bringing me down / upsetting me."
- ☀ "Man, I wasn't prepared for this conversation to take such a negative turn."
- ☀ "Say, Arthur, I'm not sure if you've noticed, but every comment you made in our meeting earlier was negative or some kind of complaint. What's this really about?"
- ☀ "You know, when our exchanges linger on negative topics, it just drains me."
- ☀ "Wouldn't it be far more productive to reframe this conversation and talk about what's going well these days?"

Be warned. No matter what you say, the D&D might continue on.

D&D Strategy #2: Avoiding or *Minimizing* Contact

Sometimes the best way to deal with a D&D is…to *not* deal with them. Not in a stick-your-head-in-the-sand kind of way, but as an actual coping strategy.

Stop seeking out negativity

What? Why would anyone in their right mind *seek out* negativity?

Oh, come on. Be honest.

Ever caught yourself yearning for a little drama? Wanting to hear the dirt, get the scoop, be in the know, or take in all the juicy details? Ever found yourself wallowing in the dark side of things? Remember the line from the movie, "Steel Magnolias"? "If you don't have anything nice to say, come sit by me!" So memorable! Misery does, indeed, love company.

Careful here.

That oh-so-human negativity bias wants to pull you into its evil clutches again.

When it happens to me and I'm being seduced by drama I could easily avoid, I remember the wise words of my dear friend Cindy: "Don't meet trouble halfway."

Albert Einstein had a similar suggestion: "Stay away from negative people. They have a problem for every solution."

And, finally, author and teacher Nancy Oelklaus, Ed.D., wisely advises, "What you focus on gets stronger."

Stop seeking out and encouraging the negativity! Go to the light!

Choose your battles

Ever fallen for this one? A D&D sets us up with a negative comment or a gripe. Before we know it, we've taken the bait and responded in a defensive or chiding way. The resulting squabble or blow-up leaves everyone involved (and within earshot) feeling hurt, upset, and drained.

Was it worth it? Heck, no. It would have been best to neither react nor engage. Zipping your lips and walking away would have been wiser.

Knowing this, when a D&D is trying to get a reaction out of you, try one of these "I'm not going there" moves:

- Stay silent—do not say one word. Not. Even. One.
- Neutralize your expression. (Don't roll your eyes, raise your eyebrows, or purse your lips. Don your best poker face.)
- Let the silence and non-reaction speak for itself.
- Swiftly change the subject to something pleasant.

- ☀ Walk away if necessary. Leave the room or vicinity.
- ☀ Refuse to waste your time or energy.

It feels really good when you can pull this off consistently. Plus, your non-participation will speak volumes.

Minimize your exposure

Once you recognize that a person is a chronic D&D, vow to reduce or even eliminate your exposure to their prickly energy. Don't engage. Don't go where they go. Don't take their calls. Practice avoidance at all costs.

See them coming down the street or making their way across the room or down the hallway? Change directions. Duck and run. Evade. Dare I say, hide in the shrubs or in the broom closet!

You are not obligated to deal with D&Ds socially.

Do whatever it takes to keep them out of your positive sphere.

True story. Several years ago, I went as far as to use the "call block" feature on the phone number of an acquaintance who had mistakenly and prematurely believed I was her #1 BFF. I had met her at a social event, and we had had a cordial conversation. But suddenly, she thought that meant we were inseparable and best pals. I mean *besties*. It was creepy.

This person began randomly calling me, often multiple times each day, to share updates regarding her career and personal life, as well as random thoughts and her latest dramas.

At first, I did my best to be a good listener. Yet she wasted hours of my time and ruined one too many happy moments and productive days.

Plus, it was clear she was thriving on venting and sharing details of her personal life that should have stayed, well, *very personal.*

It was weird and draining.

I tried many times to offer friendly hints that I was busy and had to limit our time on the phone—and that I had other people in my life. Like my family, for instance. These hints made no impact whatsoever. I also mentioned that some of the topics she brought up were really none of my business.

The chronic calls continued as if I'd said nothing. If I didn't pick up, this person would try multiple times and then leave long, rambling voice messages that clogged up my voicemail system. Things were drifting rapidly into slightly troubling, even "stalking" territory.

I finally had no other choice. I blocked her number on my home, office, and mobile phones. I kept my window blinds closed and prayed she wouldn't show up on my doorstep. Thankfully, she did not.

The call-blocking measure was dramatic, to be sure. But it worked. I'm sure I hurt and offended her, which is unfortunate. No regrets on my part. She was not only a D&D, but she was a persistent one.

> Way back in 1736, the brilliant Founding Father Benjamin Franklin wrote the wise and well-known adage, "An ounce of prevention is worth a pound of cure." He was writing about fire safety, of all things! Yet, it's appropriate and symbolic. D&Ds have the power and potential to spark a bonfire of distress in your life. Prevention is the key. Do whatever you need to do!

D&D Strategy #3:
Deflecting and Exiting

You may recall that we covered the general concept of managing and exiting conversations in Chapter 26. (Remember "Please forgive me…"?) However, deflecting and exiting an interaction with a big-time, hard-core D&D rightly deserves its own space in this book. Sort of like moving from "Exiting 101" to the more intense curriculum of "Advanced Studies in Emergency Extrication."

With that said, carry on…

Here's what we know.

There are D&Ds you can avoid or get away from quickly. And then there are others you have little choice but to face regularly.

These include family members, neighbors, co-workers, classmates, customers, or the disgruntled seatmate on a three-hour flight. When there's no escape hatch (or parachute), you need to be assertive in fending off the negativity.

Listen, acknowledge, then exit

This one's generous yet quite effective if you do it decisively and don't weaken. When the D&D approaches and commences their rant, respond with the lightest touch of empathy or sympathy. That's right, listen for a few seconds while nodding or shaking your head in complete acknowledgement, maybe offering a look of sincere concern.

Then use one of these sympathetic phrases before making a *quick exit:*

- ☀ "Gosh, I'm so sorry to hear that."
- ☀ "Man, that's rough."
- ☀ "You have my sympathies."
- ☀ "Well, that's a shame."
- ☀ "Sorry to hear it."
- ☀ "I'll keep my fingers crossed and hope things take a positive turn soon."
- ☀ "Hopefully, you'll find a quick solution for that."
- ☀ "Hmmm…"

Now. Walk. Away.

Or you can be stealthier, like talent recruiter Sherry Jenkins McHale. When Sherry worked in an office environment as a marketing executive, she had a clever way of dealing with a chronic complainer who plopped down in one of her office chairs. She'd listen for a brief minute, then stand up and grab a nearby water bottle or coffee cup that "needed refilling." (Wink, wink.) She'd gesture for the complainer to follow her. Somewhere between her office and the breakroom, she'd wrap up the exchange and move on with her day.

Yet another strategy: When the D&D approaches and breathlessly begins to share her drama and extensive list of problems and complaints, stop them in mid-sentence and say, "Gosh, is this going to take a whole minute? Or two?" This is the clear signal that you're willing to listen, but only briefly.

Here it makes sense to weigh in on the basic differences between empathy and sympathy.

Empathy involves trying to imagine or understand the feeling the other person is experiencing. Really getting in the trenches with them.

Sympathy is showing sorrow or concern for the other person, but not actually "going there."

Which one really works with a D&D? Usually a dash of sympathy fits the bill nicely.

As my friend Dawn's hilarious dad used to say when a person was taking on someone else's problems or drama in an excessive fashion: "You don't have to live the part."

He was right. You don't.

Go for controlled, neutral exposure (with a dab of disinterest)

This strategy is all about stoic tolerance. You may even need to don your imaginary force-field cloak. The key here is to minimize signals that could hint toward any interest or engagement *whatsoever*. Once again, your best poker face is a necessity. You might also glance at your watch, check your phone, or even pause to scribble a few thoughts on a nearby notepad.

In short, ignore the D&D as best you can. Look disinterested. Do not get sucked in. Then find a smooth way to exit their sphere as quickly as possible!

But wouldn't this make us a rude person and a terrible listener? Well, yes, actually. It would. Absolutely. Guilty as charged. Here, it's perfect!

Remember, we're talking about mercenary and predatory D&Ds. The saboteurs who regularly and consistently hijack and attack our time, energy, focus, peace of mind, positivity, productivity, health, and life span!

Who's really the rude one here?

Redirect with a new question

Some call this "The Bridge" or the "Distraction Method." It's really just managing and shifting the conversation. When a D&D is on a negative tear, listen for a bit if you want—totally optional. Then quickly chime in (yes, full-on interrupting) with something that totally changes the topic and shifts the energy.

- "Hey! Did you catch the game last night?"
- "When did you say you're going on vacation?"
- "By the way, what color did you decide to paint your house?"
- "Wow! That outfit looks great on you!"
- "Oh, I meant to ask you…"
- "You know, that reminds me…"
- "Hey, I've always wondered…"
- "Man, aren't these cheeseburgers delicious?"
- "Look up there! Isn't that Halley's Comet again? Wow!"

As a reminder: This technique can also shift a dreary, small-talk-y or going-nowhere chat into a much more interesting one by inserting a zinger question or comment that radically shifts everyone's energy and thought process.

Yes, it's abrupt. And it may seem rude. But when people or topics turn excessively negative, dreary, or draining, you are free to take charge and move the exchange toward a much better place.

Use a solution-oriented approach

This one's all about remembering who owns and is responsible for correcting a negative situation. But first, a little anecdote that reveals a short and simple solution a friend shared with me.

Early in his management career, Concordia University Texas' Donald Christian (you may recall I've mentioned him before) set a policy for dealing with staff members who came to him with problems, complaints, and grievances. He didn't want to get sucked into solving problems other people were hired to manage. He cleverly placed a label on his desk drawer—right in front of him in bold, black letters where only he could see it, but others could not.

The label read: "So what are YOU going to do about it?"

By using these simple but powerful words whenever staff members came to him with troubles, Don could hold them accountable. It also empowered them to find their own solutions and be more resourceful and creative. Most importantly—hallelujah!—the message on the label kept any D&D behavior at bay.

Here are more sample scenarios for how to get a D&D on a solution-oriented track:

Example 1

> **Complaining Carl:** "My doctor misdiagnosed my illness and gave me the wrong medication. Now I feel even worse!"
>
> **You:** "Wow, that's awful, Carl. Sounds like you need to make some calls or another appointment with your doctor to straighten that out. Or find a new doctor."

Example 2

> **Negative Nellie:** "I'm so frustrated with my job. My boss is just awful. My co-workers are even worse. I hate Mondays. I'm tired before I even get there..."
>
> **You:** "You sound really unhappy, Nellie. What's your plan for finding another position that's more satisfying?"

Example 3

> **Grumpy Gus:** "This client is so obnoxious. Completely uncooperative. Every interaction is a total train wreck."
>
> **You:** "Well, what do you think you should do about it?"

Example 4

> **Sour Selina:** "The prices went up. The manufacturer was running behind. Now they're telling me the product was damaged in shipping! Really?!?"
>
> **You:** "Hmmm..."

Or, as the Big Lebowski would say, "Bummer, man."

When we don't have the option to avoid D&Ds, we definitely need tools like the ones you've just read about to manage their impact. Keep your acknowledging statements, redirecting questions, and account-ability responses handy! And practice, practice, practice. It does get easier.

Up next, ways to meet a D&D head on.

D&D Strategy #4:
Proactively
Engaging

This strategy is reserved for the brave, the bold, and the endlessly saintly people who are courageous enough to tackle the D&D negativity problem head-on with hopes to resolve it (and anything causing it), once and for all.

Maybe that's you?

First, ask yourself whether it's worth it to "stir the pot" or "poke the bear." Do you really want to get involved at close range? Are you truly equipped to endure and survive this? Is this a hill you want to die on?

If your situation, your job, or your relationships have gotten so bad, you may have no choice but to try.

Are you in that boat? If you think you have the spine, the fortitude, and the patience to proactively engage with the D&Ds in your life, the following strategies may help guide your path. May the force be with you!

Hear them out

This option sounds totally insane, especially if you're already at the end of your rope with a D&D's negativity. And, quite honestly, it may not work for everyone or every situation. But there are times when it might pay to brace yourself, settle in, and be fully present as you listen to everything a D&D has to say.

That's right. Let 'em spill it all and completely purge their head, heart, soul, and gripe list. You may want to have a pen and notepad on hand to document all the details.

Maybe begin with something like, "What's on your mind, Simone? I'm here to listen."

Then listen, document, and clarify as you go.

- "So, I'm hearing you say _____. Is that correct?"
- "Go on…"
- "Your next point?"
- "Keep going…"
- "What else?"
- "Is there more?"
- "Is that everything?"
- "Any final thoughts?"

Do your best to thoroughly pull out everything that's on their mind, perhaps even exhaust them. (Hopefully, you will outlast them.)

Remember: Welcoming the complaint discussion isn't for the weary or faint of heart. Hang on for dear life, and don't be afraid to help manage the discussion when needed.

- ☀ "Tony, we've already covered that point."
- ☀ "Bella, you've said that several times now. Let's move on."
- ☀ "Isaac, I believe you mentioned that earlier."

Eventually they will run out of steam (and, hopefully, complaints).

But with a chronic D&D, who can really be sure?

Throughout this process, keep in mind that there are often grains of truth within negative comments or complaints. Listen for these. Acknowledge and capture them.

But once again, proceed with caution!

Full disclosure: This strategy could backfire and set a new precedent for what a D&D expects of you *every single time* they have a complaint or are in the mood to grumble and grouse. Unless you are trained in handling this sort of thing, your subsequent conversations could leave you worse off than when you began.

Stand firm and communicate clearly: "This is a one-time thing."

You might even find it appropriate to mention the nine-word miracle statement you read about earlier: "So, what are you going to do about it?"

Daniel Stillman, facilitator and author of *Good Talk: How to Design Conversations That Matter,* says he has an understanding heart for people who are potentially D&Ds.

"I don't believe that difficult people exist," Stillman says. "Often, challenging people just have unmet needs. Digging more deeply into what's going on with them can help you empathize with them and design a radically transformative strategy."

This can be true.

To that end, my friend Steven used the "hear them out" technique successfully while heading up the board of a professional association. A D&D in the group frequently hijacked otherwise-productive meetings with dramatic outbursts, complaints, and negative comments. There was backbiting, triangulation, and more complaining and drama behind the scenes. This strife was taking a toll on the board and the organization, not to mention its ability to get anything done.

Finally, Steven decided to proactively engage. He invited the D&D out for lunch with the goal of being fully present, listening, documenting, and addressing the full scope of the board member's complaints.

Not surprisingly, the meeting lasted several hours. And, per Steven, it was thoroughly exhausting. But the good news is, he got every last issue and problem on paper.

As it turns out, many of the issues were valid. Best of all, the D&D felt heard and respected. The board member gained valuable feedback and insight on how the passive-aggressive behavior and negativity were impacting the team and its work. This shows that situations can be difficult, but how we handle them matters as well.

Strive for clarity

Sometimes when a D&D descends upon you, their complaints will be not only numerous, but also ranty, scattered, and highly emotional. Much like when a three-year-old throws a tantrum—especially one that's a total blow-up and completely unexpected.

In situations like this, it can be difficult to know exactly what's going on or why. You can get to the source of the explosion by asking one of these questions:

- "Wow, I can see you're really upset. Can you please tell me more specifically why you're feeling this way and what happened to set you off?"
- "Oh man, I can see you're angry. What's going on?"
- "I'm not following you on what's happening here. Can you please get more specific?"
- "I can see you're upset. What are you really needing from me here?"

Sometimes the D&D won't know. Or the list is so long and convoluted that it's hard for them to communicate. If that's the case, ask them to take some time to gather their thoughts and come back when they are clear and calm. In contrast, they may be able to articulate the problem on the spot. Then you can decide what next steps are appropriate.

If that doesn't work...

Ask how you could be of assistance

Some people could genuinely use our help, wisdom, and objectivity. Others are just seeking attention or being cranky for the sake of... being cranky.

James Blackwell Gordon, CEO of Successful Life Sailing, a man known for his cheerful, sincere, and helpful personality, offers an effective way to weed out those who truly need (and want) help, as opposed to the drama-driven D&Ds.

"I listen to the complainer for a few moments," Gordon says. "Then I ask, 'How can I help you?' If they go right back into their complaining, I know not to waste my time and leave the conversation."

Collaborate on finding a solution

Another tactic: Offer some quick, specific advice or suggestions. See if they bite. But remember that advice-giving is generally not taken well unless it's requested. Anticipate that the textbook D&D may discount any and all of your ideas as inappropriate, irrelevant, or useless.

They may even hurl this thorny classic at you: "How could you possibly understand?"

This is your cue to ask what ideas they have for solving the problem. (As in, "So, what are you going to do about it?" Priceless!)

You might also help the D&D move in a positive direction and think bigger by asking a visionary question:

- "What would 'success' or 'great' look like?"
- "What are you really hoping for here?"
- "If you could snap your fingers and create any outcome you want, what would that be?"
- "What would make you happy?"

Often, they won't even know. Or they will say it's far too complicated to go into. Or it's flat-out impossible. (Hint: It's probably time to recommend some professional guidance.)

But let's assume for a moment they really do know what they want. You can attempt to spur them into action.

- "What's involved in making that happen?"
- "So, what's your first / next step here?"
- "What could you do to build momentum on this?"

Another angle: Gauge how motivated they are to make changes or improvements. (Many D&Ds just love to complain and never take action.)

Try asking this question: "On a scale of 1 to 10, how motivated are you to make this happen?"

If they say "10" (that's maximum motivation right there!), find out what they need from you and urge them to begin.

If they say "5," find out why they aren't "all in." Maybe it's really only a "2" or a "0." Which would mean they don't actually want what they say they want. If that's the case, discussion over.

Helping D&Ds see their own problem-solving motivation (or lack thereof) can help provide much-needed clarity and even defuse or dismiss the complaint.

You could also ask: "Why is this such an issue for you?"

And then there are people who will find something to rant about, regardless of the topic. Even matters beyond their control.

In his best-selling book, *The Subtle Art of Not Giving a F*ck*, Mark Manson asks a brilliant and candid question, which I'll paraphrase: How many things can and should we really worry about and possibly try to control?

Manson makes a great point. Not everything in life has to be our responsibility or a Red Alert DEFCON Five Emergency. And if we're honest, many issues are not even worth worrying, talking, or complaining about.

American speaker and author Byron Katie puts it this way:

There's...

Your business.

My business.

God's business.

Which is it?

Now let's talk accountability.

What if, miracle of miracles, you succeed in helping the D&D establish a game plan for solving their problem? Expect action and a commitment. Additionally, mention that your "fee" or payback for supporting them through the process is this: The constant negativity and complaining must stop!

Good luck with that... but it's worth a shot!

One added footnote here. Yes, helping someone get to the root of a problem can be enlightening and healing. But, unless you're a certified or licensed professional, being someone's therapist is not your job.

Express your disagreement graciously

What if you really feel compelled to offer your perspective or your opinion with a ranting D&D? It's not always a good idea and often pointless, to be sure. But sometimes, when clear heads can prevail, this strategy could be effective.

Be warned, as noted by the ever-practical Thomas Paine: "To argue with a person who has renounced the use of reason is like administering medicine to the dead."

Still, there are moments when we may have to say *something* to get the madness to stop. Or to defend ourselves.

The following phrases, categorized for your convenience, can help you express your disagreement clearly while holding your ground in a courteous way.

What to say when...

You disagree:

- "I hear what you're saying, but I see it differently."
- "I'm going to gently / respectfully disagree with you."
- "Well, that's one way to think about it."
- "I have my own thoughts on that."
- "Interesting! Although I don't personally share that view."
- "I agree with some of what you've said, but not all of it."
- "That's not at all how I see it."
- "I'd have a tough time getting on board with that."
- "Hmmm... That's a different perspective, but I disagree."
- "I don't find that to be true."
- "I'm not sure it works that way."
- "I'm afraid I don't see it from that angle."
- "This may not be the popular view, but here's how I see it..."

You disagree, but you want to keep the discussion going in a civilized manner:

- "I'm happy to debate / discuss this if we can agree to do it without getting heated."
- "I'm willing to have a respectful and balanced dialogue about this. Can we do that?"

You want to defuse the discussion and just let it go:

- "You could be right."
- "You might be correct about that."
- "Hmmm...interesting."

When you don't want to take a side or make a decision:

- "I'm going to need some time to think about that."
- "I don't really know the answer to this."
- "This is something I'd have to sleep on."
- "Some issues just can't be solved in one conversation."

It's clearly time to move on:

- "How about we agree to disagree and switch to another topic?"
- "I'm really not interested in arguing about this."
- "It's time to talk about something else."
- "I'm sensing this conversation is over..."
- "There's probably no point in continuing this discussion."
- "On that note, it's time for me to go."

When in doubt or at a loss about what to say or do, ask yourself how your wisest and most gracious friend, colleague, or mentor would respond in this situation.

Have an exit strategy ready

Hopefully you remember the tips from Chapter 26, but a quick refresher never hurts. Especially when D&Ds are involved!

Let's say none of your efforts to engage and defuse are fruitful. What's more, your D&D is dramatically hogging the spotlight while simultaneously wallowing in the quicksand of negativity. At this point, you have every right to end the interaction and walk away.

Remember, continuing to listen to the droning and the drama is hazardous to your health!

Save yourself. Your time and energy are better spent elsewhere.

Feel like you should err on the side of being gracious as you leave? **Interrupt at the very first micro-second of opportunity and say something like:**

- "Please forgive me… I really need to go."
- "Please forgive me… It's time for me to head out."
- "Please forgive me… I need to step away."
- "Please forgive me… I really need to get back to work."

Less gracious options:

- "I believe I've had quite enough of this discussion."
- "Look at the time! Gotta go."
- "On that cheery note, I need to make a call."
- "Time to go / head out / move along / say goodbye."

Then go, go, GO!

Oh, but wait! Here's one more way to shake up (and wrap up) a toxic D&D rant. Do the absolutely unthinkable. Interject with this phrase:

"Would you like to hear my thoughts?"

Witnessing the look on the D&D's face when you say this and then hearing their answer could be priceless.

Typically, a D&D is not one bit interested in what you have to say. If that's the case, that's your free ticket out! Conversation over!

- ✳ "Well, if you're not interested in what I think / my thoughts / my perspective, then it appears we're finished here."
- ✳ "Since this has become more of a lecture / rant than a conversation, I really need to move along."

But what if—shocker!—they want to hear your opinion? Great! Make a calm and concise statement that summarizes your thoughts.

Skip any additional discussion or debate, which would go absolutely nowhere.

Then excuse yourself or switch to a new topic.

Hopefully, these strategies, tips, and techniques will give you plenty of options to manage the D&Ds in your life. You may have to try and blend together different approaches with different people at different times. But at least you have some tools to help you endure less of their toxic presence.

Staying Out of the D&D Quicksand

Before I wrap up this section, I feel compelled to add the tiniest of footnotes and a gentle word of caution:

Please don't accidentally become the D&D that everyone else is avoiding!

You just laughed, didn't you?

Most people follow that up with: "Me? Oh no! I'm a positive person. Nobody would ever describe me as a Drainer or Downer."

You might be right. (See what I did there?) And yet, as I've mentioned before, negativity is contagious. Plus, we have that annoying negativity bias. And we all have less-than-perfect days.

Becoming a D&D is like falling into a giant pit of quicksand.

It's almost impossible to crawl back out of it once it's got you in its clutches. You may not even notice you've fallen in!

So here are some things you can do to help stay upbeat and avoid D&D territory:

Don't ruin positive conversations

Remember back in Chapter 14 where you vowed to start all conversations on a positive note? Check and check!

On a related subject, please don't be the one who begins conversations on a guilt-inducing note (as in, "I never hear from you anymore..."). Furthermore, promise not to besmirch otherwise positive, fun, interesting, or lively conversations with a sarcastic, negative, or mean comment.

Want to know a funny name for this? "The Turd in the Punchbowl." (I know. So gross.) But a random negative comment tossed into an otherwise positive exchange creates the same effect. Don't be the person who drops one.

A few examples:

Chatting Group is discussing different brands of blue jeans they like.

Turd in the Punchbowl: "Ugh. I feel so fat in all my jeans."

Chatting Group is discussing places they'd like to travel to one day.

Turd: "I'd never go to that country. I've heard everyone there is so rude and the food is awful."

Chatting Group is discussing modern art.

Turd: "My five-year-old can paint better than most modern artists I've seen."

A close relative to the Punchbowl Turd is a phenomenon called "narrative shopping"—a term coined by corporate CEO Robert Glazer in his *Friday Forward* blog.

Here, people are conversing on a relatively pleasant or neutral topic, and someone feels compelled to steer the conversation to their favorite controversy, pet peeve, issue, rant, or other unpleasant topic. This can happen gradually or abruptly. It occurs regularly in the media and in politics.

Glazer explains that narrative shoppers like to "look for places where they can insert their narrative, whether it is vaguely related, tangential or, in some cases, not related at all."

Let's say you're describing the delicious roast you made the other night. The conversation suddenly shifts into an angry lecture on the scourge of animal cruelty or corporate farming.

Or your neighbor calls to check on you, but within seconds the conversation reverts to a litany of his latest gripes about what's happening with your HOA.

Or you nonchalantly note that you're a bit late because you had to go gas up your car. Before you know it, you're in the midst of a tirade on how carbon-based fuels and greenhouse gasses are killing the planet.

A big red flag is when you're internally asking yourself, "How the heck did we end up on this topic???" or "Whaaaat...?"

Pay attention and note how often conversations get hijacked or manipulated in this way. No matter what the opening topic, the narrative shopper finds a way to shift the discussion to their favorite soap box.

This brings to mind an old adage: "When you have a hammer, everything becomes a nail."

Don't be the source of negative contagion

Starting now, monitor yourself during interactions. Pay attention. Notice. Be mindful and aware of the mood, attitude, and vibe you are offering others. Are you being a D&D? Did you accidentally take the discussion down a negative, whiny, or toxic path? Are you the Punchbowl Turd or the Narrative Shopper? Can you catch yourself and make a quick shift to something brighter?

Certainly, it's okay to say how you're feeling, with a preface such as:

- ※ "Gotta be honest, I'm having a rough day."
- ※ "Have to tell you, I'm feeling annoyed and irritable about this whole situation."
- ※ "Honestly? This is a bit of a hot button for me."

No one is saying you can't ever express yourself or vent freely for a few moments. But don't become the D&D who does it chronically and continually. And if you are dealing with problems that are complex or overwhelming, by all means, seek professional help in dealing with them.

That said, we have to remember that we are all responsible for our own thoughts, moods, and words. Both internally and externally. These do indeed impact our presence and conversations.

"The kindness, honesty, humility, and grace you show yourself will be shown to others," writes John Jantsch in *The Self-Reliant Entrepreneur.* "And, conversely, the rage, blame, mistrust, and suffering you bear will become how others experience you."

Sometimes our demeanors, body language, and facial expressions say it all before we ever say a word.

"We speak before we speak," writes philosopher Mark Nepo, "with eyes and lips, in how we tip our heads... We tell our whole story before we even open our mouths."

What are we generating in our own heads and hearts? What are we contributing? Cheery, complimentary, warm, and positive words and body language? Or angry, critical, sad, complaining, and negative ones?

If you catch yourself in a negative loop (yes, even about the D&Ds in your life) and then refuse to do anything to correct the situation— uh-oh!—you've become one of them!

I've been there, and I bet you have, too.

I was having coffee one day with a close (and, thankfully, honest and caring) friend. Not sure how it happened, but I got hooked on a topic that really got my knickers in a knot. Apparently, I vented a bit too long and with a little too much fury on this issue.

My friend called me on it. And, as a good friend would do, she knew it was out of character for me and wanted to find the root cause.

"Wow, Patti, I haven't seen you this bent out of shape in a long time. You okay? Do you need to talk to someone about this?"

"Me?" I thought. "I'm great. What is she talking about?"

Later, when I reflected on what I had said and the vehemence with which I had said it, I realized my friend was right! And I was grateful. A swift apology followed, as well as some serious reflection time and work on my own "stuff."

This brings to mind the words of spiritual teacher Eckhart Tolle: "When you complain, you make yourself a victim. Leave the situation, change the situation, or accept it. All else is madness."

TRY THIS!

Controlled griping.

Have a problem or gripe? Need to vent? Get intentional. Choose (and limit) the people with whom you share it. There's no need to repeat the same complaint, problem, or sad story over and over again with everyone you meet.

Facilitator and leadership consultant Karen Snyder says she purposefully chooses to share her everyday complaints and troubles (such as fender benders, annoying bosses, and work issues) with only three people. That's right, just three. These are carefully selected and trusted confidantes whom she believes will not only listen compassionately, but might also be able to share wisdom and valid suggestions for how she could reframe, cope with, and solve her problems.

Snyder emphasizes that, in the case of big issues and tragedies (such as the loss of a loved one or a debilitating illness), getting ongoing support from loved ones, trusted friends, and professionals is essential. She also adds that the process of working through those heavy burdens shouldn't be rushed.

Who would you choose to be in your close circle for "controlled griping"?

_____

_____

_____

_____

How to open a problem-centered conversation in a productive way:

- ❊ "I'm having a challenge with _____. Could I share it with you so I can get a neutral perspective?"
- ❊ "I'm struggling with _____ these days. Have you ever experienced anything similar?"

◂▴▸

Don't participate in gossip

This one is worth a mention, and it should be simple, right? Not so much. It's easy to get lured in by tempting, juicy tidbits of news that might be a little scandalous or even outrageous. (These exchanges often begin with someone uttering the words, "I heard...") The problem is, listening to or sharing that information is often negative, destructive, and a waste of time and energy. Can we be sure it's true? Is it even our business? And what's the purpose of passing it along?

Gossip can include:

- ❊ Sharing privileged information or something meant to be held in confidence.
- ❊ Passing along rumors or unverified information that may not be true or might be exaggerated or misinterpreted.
- ❊ Making cruel, judgmental, or disparaging comments about someone not present.

TRY THIS!

Call out gossip for what it is.

What can you say if you find yourself in the midst of a gossip session? Here are some ideas:

- ☀ "You know, we don't really know the facts about what happened just yet, so let's not talk about it or spread rumors that may not be true."
- ☀ "I don't really think that's any of our business."
- ☀ "Hmmm. This sounds like gossip to me. Let's talk about something else."
- ☀ "Where exactly are you going with this?"
- ☀ "What's your point in sharing this information?"

Can you think of any other phrases you might use to stop gossip in its tracks?

_____

_____

_____

_____

◂▴▸

Gossip can also take the form of ***triangulation***. Here, two people share information or say negative things about a third person not present (who should, in all fairness, be involved).

Solutions? Say something like:

- "It doesn't seem fair that we are complaining about Richard when he's not here to clarify his position or defend himself."
- "Shouldn't you be talking to Jen directly about this?"
- "This is really a discussion for you and Alexa to have directly."

Then there is the diabolical duo of **projection** and **spontaneous trait transference.**

Projection:

Whatever you judge or criticize in others is often something you judge or criticize within yourself. In other words: *You spot it, you got it.*

Spontaneous trait transference:

You go on and on to Person A about Person B's faults. Meanwhile, Person A is subconsciously placing these negative traits on you, as well.

Both are valid reasons to resist saying anything about others that you wouldn't want said about you.

Give every conversation one of these tests

Before you begin or jump into a conversation, weed out any hints of gossip by making sure the topics conform to the trusted guidelines that follow:

The Rotary Four-Way Test:

1. Is it the truth?

2. Is it fair to all concerned?

3. Will it build goodwill and better friendships?

4. Will it be beneficial to all concerned?

Socrates' Rules:

1. Is it true?

2. Is it necessary?

3. Is it kind?

And, of course, there is this common-sense advice: Sometimes the less said, the better. Just imagine how much more pleasant the world would be if everyone followed this advice!

Seems like a perfect time to segue to a related topic.

Don't be an oversharer

That's right. We're talking TMI—short for "Too Much Information."

There's oversharing about *others*, which is gossiping and leaking confidential information. Then there's oversharing about *ourselves*.

If you've ever been on the receiving end of TMI, you know why it can be a problem.

What exactly qualifies as TMI? How do we decide what does and doesn't land in this zone?

In general, TMI is anything that's really personal, private, awkward, overwhelming, upsetting, or totally inappropriate for the person, the situation, or the setting.

A few examples:

Too much detail.

All you did was toss out a conversation starter such as, "What are you working on?" The other person launches into an excruciatingly long and highly detailed description of every aspect of his job, company, endeavor, or latest project. What you really wanted was just the quick version.

Too personal, graphic, gross, or upsetting.

You asked someone you recognize in line at Target if she was having a good day. She proceeds to share the results of a recent medical procedure that was … really personal. And kind of gross. You'll never be able to look at her the same way.

Just too much.

You're seated on an airplane next to a lovely person who begins to run down an extensive list of every single child, grandchild, and pet in their family. This includes facts about their birthdays, birthplaces, favorite activities and accomplishments, and a multitude of other details about each one that you don't find one bit interesting or any of your business.

Something that a professional should help sort out.

Most of us aren't emotionally equipped or sufficiently trained to hear about or discuss issues that are horribly traumatic. When someone is grappling with situations like that, a professional is a much more suitable option.

Specific TMI could also include details about:

- Bodily functions, grooming, and health (ours or those of our family members, pets, or livestock).
- Love lives, especially intimate details that should remain ... well, intimate.
- Finances and economic situations.
- Alcohol or drug problems.
- Indiscretions and less-than-healthy habits.
- Private information about friends, family, or colleagues.
- Confidential company information.
- Latest crime spree.

The bottom line is, don't become the person known for oversharing.

Ask yourself: Could this information be perceived as disturbing, crass, offensive, or just ... too many details for polite company? If you're not sure, don't share!

At its least offensive, TMI is a total timewaster and makes others feel uncomfortable. At its worst, TMI can ruin conversations and events, end friendships, repel colleagues and, in some cases, even get us fired.

Think of others, but don't neglect your own self-care

Listening to a constant flow of negativity and complaining—from *anyone*—can take a lot out of us. Worse yet, it can sometimes leave an awful, sticky residue. If we don't intentionally make time to relax, recharge, *take a shower* (literally and metaphorically), and care for our own mental health, we run the risk of sliding down that slippery slope into D&D territory ourselves.

How can we tend to ourselves, so we don't end up like the chronic complainers who drive us crazy? I've got several suggestions:

- By removing, avoiding, and managing our exposure to D&Ds—that's how!
- By proactively seeking out and spending time with positive friends or peers.
- By putting self-care on our agendas to help neutralize the impact of negative experiences (and people) in our lives.
- By going back to the strategies and ideas in this book for inspiration.
- Or by trying one of the techniques coming up next.

NOTES:

_____

_____

_____

_____

_____

_____

_____

_____

TRY THIS!

Feeling the "ick" after being around negativity?

Sit up straight with your arms and shoulders relaxed and palms up. Close your eyes, take a few easy breaths, and visualize letting go of the strain, frustration, and negativity. This is a position known to relax your shoulders, ease tension, release negative energy, and help you "open up" to more positive feelings.

◂▴▸

TRY THIS!

Wash the negativity away.

I've mentioned taking a shower a couple of times to be funny, but water is cleansing, literally and emotionally. If you don't have time for a shower, bath, or swim, simply run water over your hands and forearms. Yes, try it! Many healers swear by this cleansing technique.

◂▴▸

The +/−/0 Test.

Pay attention to how you feel after spending time with certain people. Are they pleasant, energizing, and inspiring? Give them a "+." Are they negative, draining, or frustrating? Give them a "−." Are they neither? Just "meh"? Give them a "0." Make it a priority to spend more time with the "+" people in your life.

Hopefully, these suggestions will help protect you from becoming someone who makes others want to hide behind the drapes. Nobody wants to be that person!

◂▴▸

A few final reminders about dealing with D&Ds:

- First and foremost, life is short and time is precious.
- We are ultimately in charge of our own happiness, positivity, and well-being.
- We are also responsible for managing our lives, as well as creating and maintaining our outlook on the world around us.
- We are in charge of deciding whom and what we allow into our lives.
- We have the right to do whatever it takes to generate, protect, and preserve our own positive state of mind, energy, focus, health, and productivity so we can become the best possible versions of ourselves.

Hold firm to your truth and your positivity. Someone else's negativity is about them and how they see themselves and the world. You can't fix or change them or make them happy if they don't want to be. But you also don't have to engage with or get stuck in the presence of people who regularly upset you or drag you down.

As author and teacher Julia Cameron noted in two of her books, *The Artist's Way* and *Finding Water*, "We cannot control everyone around us, but we can learn whose company is good for us and whose company causes us to shrivel and shrink."

I don't have to give it to you, but here it is anyway:

I grant you permission to honor and take care of the Most Important Person in Your Life: YOU.

I'm also sending up a personal wish and prayer for your success. You amazing person, you!

. . . .

While there are a lot of D&Ds roaming around out there (and you need to know about them), I hope you'll remember that the vast majority of people in the world have the potential to be pleasant (or at least interesting) conversation partners.

So, with that, it's time for me to wrap up and summarize.

Conclusion

It's been lovely chatting with you!

I can honestly say I had a marvelous time—and learned a lot—in the process of researching, writing, and publishing this book. I also enjoyed imagining you reading and benefiting from it! So I hope you've found value and were mildly entertained as you read.

And, hey! Congratulations for making it all the way through!

Now, please indulge me as we recap the highlights.

Section One revealed the compelling reasons why positive, friendly socialization—from brief daily greetings to deeper, more meaningful discussions—make our lives and careers so much better and richer. Plus, you just never know where a conversation will lead!

When you have those moments when socializing becomes scary, tedious, or frustrating, I encourage you to go back and give this section a quick review. We all need that pep talk now and then!

Section Two shed light on the many barriers that can prevent you from interacting and enjoying quality conversations. These barriers and obstacles are everywhere! Which means you have to stay ever vigilant, lest they transform you into an antisocial hermit.

Section Three gave you the opportunity to build your self-awareness and design your unique Vision for what better conversations—greater social success—could look like for you. You also read about the power of setting and acting on the intentions and attitudes that can make your unique Vision a reality.

Revisit and update what you write in this section often. Trust me, your tastes and desires may shift over time and as you gain more experience.

Section Four gave you a virtual packing list of conversation tools and essentials. Used generously, they can do so much more than simply improve your conversations. They can change your life and how others experience you! We can't master these overnight, so ongoing practice is key.

Section Five shared some specific instructions for how to prepare for and move through your everyday social encounters while becoming a lot more confident and at ease during social events.

Section Six might have surprised you. Many people don't realize just how critical good listening skills are for good conversations, how many levels of listening exist, and what standard listening rules and guidelines are. Now you're in the know!

Section Seven wrapped things up with some solid and savvy advice for how to spot the Drainers and Downers in your life, the heavy toll these people can take on our lives and careers, and how to have a lot fewer negative and soul-sucking conversations. Knowing what to do when you encounter D&Ds (and not becoming one yourself) means you'll have more time, energy, and focus for the good conversations you're meant to have and enjoy. Ah, what a delicious relief!

Now, two more helpful reflections and exercises you might enjoy and find valuable.

TRY THIS!

Connect and reflect.

Grab your journal or seek out someone who has also read this book. Then explore, reflect on, and/or discuss the following questions. These might be handy in helping you assess where you are, where you want to go, and what you need to practice to get there.

* What were some significant surprises or aha! moments you experienced while reading this book?
* What's new, different, or better about your attitudes toward conversation?
* What are your three biggest takeaways at this moment?
* What are you most excited about trying, practicing, or doing differently?

Based on what you've read in this book:

* What should you keep doing? (Because it's working!)
* What should you stop doing? (Because it's not!)
* What should you start doing? (Because, what the heck, it might work!)
* What are your next, small steps toward being the conversationalist you'd really like to be?

◄▲►

It's time to talk.

Make a list of people you enjoy having conversations with. It can be as short as three or as long as 100 or more. Now, what can you do to engage them in conversation and practice (or even discuss) what you've learned in this book?

_____

_____

_____

_____

◄▲►

As a final footnote, I thought you'd enjoy a wonderful passage from the novel *Moon Palace* by Paul Auster (a very enjoyable read, by the way). His words delightfully sum up the essence of great conversationalists and what they do to make others feel good in their presence.

> *Bit by bit, I found myself relaxing into the conversation. Kitty had a natural talent for drawing people out of themselves, and it was easy to fall in with her, to feel comfortable in her presence.*
>
> *As Uncle Victor had once told me long ago, a conversation is like having a catch with someone. A good partner tosses the ball directly into your glove, making it almost impossible for you to miss it; when he is on the receiving end, he catches everything sent his way, even the most errant and incompetent throws.*

That's what Kitty did. She kept lobbing the ball straight into the pocket of my glove, and when I threw the ball back to her, she hauled in everything that was even remotely in her area: jumping up to spear balls that soared above her head, diving nimbly to her left or right, charging in to make tumbling, shoestring catches.

More than that, her skill was such that she always made me feel that I had made those bad throws on purpose, as if my only object had been to make the game more amusing. She made me seem better than I was, and that strengthened my confidence, which in turn helped to make my throws less difficult for her to handle.

In other words, I started talking to her rather than to myself, and the pleasure of it was greater than anything I had experienced in a long time.

Imagine if we could all be a little more like Kitty.

Appendix

....

Conversation-Starting Questions by Category

At a professional event

- What brought you here today?
- What made you decide to attend this event?
- Have you attended one of these before? What was it like?
- What do you hope to get out of this event?
- Have you heard the speaker before?
- How did you hear about this event?
- How are you connected to _____ ? (the host, organizer, person you were just introduced to)
- What's your career story? How did you get into that line of work / industry / profession? (After you've asked, What do you do?)
- What do you love most about your work?
- What's your typical workday like?
- Are you working on something interesting right now?
- What's most meaningful or fun about what you do?
- What was your best job and your worst job?
- What did you learn from those?
- What has been a favorite experience related to your job?
- What's the best thing that happened to you today?

- What's next for you?
- What business books have most impacted or inspired you?
- Who do you go to when you need wise advice?
- What's the best business advice you've ever received?
- How do you manage work / life balance?

At a coffee shop, restaurant, or bar

- Have you ever been here before?
- What do you like best about it?
- Any tips on the best thing to order?
- Have you ever tried the _____?
- What's your favorite drink / entrée / dessert?
- What other places like this do you enjoy or recommend?
- Have you met or had conversations with any interesting people here?
- What's your favorite question to ask random people you've met here?

At the gym

- How long have you been a member?
- What's your typical workout / way to exercise?
- What's your favorite part of the workout?
- Do you ever work with a trainer or a group?
- Do you take any of the classes? Which ones are your favorites?
- What do you think is the biggest benefit you receive from exercising?
- Are you training for an event? If so, which one?

- Any workout tips you'd like to share?
- What motivates you to come to the gym / keep up a regular workout routine?

At the dog park or if you see someone walking their dog

- What kind of dog is that?
- How old is he / she?
- What's the dog's name? How did you choose that?
- Where did you get him / her?
- Do you have other pets? Do they get along?
- What do you enjoy most about having a dog?
- What's one of your dog's most interesting personality quirks or habits?
- If your dog could talk and had the voice of a celebrity, whose would it be?

When talking to a receptionist, server, bartender, or clerk

- How's your day going so far?
- What do you enjoy most about working here?
- Met any interesting people today?
- Any celebrities or VIPs ever come in here?
- What's the weirdest or most memorable thing that's ever happened to you on the job here?
- What are the crowd-pleasing items on the menu?
- What would you recommend I order?
- What's your favorite cocktail / drink to make?
- What do you enjoy doing when you're not working here?

If you're traveling (airplane, train, bus, etc.)

- Where are you headed?
- Where is home for you?
- Traveling for business or pleasure?
- Where are you from originally?
- What's the most interesting place you've visited?
- If you could spend 90 days traveling anywhere, all expenses paid and no worries about work or family, where would you go?
- Would you travel solo or with someone?

At a social gathering (party, wedding, etc.)

- How do you know the host or guest of honor?
- Do you know any of the other people here?
- Do you live here or are you visiting from out of town?
- How long have you lived there?
- What do you do when you aren't attending social gatherings?
- Do you have a favorite story about the host or guest of honor?

At a gathering when you want to shake things up

- What's your favorite unusual question to ask people?
- What's the funniest or most unusual question anyone has asked you at a social gathering?
- What was your most profound childhood experience?
- Who is (or was) the love of your life?
- What's your most passionate belief?
- What would you do differently if you discovered you only had 30 days to live?

- Who is on your Mount Rushmore?
- What are three things that bring you joy?
- What's your favorite part of the day?
- What do you think about when you can't sleep?
- Do you ever have weird dreams?
- Do you dream in color or black and white?
- Have you done something cool for someone else recently?
- What are three things on your bucket list?
- What's your favorite room in the house?
- What's a big goal for you in the coming year?
- What was your biggest life lesson from the past year?
- What's something you recently changed your mind about?
- What do you enjoy learning most about people?
- What are you most curious about?
- What teachers most influenced you and how?
- What three items do you always keep in your fridge?
- When was the last time you did something for the first time?

At any event where you want to find "buried treasure"

- What books are on your nightstand?
- What movie do you think everyone should watch before the age of 21?
- What movie have you watched the most and never tire of?
- When do you feel the most creative?
- What gives you the chuckles?
- What's something I should know about you?

- What's the scariest decision you've ever made or step you've had to take?
- What's the one thing that has made the biggest difference in your life?
- If you could go back and do one thing over again, what would it be?
- What's your favorite wise quote?
- What's your best advice to give me right now?
- Do you have any interesting / quirky / famous family members?
- Who's the most famous person you've ever met? What was that like?
- Which one of your teachers or older relatives has influenced you the most?
- What are some of your happiest childhood memories?
- Are you a plaid, stripes, polka dots, or floral person—and why?
- How did you know your spouse or significant other was "the one"?
- When was the last time you felt true awe?
- Who do you think is your biggest fan?
- What was your favorite vacation / trip ever?

As a wrap-up and bridge to the next connection

- This was really enjoyable. Would you like to meet again sometime to continue this discussion?
- Could I introduce you to_____? She would be a great resource for you.
- If you'd be willing to share your contact information, I can follow up with you next week to talk more about that.

More useful (and powerful) phrases and questions to sprinkle into your conversations

- I wonder...
- May I share an example / story?
- Let me turn the question around and ask you...
- Help me understand...
- How do / did you feel about that?
- What about you?
- What are your thoughts?
- That's interesting. Can you share more?
- Tell me...
- Tell me something good / interesting about...
- This conversation has made me feel...
- That reminds me of...
- Actually, I think I've changed my mind about...
- Could you go back and clarify...
- That's an interesting observation...
- I don't know the answer to that, although...
- Yes, and... (rather than Yes, but...)
- I can only imagine... (rather than I know...)
- I've observed...
- I appreciate you / this / what you just said because...

References
and Resources

· ·

~ Articles ~

"3 Conversation Tricks to Make People Remember You" by Hanna Brooks
    Olsen: CreativeLive (November 14, 2014).
"3 Steps Toward More Meaningful Conversations" by Fredrik Lyagen:
    LifeHack.
"3 Tips to Have Better Conversations" by Tim Herrera: *New York Times*
    (September 16, 2018).
"4 Reasons Highly Intelligent People are Often Socially Inept" by Sean
    Cooper: The Shyness & Social Anxiety Guy.
"4 Things Emotionally Intelligent People Don't Do" by Nick Wignall:
    Medium.com (April 4, 2020).
"5 Characteristics of Bad Listeners" by Eve Ash: SmartCompany.com
    (February 21, 2017).
"5 Personality Traits of Extroverts" by Kendra Cherry: VeryWellMind.com
    (July 9, 2017).
"5 Reasons Some People Insist on Telling You Every Detail of Their Personal
    Lives" by Amy Morton: *Inc. Magazine* (July 1, 2016).
"5 Steps for Dealing with People Who Talk Too Much" by F. Diane Barth,
    L.C.S.W.: *Psychology Today* (April 22, 2012).
"5 Tips for Handling Toxic People in the Workplace" by Larry Kim: *Inc.
    Magazine.*
"5 Ways to Have Great Conversations" by Harvey Duetschendorf: *Fast
    Company* (March 24, 2014).
"5 Ways to Make Small Talk More Meaningful" by Jennifer Granneman:
    LinkedIn (July 28, 2016).
"6 Ways to Become a Better Listener" by Stephanie Vozza: *Forbes* and *Fast
    Company* (March 17, 2017).
"6 Ways to Build Rapport with Clients and Colleagues" by the Young
    Entrepreneur Council: *Inc. Magazine.*

"6 Ways to Deal with Chronic Complainers" by Gwen Moran: *Forbes* (August 18, 2016).

"6 Ways to Show People You're Really Listening" by Jacqueline Whitmore: Entrepreneur.com (October 27, 2015).

"7 Bad Public Speaking Habits That Immediately Destroy Your Likability" by Richard Feloni: *Inc. Magazine*.

"7 Common Habits of the Best Listeners" by Travis Bradberry: *Inc. Magazine* (April 13, 2016).

"7 Things to Say When a Conversation Turns Negative" by Kathleen Kelley Reardon: HubSpot (May 11, 2016).

"7 Tips for Finding Your Tribe" by Lissa Rankin, M.D.: LissaRankin.com.

"7 Ways to Cope with People Who Want to Bring You Down" by Andrea F. Polard, Psy.D.: *Psychology Today* (July 24, 2018).

"7 Ways to Deal with a Chronic Complainer" by Tim David: *Psychology Today* (July 30, 2015).

"7 Ways to Make Small Talk Work for You" by Susan Krauss Whitbourne, Ph.D.: *Psychology Today* (September 6, 2014).

"8 Questions to Ask Someone Other Than 'What Do You Do?'" by David Burks: *Harvard Business Review* (January 30, 2018).

"8 Types of People Who Will Rob You of Your Happiness" by Jessica Stanton: *Inc. Magazine* (March 2, 2017).

"9 Mistakes That Make You a Bad Listener" by Amy Morin: *Inc. Magazine*.

"9 Simple Phrases to Improve Your Relationships" by Susan Zelinsky: The Zen of Business (May 26, 2009).

"10 Behaviors of Genuine People" by Steve Tobak: *Entrepreneur* (March 16, 2015).

"10 Big Rules of Small Talk" by Jennifer Tung: *Real Simple* (May 17, 2017).

"10 Characteristics of Likable People: Are You One of Them?" edited by Alex Chris: ManageYourLifeNow.com.

"10 Myths About Introverts" by Carl King: CarlKingdom.com.

"10 Powerful Phrases That Will Improve Your Leadership" by Daniel Threlfall: TeamGantt.com (December 10, 2018).

"10 Questions to Ask to Spark Stimulating Conversations" by Marcel Schwantes: *Inc. Magazine*.

"10 Reasons You're Talking Too Much and What to Do About It" by Deborah Grayson Riegel: *Inc. Magazine*.

"10 Rules of a Great Conversationalist" by Celestine Chua: PersonalExcellence.com.

"10 Ways to Deal with Negative or Difficult People" by Lori Deschene: Tiny Buddha.

"11 Habits of Ridiculously Likable People That You Can Teach Yourself" by Travis Bradberry: LinkedIn *Business Insider* (May 22, 2019).

"11 Questions Interesting People Always Ask to Spark Great Conversations" by Marcel Schwantes: *Inc. Magazine.*

"13 Simple Ways You Can Have More Meaningful Conversations" by John Hall: *Forbes* (August 18, 2013).

"16 Secrets to Being Exceptionally Likable" by Lolly Daskal: LollyDaskal.com.

"18 Ways to Improve Your Body Language" by Henrik Edberg: Positivity Blog (January 20, 2021).

"20 Odd Questions" featuring Pharrell Williams by Jacob Gallagher: *Wall Street Journal* (August 5-6, 2017).

"36 Questions that Lead to Love" by Daniel Jones: *New York Times* "Modern Love" Column (January 9, 2015).

"Active Listening: The Art of Empathetic Conversation" by Birgit Ohlin: BirgitOhlin.com (December 6, 2016).

"Active Social Life May Delay Memory Loss Among U.S. Elderly Population": News release from Harvard's T.H. Chan School of Public Health (May 29, 2008).

"Are You Really Listening or Just Waiting to Talk?" by Caren Osten: *Psychology Today* (October 5, 2016).

"The Art of Gracious Leadership" by David Brooks: *New York Times* (August 26, 2016).

"The Art of the Dinner Party": *New York Times Magazine* (October 29, 2017).

"Be Excellent to Each Other" by Deborahann Smith: *O Magazine* (December 2003).

"The Benefits of a Little Small Talk" by Jennifer Breheny Wallace: *Wall Street Journal* (September 30, 2016).

"The Benefits of Being a Gracious Leader" by Willy Steiner: Executive Coaching Concepts (September 15, 2016).

"The Benefits of Talking to Strangers" by Jane E. Brody: *New York Times* (August 2, 2020).

"Brian Grazer's Curious Conversations" by Alexandra Wolfe: *Wall Street Journal* (April 20, 2015).

"Can Conversations Add 15 Years to Your Life? The Science Says Yes" by Diana Rau: *Forbes* (July 31, 2020).

"Can You Get Smarter?" by Richard A. Friedman: *New York Times* (October 25, 2015).

"Charisma, Quantified" by Dana Wechsler Linder: *Wall Street Journal* (October 13, 2017).

"Close Friends Linked to a Sharper Memory: Maintaining Strong Social Networks Seems to Be Linked to Slower Cognitive Decline" by Kristin Samuelson: *Northwestern Now* (November 1, 2017).

"The Closing of the Academic Mind" by Amy Wax: *Wall Street Journal* (February 17-18, 2018).

"Confronting the Negativity Bias" by Rick Hanson, Ph.D.: *Psychology Today* (October 26, 2010).

"Connect: Practice Appreciation for Your Fellow Human Beings" by Frank Lipman, M.D.: *Experience Life Magazine.*

"Connect, Then Lead" by Amy J.C. Cuddy, Matthew Kohut, and John Neffinger: *Harvard Business Review* (July–August 2013).

"Connection Roadmap: The Three Levels of Conversation" by Robert MacNaughton: Integral Centered Leadership (December 20, 2014).

"Conversation Etiquette" by Debby Mayne: *The Spruce* (April 4, 2017).

"Conversational Narcissism": PhilosophicalSociety.com.

"Curiosity and Pathways to Well-Being and Meaning in Life: Traits, States & Everyday Behavior" by Todd Kashdan of George Mason University and Michael F. Steger of the University of Louisville (September 2007).

"David Whyte on Welcoming Humiliation" by Lindy Alexander: *DailyGood* (May 23, 2018).

"Dealing with Negative People" by Raj Raghunathan, Ph.D.: *Psychology Today* (March 19, 2013).

"A Diagnosis for American Polarization" by Andrew Hartz: *Wall Street Journal* (November 4, 2020).

"Did Campfire Talk Spark the Rise of Human Culture?" by Melvin Konner: *Wall Street Journal* (October 15-16, 2016).

"Do You Make These 10 Mistakes in Conversation?" by Henrik Edberg: The Positivity Blog (March 22, 2021).

"Does Similarity Lead to Attraction and Compatibility?" by Jeremy Nicholson, M.S.W., Ph.D.: *Psychology Today* (September 26, 2017).

"The Dunning-Kruger Effect Explains Why Society is So Screwed Up" by Chuckles Freely: The Happy Neuron and Medium.com (May 12, 2020).

"The Dynamic Communicator" by Stacy Kaiser: Live Happy (April 10, 2014).

"Finding Your Tribe—Tips for Connecting with Like-Minded Souls" by Bernadette Logue: TheDailyPositive.com.

"Five Characteristics of Bad Listeners" by Eve Lash: *Smart Company* (February 21, 2017).

"Five Things Jerry Seinfeld Teaches Us About the Art of Great Conversation" by Bruce Weinstein: *Forbes* (July 7, 2018).

"For the First Time in My Life I Didn't Have Any Friends" by Ruth Whippman: *Good Housekeeping* (February 2017).

"For the New Year: Say No to Negativity" by John Tierney and Roy F. Baumeister: *Wall Street Journal* (December 28-29, 2019).

"Friendship Is Good for You—Unless It Is Strained" by Robert M. Sapolsky: *Wall Street Journal* (September 10-11, 2016).

"Getting Along with Co-Workers Can Significantly Increase Your Life Span": Peer-Reviewed Publication of American Friends of Tel Aviv University (August 4, 2011).

"Giving People Advice Rarely Works—This Does" by Thomas G. Plante, Ph.D., A.B.P.P.: *Psychology Today* (July 15, 2014).

"Good Friends Might Be Your Best Brain Booster as You Age" by Judith Graham: *Kaiser Health News* (December 25, 2017).

"A Guide to Having More Meaningful Conversations" by Erin Falconer: PickTheBrain.com (February 25, 2008).

"Happiness is Other People" by Ruth Whippman: *New York Times* (October 27, 2017).

"Harvard Researchers Say This Mindset Matters Most: Follow 'Rule of 4' Questions to Be More Likable (and Make a Better First Impression)" by Jeff Haden: *Inc. Magazine* (April 19, 2021).

"The Health Benefits of Finding Your Tribe" by Lissa Rankin, M.D.: *Psychology Today* (September 11, 2012).

"Here's a Simple Trick to Make People Like You in 2 Seconds" by Shana Lebowitz: *Business Insider* (December 12, 2015).

"Here's the Science Behind Why Small Talk Is So Awkward—And So Essential" by David Nield: ScienceAlert.com (July 27, 2016).

"How Curiosity Creates Real Conversation" by Kevin Eikenberry: *Leadership & Learning* (August 1, 2016).

"How Do You Respond to a Compliment? Why it Matters" by Wendy L. Patrick: *Psychology Today* (November 11, 2019).

"How Introverts Can Command Attention on Any Professional Stage" by Jane Finkle: ThinDifference.com (September 28, 2019).

"How Negative News Distorts Our Thinking" by Austin Perlmutter, M.D.: *Psychology Today* (September 19, 2019).

"How Small Talk with Almost-Strangers Profoundly Affects Your Happiness" by Jamie Friedlander: Vice (May 7, 2019).

"How Smartphones Are Affecting Our Relationships" from the Association for Psychology Science (February 11, 2019).

"How to Accept a Compliment" by Carolyn Bucior: *New York Times* (May 20, 2018).

"How to Be a Better Listener" by Adam Bryant: *New York Times*.

"How to Be a Better Listener" by Sunny Sea Gold: Scientific American Mind (September 1, 2015).

"How to Become a Better Listener: Seven Steps to Gaining Understanding & Respect" by Marty Nemko, Ph.D.: *Psychology Today* (May 31, 2014).

"How to Become a Master at Talking to Strangers" by Joe Keohane: *Entrepreneur* (July 2021).

"How to Dazzle in Conversation: Tips to Nurture Close Relationships or Shine in New Ones" by Abigail Fagan: *Psychology Today* (December 2019).

"How to Deal with Blamers": PairedLife.com (June 18, 2019).

"How to Deal with Chronic Complainers" by Guy Winch, Ph.D.: *Psychology Today* (July 15, 2011).

"How to Deal with Chronic Complainers" by Patrick Allan: LifeHacker (October 8, 2019).

"How to Deal with People Who Just Won't Stop Talking" by Susan Krauss Whitbourne, Ph.D.: *Psychology Today* (August 5, 2017).

"How to Have Better Conversations with Your Partner and Just About Everyone Else" by Andy Reynolds, M.S.W., L.C.S.W.: The Gottman Institute.

"How to Have Curious Conversations": The Institute of Curiosity (April 29, 2015).

"How to Have More Engaging Conversations in Everyday Life" by Jonah Engel Bromwich: *New York Times* (October 17, 2016).

"How to Host a Jeffersonian Dinner": PurposeGeneration.com (May 29, 2015).

"How to Know if You Talk Too Much" by Mark Goulston: *Harvard Business Review* (June 3, 2015).

"How to Know if You're a Bad Listener" by Michael Gelb: Entrepreneur.com (September 27, 2017).

"How to Make Every Interaction More Meaningful and Memorable" by Jeremy Chandler: ThinDifference.com (October 3, 2019).

"How to Make Small Talk Using the FORM Technique": PsychologistWorld.com.

"How to Make Small Talk with Strangers: My 21-Day Happiness Experiment" by John Corcoran: The Art of Manliness (September 25, 2021).

"How to Stop Your Brain's Addiction to Bad News" by Jerry Mackay: *Fast Company* (November 19, 2018).

"How to Talk to Strangers" by Kio Stark: *New York Times* (September 18, 2016).

"How to Talk to Strangers: Terry Gross's 40-Year Master Class in the Art of the Interview" by Susan Burton: *New York Times Magazine* (October 25, 2015).

"How to Tell If You're a Conversational Narcissist" by Christine Schoenwald: YourTango.com (July 8, 2018).

"Humblebragging: A Distinct—and Ineffective—Self-Presentation Strategy" by Ovul Sezer (University of North Carolina—Chapel Hill) and Francesca Gino and Michael I. Norton (Harvard Business School): *Journal of Personality and Social Psychology*, American Psychological Association (September 2017).

"I Am Not An Introvert. I Am Not An Extrovert. I Am an Ambivert." by Shashi Camling: HuffPost.com (March 23, 2017).

"If You Want People to Listen, Stop Talking" by Peter Bregman: *Psychology Today* (May 26, 2015).

"The Importance of Feeling Heard" by Alice Chan, Ph.D.: *Lead from Your Heart* at DrAliceChan.com (September 3, 2013).

"The Importance of Responding to Compliments" by Wendy L. Patrick: Newsmax.com (November 12, 2019).

"The Importance of Social Connection": Mindwise.org.

"In Defense of Small Talk" by Ruth Graham: CultureBox.com (February 25, 2016).

"The Intimidation Factor" by Jennifer Latson: *Psychology Today* (October 2019).

"Introversion vs. Shyness: The Discussion Continues" by Sophia Dembling: *Psychology Today* (October 10, 2009).

"The Introvert's Guide to Making Great Connections": ProductiveFlourishing.com (September 12, 2011).

Job Jibber Jabber: "What People Who Belong to Various Associations are Often Asked When They Share What They Do" compiled by Ben Schott: *New York Times Sunday Review* (August 2, 2013).

"Job Seeker's X-Factor: Chemistry" by Sue Shellenbarger: *Wall Street Journal* (November 30, 2016).

"Laughter: The Best Medicine" by Hara Estroff Marano: *Psychology Today* (June 9, 2016).

"Leadership is a Conversation" by Boris Groysberg and Michael Slind: *Harvard Business Review* (June 2012).

"The Least Empathetic Thing to Say" by Jessie Stuart: *Wall Street Journal* (April 10, 2020).

"Listening" by Margaret Wheatley: Workshop Handout (2001).

"The Lives They Lived: Mavis Galant" by Rosemary Mahoney: *New York Times Magazine* (December 25, 2014).

"The Love Connection" by Nichole Frehsée: *O Magazine* (February 2013).

"Make Your Meetings a Safe Space for Honest Conversation" by Paul Axell: *Harvard Business Review* (April 11, 2019).

"Making Friends as an Adult" by Jessie Sholl: *Experience Life Magazine* (April 2014).

"The Me, Me, Me of Social Media Might Make You End Up Alone, Alone, Alone" by Michael Jascz: *Huffington Post* (June 29, 2016).

"Mindful Listening: Using Empathy to Listen Instead of Offering Advice" by Elizabeth Dorrance Hall, Ph.D.: *Psychology Today* (March 31, 2017).

"Mistakenly Seeking Solitude" by Nicholas Epley and Juliana Schroeder: *Journal of Experimental Psychology* (July 14, 2014).

"Most Googled: Why Don't Londoners Talk on the Tube?" by El Hunt: TimeOut.com (January 27, 2020).

"The Negative People in Your Life Are Literally Killing You" by Jessica Stillman: *Inc. Magazine* (October 13, 2016).

"Negative Thinking: A Dangerous Addiction" by Nancy Collier: *Psychology Today* (April 15, 2019).

"Networking 101 for Introverts" by Katharine Brooks, Ed.D.: *Psychology Today* (October 31, 2010).

"Networking for Actual Human Beings" by David Burns: *Wall Street Journal* (April 21-22, 2018).

"The Neurochemistry of Positive Conversations" by Judith E. Glaser and Richard D. Glaser: *Harvard Business Review* (June 12, 2014).

"New Research Shows We're All Bad Listeners Who Think We Work Too Much" by Samantha Cole: *Fast Company* Online—The Future of Work (February 26, 2015).

"New Sentences" (Mount Rushmore Questions) by Sam Anderson: *New York Times Magazine* (July 15, 2018).

"Nice People Really Do Have More Fun" by Arthur C. Brooks: *Wall Street Journal* (October 20, 2016).

"Not All Conversations are Born Equal: Find the Good Ones" by Andy Mort: AndyMort.com (May 4, 2015).

"Not an Introvert, Not an Extrovert? You May Be an Ambivert" by Elizabeth Bernstein: *Wall Street Journal* (July 27, 2015).

"Now Hear This: Most People Stink at Listening" by Bob Sullivan and Hugh Thompson: *Scientific American* (May 3, 2013).

"One Simple Habit That'll Make You Great at Conversations" by Charlie Houpert: *Thought Catalog* (January 18, 2014).

"An Open Letter to People Who Talk Too Much" by Sophia Dembling: *Psychology Today* (April 20, 2017).

"Our Brain's Negative Bias" by Hara Estroff Mara: *Psychology Today* (June 9, 2016).

"The Perils of Listening Well" by Sophia Dembling: *Psychology Today* (July 6, 2020).

"The Pleasure of Not Being Perfect" by Roger Housden: *O Magazine* (December 2005).

"Positive Social Support at Work Shown to Reduce Risk of Diabetes": Peer-Reviewed Publication of American Friends of Tel Aviv University (May 9, 2013).

"The Power of Curiosity" by Todd Kashdan: *Experience Life Magazine* (May 2010).

"Practice Better Listening" by Kate Murphy: *New York Times* (May 17, 2020).

"Prepare for Social Interaction When You Don't Feel Up to It" by Andy Mort: AndyMort.com (July 20, 2015).

"The Questions of a Lifetime" by David Epstein: *Wall Street Journal* (May 13-14, 2017).

"Remember, It's OK to Set Boundaries" by Julie Fingersh: *New York Times* (August 23, 2020).

"The Right Way to Have Difficult Conversations" by Celeste Headlee: *Wall Street Journal* (September 9-10, 2017).

"Save Yourself from Tedious Small Talk" by Sue Shellenbarger: *Wall Street Journal* (May 24, 2017).

"The Science and Art of Listening" by Seth S. Horowitz: *New York Times* (November 9, 2012).

"The Science of Why We Talk Too Much and How to Shut Up" by Lydia Dishman: *Fast Company* (June 11, 2015).

"The Secret to Revealing Your Secrets" by Susan Krauss Whitbourne, Ph.D.: *Psychology Today* (April 1, 2014).

"Seven Tips for Making Good Conversation with a Stranger" by Gretchen Rubin: GretchenRubin.com (May 20, 2009).

"Share Your Ideas, Even the Crazy Ones" by Adam Bryant interviewing Joe Andrew for his Corner Office column: *New York Times* (June 25, 2017).

"Six Reasons Small Talk is Very Important and How to Get Better at It" by Brett Nelson: *Forbes* (March 30, 2012).

"Six Science-Based Reasons Why Laughter is the Best Medicine" by David DiSalvo: *Forbes* (June 5, 2017).

"Six Story-Sharing Questions for this Holiday Season" by Eric Torrence: ThinDifference.com (November 29, 2018).

"Skip the Small Talk: Meaningful Conversations Linked to Happier People" by Melinda Wenner Moyer: *Scientific American Mind* (July 1, 2020).

"Smooth Encounters" by Mary Loftus: *Psychology Today* (April 2013).

"Social Interactions and Well-Being: The Surprising Power of Weak Ties" by G.M. Sandstrom and E.W. Dunn: *Personal Psychology Bulletin* (July 2014).

"Souls Knit Together" by Justin Foster: FosterThinking.com (April 27, 2020).

"Stop Asking 'How Are You?': Harvard Researchers Say This is What Successful People Do When Making Small Talk" by Gay Burnison: CNBC *Make It* (March 21, 2019).

"Stop Googling. Let's Talk" by Sherry Turkle: *New York Times* (September 26, 2015).

"The Surprising Boost You Get from Strangers" by Elizabeth Bernstein: *Wall Street Journal* (May 13, 2019).

"Survival of the Friendliest" by Brian Hare and Vanessa Woods: *Scientific American* (August 2020).

"Taking a Deeper Look at the 'Negative Person'" by Carrie Barron, M.D.: *Psychology Today* (November 24, 2016).

"Talkaholics Hurt Their Careers, Firms Say" by Joann S. Lublin: *Wall Street Journal* (December 14, 2017).

"Teach this Trait and Your Customer Service Marks Will Soar" by Vanessa Merit Nornberg.

"Team Building Icebreaker: Finding Three Things in Common": StarfishTaylor.com.

"This is How to Make Close Friends: Four Surprising Secrets from Research" by Eric Barker: Barking Up the Wrong Tree (February 19, 2017).

"This Is the Key to Mastering Small Talk, According to Harvard Researchers" by Brittany Wong: *Huffington Post* (June 20, 2017).

"Tight Club: The First Rule of Networking Events is Don't Talk About How Much You Hate Networking Events" by Jacqueline Detwiler: *American Way Magazine*.

"To Be A Better Leader, Ask Better Questions" by Hal Gregersen: *Wall Street Journal* (May 14, 2019).

"To Give or Not Give Advice" by Sharon K. Anderson: *Psychology Today* (May 10, 2012).

"Toxic People: How to Recognize and Avoid Them" by George S. Everly, Jr., Ph.D., A.B.P.P., F.A.C.L.P.: *Psychology Today* (November 3, 2019).

"Toxic Venting: When to Stop Listening" by Judith Acosta, L.I.S.W., C.C.H.: *Huffington Post* (November 17, 2011).

"The Tribes" by Ligaya Mihan: *New York Times Magazine* (April 19, 2020).

"Use Social Media to Help Mental Health and Relationships" by Pam Moore: WebMD (June 13, 2022).

"A Victory for Office Small Talkers" by Rachel Emma Silverman: *Wall Street Journal* (October 28, 2014).

"We're Finnish. Small Talk is Hard. We are Taking Lessons." by Alistair MacDonald: *Wall Street Journal* (May 29, 2019).

"What are Common Introversion Traits?" by Kendra Cherry: VeryWellMind.com (July 15, 2018).

"What Great Listeners Actually Do" by Jack Zenger and Joseph Folkman: *Harvard Business Review* (July 16, 2014).

"What is the Impact of Your Communication Style on Others?" by Deborah Easton: Your Training Partner, Kent State University Center for Corporate and Personal Development—Kent.edu (June 14, 2016).

"What it Means to be Gracious" by Arthur Dobrin, D.S.W.: *Psychology Today* (February 11, 2014).

"What Makes a Conversation Memorable and Meaningful" by James Ware: MakingMeetingsMatter.com (March 2015).

"What Makes People Charismatic and How You Can Be, Too" by Bryan Lark: *New York Times* (August 15, 2019).

"What's in Your Positive Emotions Toolkit?" by Vivienne Dutton: PositiveChangeGuru.com (September 10, 2015).

"When You're In a Relationship with a Blamer" by Nancy Collier, L.C.S.W.: *Psychology Today* (December 1, 2015).

"Why Do Londoners Never Talk On the Tube (London Underground)?": Quora.com.

"Why Do We Like People Who Are Similar to Us?" by Gwendolyn Seidman, Ph.D.: *Psychology Today* (December 18, 2018).

"Why Don't You Want to Feel Better?" by William Berry, L.M.H.C., C.A.P.: *Psychology Today* (May 18, 2014).

"Why Giving Advice Doesn't Work" by Mark Murphy: *Forbes* (October 13, 2015).

"Why I Sit on the Streets and Listen to Strangers" by Heather Monro: LinkedIn (November 11, 2019).

"Why Listening is Better Than Talking" by Margaret Hefferman: CBS News (January 15, 2013).

"Why People Give Unsolicited Advice (Though No One Listens)" by Seth Meyers, Psy.D.: *Psychology Today* (December 31, 2017).

"Why Small Talk Is So Excruciating" by David Roberts: *Vox* (October 28, 2017).

"Why We Ignore Friends to Look at Our Phones" by Dan Ariely: *Wall Street Journal* (April 28-29, 2021).

"Why We Love Talking About Ourselves" by Samantha Boardman, M.D.: *Psychology Today* (March 7, 2017).

"Why We'd Rather Talk Than Listen" by Mark Goulston, M.D., F.A.P.A.: *Psychology Today* (September 5, 2013).

"Why You May Talk Too Much and Not Know It" by Will Yacowicz: *Inc. Magazine*.

"Why You Should Make Time for Self-Reflection (Even If You Hate Doing It)" by Jennifer Porter: *Harvard Business Review* (March 21, 2017).

"Would You Rather Be Right or Would You Rather Be Happy?" by Dan Mager, M.S.W.: *Psychology Today* (July 24, 2014).

"You are Either Listening or You're Not" by Andrew Forsthoefel: OnBeing.org (May 9, 2017).

"You Have Power Over Your Brain Chemistry" by Loretta G. Breuning, Ph.D.: *Psychology Today* (October 20, 2016).

"You're More Likable Than You Think" by Dan Ariely: *Wall Street Journal* (October 2-24, 2021).

"You're Not Listening. Here's Why." by Kate Murphy: *New York Times* (February 11, 2020).

∼ Books ∼

11 Laws of Likability by Michelle Tillis Lederman: AMACOM, American Management Association (2012).

Advocacy: Championing Ideas and Influencing Others by John A. Daly: Yale University Press (2011).

The Art of Creative Thinking by Wilfred A. Peterson: Hay House (1991).

The Art of Gathering: How We Meet and Why It Matters by Priya Parker: Riverhead Books (2018).

The Art of Possibility: Transforming Professional and Personal Life by Rosamund Stone Zander and Benjamin Zander: Penguin Books (2000).

Aspire: Discovering Your Purpose Through the Power of Words by Kevin Hall: William Morrow (2009).

Banish Your Inner Critic by Denise Jacobs: Mango Publishing Group (2017).

Barking Up the Wrong Tree by Eric Barker.

Better Conversations: A Starter Guide (Free e-book): OnBeing.org.

The Book of Awakening: Having the Life You Want by Being Present to the Life You Have by Mark Nepo: Conari Press (2011).

The Book of Beautiful Questions: The Powerful Questions that Will Help You Decide, Create, Connect, and Lead by Warren Berger: Bloomsbury Publishing (2018).

Captivate: The Science of Succeeding with People by Vanessa Van Edwards: Portfolio Books (2017).

The Charisma Myth: How Anyone Can Master the Art and Science of Personal Magnetism by Olivia Fox Cabane: Portfolio/Penguin (2013).

Charm: The Elusive Enchantment by Joseph Epstein: Lions Press (2018).

Consequential Strangers: Turning Everyday Encounters into Life-Changing Moments by Melinda Blau and Karen L. Fingerman: W.W. Norton & Company (2010).

A Conversation You'll Never Forget: A Guide to Capturing a Lifestory by Mike O'Krent: SkillBites Publishing (2017).

A Curious Mind: The Secret to a Bigger Life by Brian Grazer and Charles Fishman: Simon & Schuster (2016).

The Dance of Intimacy: A Woman's Guide to Courageous Acts of Change in Key Relationships by Harriet Lerner: William Morrow Paperbacks (1989).

Discovering Your Personality Type: The New Enneagram Questionnaire by Don Richard Ruso: Houghton Mifflin Company (1995).

Don't Sweat the Small Stuff… and It's All Small Stuff by Richard Carlson, Ph.D.: Hyperion (1997).

Elements of Wit: Mastering the Art of Being Interesting by Benjamin Errett: Perigee Books (2014).

Emotional Self Mastery: The Best Book on Regaining Personal Power, Self-Confidence, and Peace by Cheryl C. Jones: Can-Do Press (2019).

Essentialism: The Disciplined Pursuit of Less by Greg McKeown: Currency New York (2014).

Everyone Communicates, Few Connect: What the Most Effective People Do Differently by John C. Maxwell: Thomas Nelson (2010).

Face to Face: The Art of Human Connection by Brian Grazer: Simon & Schuster (2019).

Fierce Conversations: Achieving Success at Work & Life, One Conversation at a Time by Susan Scott: Berkley Books (2004).

The Fine Art of Small Talk: How to Start a Conversation, Keep it Going, Build Networking Skills, and Leave a Positive Impression by Debra Fine: Hatchett Books (2005).

The Friendship Crisis: Finding, Making and Keeping Friends When You're Not a Kid Anymore by Marla Paul: Rodale (2004).

Friendship: The Evolution, Biology, and Extraordinary Power of Life's Fundamental Bond by Lydia Denworth: W.H. Norton & Company (2020).

The Gift of Fear: Survival Signals that Protect Us From Violence by Gavin DeBecker: Dell Publishing (1997).

Grow from Within: Mastering Corporate Entrepreneurship and Innovation by Robert Wolcott and Michael Lippitz (Kellogg School of Management at Northwestern University): McGraw Hill Education (2009).

Has Technology Left Us Speechless? Restoring the Human Connection in Our Digital Age by Tod Novak: Aviva Publishing (2015).

The Hiding Place by Corrie ten Boom: Bantam Books (1971).

How to Be Interesting (In 10 Simple Steps) by Jessica Hagy: Workman Publishing Company (2013).

How to Create Your Own Luck by Susan RoAne: John Wiley & Sons (2016).

How to Start a Conversation and Make Friends by Don Gabor: Legacy Publishing Group (1983).

How Winning Works: 8 Essential Leadership Lessons from the Toughest Teams by Robyn Benincasa: Harlequin (2012).

Humble Inquiry: The Gentle Art of Asking Instead of Telling by Edgar H. Schein: Berrett-Koehler Publishers, Inc. (2013).

Insight: The Surprising Truth About How Others See Us, How We See Ourselves, and Why the Answers Matter More Than We Think by Tasha Eurich: Currency New York (2017).

The Introvert Entrepreneur by Beth Beulow: Perigree Books (2015).

The Introvert's Way: Living a Quiet Life in a Noisy World by Sophia Dembling: Perigree Books (2012).

The Kindness Habit: 5 Steps to Maximize Your Happiness and Impact by Allison Clarke, C.S.P.: Freeman Publishers (2018).

Love 2.0: How Our Supreme Emotion Affects Everything We Feel, Think, Do and Become by Barbara L. Fredrickson, Ph.D.: Hudson Street Press (2013).

Man's Search for Meaning by Viktor Frankl (1946).

Marry Your Muse: Making a Lasting Commitment to Your Creativity by Jan Phillips: Quest Books (1997).

A More Beautiful Question: The Power of Inquiry to Spark Breakthrough Ideas by Warren Berger: Bloomsbury (2014).

The Power Of Curiosity: How To Have Real Conversations That Create Collaboration, Innovation, and Understanding by Kathy Taberner and Kirsten Taberner Siggins: Morgan James Publishing (2015).

The Power of Who: You Already Know Everyone You Need to Know by Bob Beaudine: Center Street (2009).

Powerful Conversations: How High Impact Leaders Communicate by Phil Harkins: McGraw Hill Education (1999).

The Ripple Effect: Maximizing the Power of Relationships in Your Life and Business by Steve Harper: SWOT Publishing (2009).

The Science of Customer Connections: Manage Your Message to Grow Your Business by Jim Karrh, Ph.D.: Career Press (2019).

The Self-Reliant Entrepreneur: 366 Daily Meditations to Feed Your Soul and Grow Your Business by John Jantsch: Wiley (2020).

Servant Leadership: A Journey Into the Nature of Legitimate Power and Greatness by Robert Greenleaf: Paulist Press (1977).

The Seven Levels of Intimacy: The Art of Loving and the Joy of Being Loved by Matthew Kelly: Fireside (2007).

Social Intelligence: The Revolutionary New Science of Human Relationships by Daniel Goleman: Bantam (2006).

To Bless the Space Between Us: A Book of Blessings by John O'Donohue: Doubleday (2008).

Trust Edge: How Top Leaders Gain Faster Results, Deeper Relationships, and a Stronger Bottom Line by David Horsager: Summerside Press (2010).

Uncertainty: Turning Doubt and Fear into Fuel for Brilliance by Jonathan Fields: Portfolio/Penguin (2012).

Vocal Power: Harnessing the Power Within by Arthur Samuel Joseph: Vocal Awareness Institute (2003).

What Got You Here Won't Get You There: How Successful People Become Even More Successful by Marshall Goldsmith: Hyperion (2008).

When Strangers Meet by Kio Stark: Simon and Schuster/TED (2016).

Women's Work Is Never Done: Celebrating Everything Women Do by B.J. Gallagher: Conari Press (2006).

You—According to Them: Uncovering the Blind Spots That Impact Your Reputation and Your Career by Sara Canaday: T&C Press (2012).

Younger Next Year and *Younger Next Year for Women* by Chris Crowley and Henry S. Lodge, M.D.: Workman Publishing (2005).

~ Other Media ~

Movie: "Remember the Titans" (2000).

Movie: "Steel Magnolias" (1989).

Online Course: "Conversation Skills: The Art of Meeting and Greeting People" by Daniel Post Senning (great-grandson of social etiquette legend Emily Post).

TED Talk: "5 Ways to Listen Better" by Julian Treasure (July 29, 2011).

~ Additional Resources ~

Alexandra Franzen: 100 Questions to Spark Conversations and Connection
    alexandrafranzen.com
Andrew Forsthoefe
    livingtolistem.com
Arthur Samuel Joseph: The Vocal Awareness Institute
    vocalawareness.com
Bureau of Labor Statistics: American Time Use Survey
    bls.gov/tus
Daniel Stillman: The Conversation Factory
    theconversationfactory.com
Drs. John and Julie Gottman: The Gottman Institute
    gottman.com
Graham D. Bodie, Ph.D.: Listening Educator & Consultant
    grahambodie.com
Gretchen Rubin: The Happiness Project
    gretchenrubin.com
Happy Brain Science
    happybrainscience.com
The Human Library
    humanlibrary.org
Institute of Curiosity: Effective Conversation Skills for Work & Parenting
    instituteofcuriosity.com
Jan Goss: Civility Consulting
    civilityconsulting.com
Jan Phillips: The Museletter
    janphillips.com
Jeff Goins: Tribe Writers
    goinswriter.com
Nurses' Health Study
    nurseshealthstudy.org
Scott Crabtree: Happy Brain Science
    happybrainscience.com

Index

"Dance Mom" experience, 161–164
on exiting conversations, 256
experience of being belittled, 168–169
experience with chronically negative person, 353–354
experience with Priya Parker, 119–120
graciousness workshop, 153
unexpected question experience, 241–242
website, 247
autism, 94

B
backgrounds, 24–25, 237
bad breath, 214–216
bad days, 321, 324
balance
    boundary violations and, 256–259
    emotional intelligence and, 108–109
    general discussion, 192
    humility and, 176–178
    listening skills and, 276, 281
banter. *See* small talk
barriers. *See also specific barriers*
    constant small talk, 230–233, 358–359
    cultural/societal messages, 85–86
    distractions/interruptions, 71–72, 218, 283
    exercises, 73, 74, 84, 94
    extreme busyness, 63–65
    false assumptions, 88–89
    general discussion, 61, 95, 391
    to good listening, 283–286
    health-related, 55, 56, 93–94
    hectic/rushed environment, 72–73
    high intelligence, 92–93
    homes/neighborhoods, 74–75
    interaction overload, 65–66
    language differences, 91
    limited opportunities to engage, 67–68
    listening skills and, 278–279
    loud music/poor acoustics, 69–70
    negative thinking, 88
    self-isolation, 66–67
    social media, 81–84
    speaking habits, 92
    stressful/toxic work environments, 76–77
    technology, 79–80, 81

demeanor, 379
depression
    general discussion, 39, 56, 94, 332
    social media and, 83–84
determination
    exercises, 130–131
    general discussion, 129, 132, 391–392
    generosity and, 164–166
    kindness and, 157–164
    setting, 209–210
digital devices, 79–80
dignity, 166, 167
dinner parties, 71, 212–213
diplomacy, 187–188
disappointments, 324
discipline, 292–293, 302
discretion, 302
diseases, 39, 55, 56, 94
dishonesty, 185, 187–188
disinterest
    chronic negativity and, 352–353, 357–358
    general discussion, 39–40
disrespect
    general discussion, 52–53
    honesty versus, 185, 187–188
    overtalking and, 283–285, 384–386
Distraction Method, 358–359
distractions, 71–72, 218, 283
"dragon breath," 214–216
Drainers and Downers. See chronic negativity
Durkheim, Émile, 41
Dyer, Wayne W., 52

E

eager-to-talk listening, 287–288
earbuds, 81
egomania, 321, 324
Einstein, Albert, 352
electronic devices, 79–80
elegance, 155
Elements of Wit (Errett), 175
emotional attacks, 187–188
emotional contagion
    chronic negativity and, 336, 378–380
    friendliness, 15–16

Venn diagrams for mapping, 28–30

G

Gallagher, B.J., 317–318
gatherings, 73, 400
generational intelligence, 108–109
generosity
    general discussion, 211
    graciousness and, 155, 164–166
    hearing others, 341
    listening skills and, 280–281, 301
geniuses, 39–40
genshai concept, 168–170
genuineness. *See* authenticity
Getz, Stan, 12–15
Gift of Fear, The (DeBecker), 86
"Gift of Listening, The" (Gallagher), 317–318
Glazer, Robert, 377
goals, 130–131, 148–150
Goins, Jeff, 43
Goleman, Daniel, 34–35, 336
"goodbye" expression, 150–151
good conversations
    characteristics, 159–160, 172–173, 210–212
    contagious nature, 15–16
    exercises, 13, 16, 20–21
    happiness and, 9, 17–19
    oxytocin and, 11–14
    role models, 16, 52–53
good impressions. *See also* emotional imprints
    10/5 Rule, 213–217
    hygiene check, 214–216
    strategies, 217
    welcoming others and, 33–35
Good Talk (Stillman), 365
goodwill, 155, 214, 336, 384
Gordon, James Blackwell, 367
Goss, Jan, 52–53, 186
gossip
    avoiding, 381–384
    general discussion, 160, 325
graciousness
    definition of grace, 153–157
    exercises, 156, 159, 166
    exiting conversations, 256–259

R

random conversations
    negative comments in, 376–378
    spontaneity, 12–15
rapport
    assuming positive, 137–139, 218
    beautiful questions and, 245–247
    small talk and, 224–226
RAS (Reticular Activating System), 117–118
Read-the-Room Rule, 311
redirecting questions, 358–359
refinement, 155
reflection, 100
Reflections on the Art of Living (Campbell), 182
Reich, Robert Bernard, 190
Reisman, Karen Cortell, 56
relationships
    active listening and, 296
    bonding, 30–31
    chronic negativity and, 335–339
    deconstructing, 23–24, 122–123
    expanding, 24–28
    general discussion, 23–35
    health benefits, 335–339
    hosting events, 26–28
    sharing memories, 31–32
    small talk and, 224–226
    success and, 37–38
    Venn diagrams for mapping, 28–30
    welcoming others, 33–35
reliability, 172–173, 184, 211, 302
"Remember the Titans" (movie), 30, 46
Remen, Rachel Naomi, 246
reputation
    active listening and, 296
    becoming a better role model, 16, 52–53
    success and, 38–39
    toxic work environments and, 76–77
resolve
    exercises, 130–131
    general discussion, 129, 132, 391–392
    generosity and, 164–166
    kindness and, 157–164
    setting, 209–210

respect
    compliments, 227–228
    general discussion, 211, 302, 316
    graciousness and, 167–168
    honesty and, 187–188
    oversharing and, 283–285, 384–386
    setting example in, 52–53
restaurants, 52, 71, 80, 398, 399
Reticular Activating System (RAS), 117–118
reverse-engineering past conversations, 23–24, 122–123
RoAne, Susan, 226
Robertson, Mike, 25
Rogers, Carl, 278
role model, 16, 52–53
Rotary Four-Way Test, 384
Rule of Hospitality, 213–214
rushed environments, 72–73

S

safety, 86, 154, 167, 179–180. *See also* self-care
Sanders, Tim, 343–344
sarcasm, 175–176
"Sarcasm in Relationships" (Dauphin), 176
Schroeder, Juliana, 14
Science of Customer Connections, The (Karrh), 266
"Secret to Dealing with Chronic Complainers, The" (Winch), 329
Sedaris, David, 242–243
Segall, Lindy, 113
selective listening, 291–293, 297
self-absorption, 67, 82–83
self-awareness
    authenticity and, 184
    social personality/type, 101–105
self-care
    from chronic negativity, 343–345, 387–390
    general discussion, 66–67
self-control, 292–293, 302
self-deprecation, 184. *See also* vulnerability
self-discovery, 49–51
self-esteem, 336
self-introductions
    10/5 Rule, 213–214
    general discussion, 142, 212–213
    strategies/tips, 217–218, 219
self-isolation, 18, 66–67

T

tablets, 79–80

tact, 185, 187–188

taglines
 general discussion, 159–160, 211–212
 kindness and, 159–160
 listening skills and, 306–307
 Vision statement, 125–126

talking about ourselves, 239, 272–273, 283–285, 324

targeted questions, 236–241

technoference, 80

technology, 79–84

"tell me…" phrase, 237–239

10/5 Rule, 213–214

ten Boom, Corrie, 19

Tereshchuk, Julie, 213

"thank you" expression, 150–151, 160

therapists, 270

thoughtful-reply listening, 288–289

Threlfall, Daniel, 39

Thurman, Howard, 182

Thurston, Baratunde R., 231

Tippet, Krista, 245

TMI (Too Much Information), 283–286, 384–386

Toker, Sharon, 56

Tolle, Eckhart, 87, 380

tone, 92, 147

tools. *See also* graciousness; Try this! exercises; *specific tools and attributes*
 authenticity, 181–188, 211, 302
 being positive, 137–139
 being a possibilitarian, 140–142
 being proactive, 142–144, 301
 being purposeful, 139–140
 caring, 146–148, 301
 courage, 145–146
 courtesy, 150–151
 curiosity, 148–150
 general discussion, 135, 392
 humility, 176–178
 humor, 174–176
 integrity, 172–173
 openness, 178–179
 optimism, 173
 patience, 197–202
 practice, 203–204

Venn diagram mapping, 29–30
Vision statement, 124, 126, 127
vulnerability, 191, 196
"24" (television series), 141

U

unanswerable questions, 246–247
uncertainty, 86–88
Uncertainty (Fields), 87
understanding
    chronic negativity, 329–333
    general discussion, 165, 167, 236, 245
    listening skills and, 269–273
unexpected questions, 240–244, 400–402
unfamiliar topics, 240
unfiltered honesty, 185, 187–188
unfortunate circumstances, 323–324
unfriendliness, 52–53
unhappiness, 331
unkind honesty, 185, 187–188
unsolicited advice, 294–295

V

Venn diagrams, 28–30, 159
venting, 294–295, 380–381. *See also* complaining
Vertical Leadership Development (Chrysalis) Program, 50
victimhood, 323–326. *See also* chronic negativity
visibility, 38–39
Vision
    asking for help, 118–121
    composing draft statement, 124
    deconstructing past conversations, 122–123
    exercises, 121–122, 123, 124, 126, 127
    general discussion, 115–117, 391–392
    imagining successful conversations, 121–122
    motivation, 127
    purposefulness, 139–140
    RAS, 117–118
    small talk and, 230–233
    strategy, 209
    tagline for, 125–126
Vocal Power (Joseph), 92
vulgar honesty, 185, 187–188
vulnerability
    beautiful questions and, 245

exercises, 191, 196
general discussion, 189–190, 193, 196, 245
listening skills and, 302
sharing openly, 191–192
taking the lead in, 194–195

W

W.A.I.T. (Why Am I Talking) Rule, 311
War of Art, The (Pressfield), 182
Washington, Denzel, 30
weak ties, 14
weather, talking about, 229–230
weighty conversations
    benefits, 17–19
    exercises, 20–21
importance of engaging in, 230–233
Weingarten, Elizabeth, 242
Weissbourd, Richard, 52–53
welcoming others
    general discussion, 142, 165, 167
    sense of community and, 33–35
West, Ron J., 50
"What Great Listeners Actually Do" (Zenger & Folkman), 280
Wheatley, Margaret, 279
"When you have a hammer…" adage, 378
Whippman, Ruth, 18
Why Am I Talking (W.A.I.T.) Rule, 311
Whyte, David, 245
Wilde, Oscar, 229
Williams, Pharrell, 178
Winch, Guy, 329–330
Winnie the Pooh, 303
wisdom
    from deep conversations, 17–19, 230–233
    general discussion, 116, 148, 236
    knowing oneself, 101–105
    listening skills and, 275–277
wit
    general discussion, 211, 227, 302
    likability and, 174–176
    quirky questions and, 242–243
    unfortunate circumstances stories, 323–324
Wolcott, Robert, 38
word choice, 92
words of thanks, 150–151, 160

workplace stress, 76–77
worries, 324
"worst-case scenarios," 256–259

Y

Yeats, William Butler, 139
Younger Next Year (Crowley & Lodge), 58
young people, 52–53
"You're More Likable Than You Think" (Ariely), 139

Z

Zeldin, Theodore, 43
Zenger, Jack, 280
Zone of Hospitality, 213–214

Acknowledgments

. . . .

This book is proof that most publishing projects don't come to life over a weekend with one person typing away on a perfect-from-the-start manuscript in an idyllic cabin by a lake in the woods. As much as I love this scenario, that's not how this book came to be.

In reality, this book is the result of a vision that morphed several times in an ongoing quest to answer questions I heard over and over again from audiences and clients. It's also the culmination of many years of reading and research, untold conversations and discussions, hundreds of sticky notes and pages of scribbled notes, and dozens of drafts.

As with my first book, *The Intentional Networker,* the countless people who made their contributions both significant and small, made all the difference in the quality of the outcome. If I fail to mention you by name, you have my sincere apologies. It's been a long, winding road. Please pat yourself on the back.

In the meantime, my sincere gratitude goes out to the following key team members for their precious time and talents in making this book come to life:

Susan Priddy—My dear friend and fellow communicator of 30+ years, developmental editor, writing coach, clever organizer, head cheerleader, conversation enthusiast, mind-reader, quality control expert, and so much more. Smart, funny, creative, detail-driven, hard-working, loyal, and very patient.

Kendra Cagle—My creative and attentive graphic designer, superb question-asker and listener. Cooperative, intuitive, enthusiastic, and an inspiring example of how to balance work and family.

Janica Smith—My wise publishing assistant. Ready to jump back in with another book and add her strategic guidance, innovative ideas, and publishing expertise.

Sara Canaday—My dear friend and colleague who is a considerate and valued listener, encourager, and advisor. She has walked this path with me from the outset and lets me know regularly that she respects and appreciates what I bring to the world. I was so pleased when she agreed to write the Foreword for this book.

Korey Howell—My photographer and friend who always makes me laugh, knows how to capture my personality, and snap the shutter at just the right time.

Amy Hufford—My website and marketing communications expert and friend of more than 30 years.

Jessica Hagy—My new friend who beautifully "draws connections between things" and provided the Venn diagram in Chapter 2.

Marjo Rankin and Russell Santana—My proofreader and indexer who did a fantastic job helping me put the final touches on the book before printing.

Then there's my incredible peer review team. These are the people who read the initial manuscript and offered constructive feedback to make it even better: Lillian Aaron, Darla Akin, Karalee Brown, Michelle Crim, Natasha Gorski, Jan Goss, Doug Hall, Debbie Herrington, Sara Jochems, Kent Nutt, Lindy Segall, Stephanie Sherman, Sam Stinson, Sarah Swanson, and Dennis Welch.

My gratitude also goes out to the many authors, journalists, experts, colleagues, and friends who answered my questions and offered their permission to share their perspectives and wisdom.

And finally, this book would not exist without the loved ones—Ryan, Rhea, and Mark—as well as precious friends, and supportive colleagues who put up with my conversation nerdiness (bordering on obsession) and urged me on to the finish line. You are the best. I love you dearly!

A huge thanks to all of you!

About the Author

Patti DeNucci

Patti DeNucci believes the quality of our conversations and connections determines our success—not how many people we know or talk to.

Patti is a corporate and conference speaker, workshop facilitator, consultant, and the author of the award-winning success guide, *The Intentional Networker: Attracting Powerful Relationships, Referrals & Results in Business*. She's known for imparting her wisdom through highly interactive and engaging presentations and workshops, which she sprinkles with her signature sense of humor and irresistible charisma.

Patti works with a wide range of organizations to help their teams and event participants learn how to converse and connect with greater purpose, polish, and productivity. She has worked with Microsoft, Rodan + Fields, H-E-B, MGM Resorts, Hewlett-Packard, and the Texas Conference for Women, among many others.

For more information visit **https://PattiDeNucci.com**.

Other Resources
from Patti:

The Intentional Networker:
Attracting Powerful Relationships, Referrals & Results in Business

Available from most retail or online book sellers.

Services include:

- Corporate and Conference Presentations
- Workshops
- Strategic Sessions
- Panel Moderation
- Coaching & Consulting

Contact

....

Patti DeNucci

www.PattiDeNucci.com
pattidenucci@gmail.com
+1 512-970-8129

- TheIntentionalNetworker
- PattiDeNucci
- pattidenucci

Did you enjoy this book and find value in it?

Please share that news with your family, friends, and colleagues. Even better, consider giving this book a positive (if not glowing and enthusiastic) review. I'd sure appreciate it!

Have feedback for me?

Please email me with your constructive thoughts at **pattidenucci@gmail.com**.

Want to stay in the loop and learn more?

Please subscribe to my newsletter at
PattiDeNucci.com
and follow me on social media.

Interested in booking me?

Please contact me to check my availability and fees at **pattidenucci@gmail.com**.

Made in the USA
Coppell, TX
19 January 2023

11361397R00272